OPENING DOORS

Opening Doors
in
Vancouver's East End: Strathcona

Compiled and edited by
Daphne Marlatt
&
Carole Itter

With a new foreword by
James C. Johnstone

Harbour Publishing

First Published 1979 as Volume VIII, Numbers 1 and 2 of *Sound Heritage*, published quarterly by the Aural History Program, Ministry of Provincial Secretary and Government Services, Provincial Archives
Reprinted by Harbour Publishing in 2011, copyright © Daphne Marlatt and Carole Itter

1 2 3 4 5 — 15 14 13 12 11

Harbour Publishing Co. Ltd.
P.O. Box 219, Madeira Park, BC, V0N 2H0
www.harbourpublishing.com

Text design by Mary White
Cover design by Teresa Karbashewski
New edition edited by Audrey McClellan
Interpreters and translators: Charles Mow, West Coast Chinese-Canadian Historical Society; Kwok Chui of SPOTA; Rocky Yang of MOSAIC; Mr. and Mrs. Alexander Wah-Sai Ho; and Taki Bluesinger.
Transcription: Lorraine Buchanan
Portrait photography and copying from family albums: Tod Greenaway (except for page 53, Carole Itter, and page 137, Taki Bluesinger)

Additional photography credits
Cover: This recently renovated Victorian on East Georgia (originally Harris Street), painted sunny yellow with bright red and black trim, today exudes a sense of joy, but this home had a sad start. Newfoundland-born carpenter Isaac Churchill built this house in 1900 for himself, his wife Emma, and their newborn son. Tragedy struck the family shortly after moving in to the house when baby Isaac died at fourteen months of age, followed by Emma a month later. Churchill left the house soon after. For a number of decades this house's neighbour, 827 East Georgia, was home to Tennessee-born Nora Hendrix, grandmother of the legendary Jimi Hendrix. Photograph by Dianne Whelan.

Back cover and page 2: Design and collage by Carole Itter. Additional photography by Tod Greenaway and Yim Lam-Leong.
Map on page 10–11: Chas. E. Goad Fire Insurance Atlas of Vancouver, 1912. Photocollage by Tod Greenaway.
Page 29, houses in the 800-block of East Georgia Street near Campbell Ave., c. 1972. Art Grice photo, City of Vancouver Archives, CVA 677-946.
All Tod Greenaway photographs used by permission of the Greenaway Estate.
Printed and bound in Canada

Harbour Publishing acknowledges financial support from the Government of Canada through the Canada Book Fund and the Canada Council for the Arts, and from the Province of British Columbia through the BC Arts Council and the Book Publishing Tax Credit.

With support from the City of Vancouver's 125th Anniversary Grants Program and the participation of the Government of Canada.

**Library and Archives Canada
Cataloguing in Publication**

Opening doors : in Vancouver's east end: Strathcona / compiled and edited by Daphne Marlatt and Carole Itter.

ISBN 978-1-55017-521-9

1. Strathcona (Vancouver, B.C.)—History. 2. Strathcona (Vancouver, B.C.)—Biography. 3. Vancouver (B.C.)—History. 4. Vancouver (B.C.)—Biography. I. Marlatt, Daphne, 1942– II. Itter, Carole

FC3847.25.O64 2011   971.1'33   C2011-901030-5

CONTENTS

FOREWORD:
OPENING DOORS IN THE TWENTY-FIRST CENTURY

The first time I ever walked through Vancouver's East End was in 1975. My guide was a new friend from university, a fellow named Paul Yee. We met on my first day at UBC. Paul had grown up and gone to school in the neighbourhood. Paul's Strathcona was nothing like the rootless modern Richmond suburb I had been living in since my dad brought our family to Vancouver in 1965. The East End's weathered old houses and corner stores obviously had their stories. Paul's Strathcona had roots—a deep and pervading sense of community and history. Its well-worn streets and unpaved, undulating back alleys reminded me of my old North Kamloops neighbourhood from my childhood—a place that I still missed ten years after being uprooted from it. I had only lived there for five years, but that is a long time when you are an impressionable pre-teenage kid, struggling with identity, working on where he belongs.

After graduating from UBC I spent some time studying in Japan. When I returned to Canada, I got a job downtown and lived in the West End. On my daily walks to and from work I would vary my route to pass by the old houses of Mole Hill or by what is now known as Barclay Heritage Square. The old houses fascinated me. Often I would use my imagination and fantasize about how the neighbourhood would look if there had been no high-rises—if all the old houses remained. Though I was grateful for the sections of the old West End neighbourhood that still remained here and there, I resented progress in all its inexorableness, and how it continued to change my neighbourhood.

It was in the early 1990s that I read a collection of short fiction by Chinese Canadian writers called *Many Mouthed Birds* edited by Jim Wong-Chu. Paul Yee, who had by that time already published *Saltwater City: An Illustrated History of the Chinese in Vancouver*, as well as a number of children's books, had a story in the anthology. I remember the evocative power of one particular short story in that collection. It was a lovingly written tale about an elderly Chinese woman who roamed the back alleys of the East End with her grandson looking for pieces of broken glass with which she planned to make a special wind chime. The first time I read it I burst into tears. The name of that compelling piece of short fiction by Wayson Choy was "The Jade Peony." It was later expanded into a nationally best-selling novel of the same name.

By 1995 I was living in the East End, not in Strathcona but in an old house on Odlum Drive, just east of Clark in Grandview Woodland. It was my first time back living in an old house since I moved away from Kamloops as a nine-year-old. Everything from the worn wooden floor boards and the creaking basement steps to the initials scratched on closet and basement walls hinted at a human history this house had witnessed. Curious as to what I could find out about the former residents of the house, I set off to the archives and took my first uncertain but excited steps into the wonderful world of researching house histories. The more I knew, the more I wanted to know. What started as a single house project ended up with me researching every house on the block on both sides of the street. I began to be curious about where people had lived before they moved to my house and where they moved to after. The builder of the house had lived on the 600-block of East Cordova, and a number of former residents had lived on East Pender and on Hawks Avenue in Strathcona. I walked and biked around Strathcona tracking down these houses. Some still stood, others had been demolished. In between looking for those houses I tried to remember the route that Paul had taken me on through the neighbourhood so many years before, and I wandered down alleys that looked like they had changed very little from the time written about in *The Jade Peony*.

By a very happy twist of fate, my partner Richard was house-sitting in Strathcona when a unit in the row house our friends lived in came up for sale. Long story short, he was able to buy the house and by October 31, 2000, we

The original occupants of these Hawk Avenue row houses were mostly working class immigrants from Britain and Eastern Canada. These were later followed by Italians, Russians, Yugoslavs, Jews from Eastern Europe, Japanese, and later, Chinese residents. The photo above was taken in the 1960s. In 1984, new owners rehabilitated the rundown houses and planted gardens where before there had been only gravel and concrete. In 2002 this section of Hawks Avenue was voted Vancouver's most beautiful block (below).TOP: MILJENKO RUSINIĆ, BELOW: JAMES JOHNSTONE

had finally moved in together in that house. It wasn't long before I was back at the archives researching not only our 1908 row house, but the four houses across the street.

Vancouver's old East End really is another world. Though I had been made aware of some of its history through my connection to Paul and reading *The Jade Peony*, it didn't take very long before I realized just how history-proud the people in this neighbourhood are. Did I know that k.d. lang had lived just around the corner on Union? Had I heard that there was a Jimi Hendrix connection to the neighbourhood? Was I aware that two world champion boxers, Jimmy McLarnin and Phil Palmer, had lived in Strathcona, one just across the street from me? Did I know that the East End produced two judges of the Supreme Court? Was I aware that my corner store had once been a bootlegger's joint selling ice cream from the front and booze out the back? Had I heard about the freeway and urban renewal plans of the '50s and '60s that almost wiped out the entire neighbourhood? What about Mary Lee Chan and SPOTA (Strathcona Property and Tenants Association) and how the determination of a grassroots East End organization was able to take on City Hall, the province and the federal government and save Vancouver's oldest neighbourhood and its precious built heritage, along with large swathes of Chinatown and Gastown, from destruction? It seemed as if I was living in a land of legend.

The more people told me about my new neighbourhood, the more I wanted to know. I went out and bought John Atkin's *Strathcona: Vancouver's First Neighbourhood* (another book that needs to be reprinted) and when I was finished reading that, I found what must have been one of the last copies of Daphne Marlatt and Carole Itter's *Opening Doors: Vancouver's East End* left for sale in a book shop on Commercial Drive. Reading *Opening Doors* really did open doors for me. At the time I was reading it, the sudden downturn in Japanese tourism brought on by the September 11 attacks left me suddenly unemployed. On the encouragement of a neighbour who thought I might be able to turn my house history hobby into some sort of job, I embarked on a search for possible clients.

One of my first jobs concerned the houses on the 600-block of Princess Avenue. After days of transcribing reams of data gleaned from city directories at the City of Vancouver Archives I settled into some bedtime reading with *Opening Doors*. As I pored over the pages, I came across not one, but three stories about people who I had come across researching the houses on the 600-block of Princess: Rabbi Nathan Meyer Pastinsky, Abram Gurevich and Rose Bezubiak. Reading those amazing stories about the lives of old-time East Enders really made the history of that block come to life. The same thing happened all over again when I researched some houses on the 800-block of East Georgia. I found an interview with Nora Hendrix, Jimi's grandmother, and Leona Risby, who lived across the street at 826 East Georgia. I also found another house where the Gurevich family lived. Over the past decade this process has repeated itself over and over and my original copy of *Opening Doors* has been read so many times it is falling apart.

I have lived in Strathcona for only a little over a decade, but somehow it feels as if I have always been an East Ender—that I have always lived in Strathcona. For me, that's the magic of the place. It is a neighbourhood that has been the first Vancouver home to successive waves of a diverse array of people from all over the world, many of them escaping a broad range of problems, some from poverty and prejudice, others from famine, pogroms, war and ethnic cleansing. East End Vancouver, even with all its challenges, was a place to live in hope, set down roots—make a new beginning. Maybe it is the cumulative effect of generations of all those hope-filled industrious people, working the soil in their backyard gardens while setting down roots of their own that makes Strathcona feel so grounding to me. The more I learn about my East End neighbourhood the more I love it—and reading and re-reading *Opening Doors* has been a huge part of that process.

Strathcona opens its doors to the entire Lower Mainland during the November East Side Culture Crawl. Crowds of art lovers visit East End studios and galleries, many in private homes, during this increasingly popular art festival. MICHAEL SCALES PHOTO

Just beyond Strathcona, summer nights bring crowds of locals and tourists to Chinatown's popular Night Market, the first of its type in North America. LOUISE FRANCIS-SMITH PHOTO

In 1993 a foundation provided grants to restore thirteen heritage porches in Strathcona, including the one at 549 Union. COURTESY PATRICK GUNN, HERITAGE VANCOUVER

The first printing of *Opening Doors* ended with the neighbourhood's victory over the forces pushing for "urban renewal" in the neighbourhood. Since that victory, Strathcona has gone through a period of renewal on its own terms. In 1971, funds were secured for a Strathcona Rehabilitation Project that not only provided street and sidewalk improvements, parks, and a variety of other public works, but also allowed homeowners to get grants and loans of up to $3,000 to rehabilitate their long-neglected homes. That same year, the year of the famous blockades by the militant mothers of Raymur, the Ray-Cam Co-operative Centre was established, developing out of a neighbourhood food co-operative set up in 1970. In 1972, the Strathcona Community Centre Association was established. The same year, SPOTA opened an office on the 800-block of Jackson Street and worked to develop five new, non-profit infill housing projects through its housing arm, the Strathcona Area Housing Society. The last of these, the Mau Dan Gardens was established in 1981.

In 1985, work began on the old city dump site south of Prior on what would become a neighbourhood showcase, the Strathcona Community Garden. Through the 1980s and '90s the process of renewal continued. In 1991, the Strathcona Residents' Association was founded as the result of a three-year community planning process sponsored by the City of Vancouver. Strathcona's special RT-3 Zoning Code, designed to protect our neighbourhood's built heritage, was established in the same year out of the same process. Two years later, the SRA Zoning Committee received a grant from the Samuel and Saidye Bronfman Foundation to restore thirteen heritage porches in the neighbourhood. The project ran from 1993 to 1996 and received heritage awards from the city as well as from Heritage BC. In 1997, the Eastside Culture Crawl began with forty-five artists in three Strathcona-area studio buildings attracting a few hundred people. Fourteen years later, the three-day art festival attracts 10,000.

The East End embarked on another period of planning for its renewal when the Strathcona Revitalization Committee was founded in 2004. The SRC was a coalition of voluntary citizen organizations of residents and businesses in the Strathcona area. The five core organizations were: Strathcona Property Owners and Tenants Association (SPOTA), the Strathcona Community Centre Association, the Ray-Cam Co-operative Centre Association, the Strathcona Business Improvement Association and the Strathcona Residents' Association. After four years of hard collaborative work, the committee made public the fruits of their labour: *Strathcona 2010: A Clear Vision for Our Community*.

One important legacy of this process was that the report identified Strathcona's boundaries consistent with the Community Centre and School catchment areas and the city-defined Business Improvement Area, in effect, reaffirming the historic borders of the East End. This is very important for Strathcona and its future because, at the time of this writing, the powers that be have been redrawing city maps, and in the process, have been trying to rewrite history. Strathcona, Vancouver's old East End, now finds itself being carved up. The oldest, most historic part of Strathcona, the part closest to the old Hastings Mill site, the part that includes Japantown, the Powell Street Grounds, the old Japanese Language School, and the Alexander Street Red Light District now lie within the so-called Downtown Eastside Oppenheimer District. This part of Strathcona contains some of Vancouver's oldest, most fragile and at-risk built heritage. For the past two years, Strathcona North of Hastings has been included in Vancouver Heritage Society's Top 10 Most Endangered list. A full and proper heritage inventory must be made before any planning for the area is allowed to proceed. Documenting and finding creative ways to preserve and promote the history and heritage of Strathcona North of Hastings and the old East Hastings commercial strip is an important first step in the rehabilitation of the area as a whole.

So the republication of *Opening Doors*, this compelling collection of East End neighbourhood memory and history, could not come at a better time. This unique book about a one-of-a-kind neighbourhood, is an invaluable resource and a precious legacy, not only for the people of this neighbourhood, but the city at

A typical SPOTA house designed by local architect Joe Wai. JAMES JOHNSTONE PHOTO

large. The editors, Carole Itter and Daphne Marlatt, had such amazing foresight in embarking on this project. *Opening Doors* is their enduring gift to the people who live and will live in Vancouver's East End. This best-of-time-capsules opens doors into a world and a time that would have been lost to us had it not been for Itter and Marlatt's vision and pioneering efforts. The stories in this book are an important part of our collective East End identity. They are the route to our roots throughout this neighbourhood. From old Hogan's Alley and the borders of Chinatown to Clark Drive, from False Creek Flats to Burrard Inlet, the East End has so many more marvellous stories yet to tell.

—JAMES C. JOHNSTONE, VANCOUVER, 2011

Strathcona Residents' Association Chair James Johnstone is an East End-based house history researcher, heritage activist and neighbourhood history walking tour guide.

The G. and T. Grocery and the apartments above at 478 Union Street in Strathcona. ART GRICE PHOTO, CITY OF VANCOUVER ARCHIVES, CVA 677-921

PREFACE

The story of East Vancouver is a success story. The immigrant residents, sometimes thought of as neglected or depressed, coalesced to make their positive feelings about their neighbourhood known to politicians and other decision makers, demonstrating their arrival at or near the mainstream of Canadian life and their ability to save their community heritage. The voices of the pioneer residents tell how so-called "Wops, Chinks, Japs, Bohunks, and Sheenies" achieved economic survival, social acceptance, and political and legal equality. Some survived the arduous process better than others, but in the 1950s, 1960s, and 1970s, when their community was faced with destruction in a program of "urban renewal," sufficient strength, will, and unity was found to save at least part of Vancouver's historical East End.

What is being discussed here is the most basic of North American experiences: immigration and assimilation. All our families (with the obvious exception of the aboriginal popularion), in one generation or another, have been strangers in the new land. When we hear these voices they are familiar and through their stories we can learn more of our own.

Daphne Marlatt and Carole Itter are two observant East End residents who have closely watched the changes taking place in the community around them. They have tape-recorded the reminiscences of a small group of people who represent the various backgrounds of the residents in this area.

A little part of the history of East Vancouver was chosen for the 1979 *Sound Heritage* issue from the verbatim transcripts of the nearly sixty interviews done by Marlatt and Itter. Selection of material was based on the ability of each reminiscence to capture the vital essence of Vancouver's East End. The Aural History Program and Sound Heritage were very pleased to help document this story. In the intervening years, the Aural History Program and the BC Provincial Archives have become part of the Royal British Columbia Museum.

—DEREK REIMER, EDITOR
REVISED 2011

ALEXANDER ST.

ALEXANDER ST.

WATER ST.

POWELL ST.

D.L. 196

CORDOVA ST. EAST (LATE OPPENHEIMER ST.)

SEE PLATE 3 (VOL.1)

CARRALL ST

COLUMBIA AVE.

MAIN ST.

GORE AVE.

CORDOVA ST. WEST

HASTINGS ST. WEST

WARD 3

HASTINGS ST. EAST

PENDER ST. WEST

PENDER ST. EAST (LATE DUPONT ST. & S. PRINCESS ST.)

SEE PLATE 4 VOL. 1

CARRALL ST.

COLUMBIA AVE.

D.L. 196

KEEFER ST.

SHORE ST. (LATE HARRIS)

HARRIS ST.

GORE AVENUE

LSE CREEK

UNION ST. (LATE BARNARD)

PRIOR ST

OLD BUILDINGS OF THE ROYAL PLANING MILL
TO BE TORN DOWN

GREAT NORTHERN RAILWAY

D.L. 196

GREAT NORTHERN RAILWAY BRIDGE

MAIN ST. (LATE WESTMINSTER AVE.)

PARK LANE

SITE FOR PROPOSED STATION
GREAT NORTHERN RAILWAY

PROPERT...
V. V. & E. RAILT...
GREAT NORT...

TO BE FILLED IN & USED FOR RAIL...

MAIN STREET BRIDGE

USE CREEK

FALSE

SCALE—100 FT TO 1 INCH

East Vancouver, circa 1912.

Top: False Creek and Strathcona district looking north from Mount Pleasant, 1904. VANCOUVER PUBLIC LIBRARY, SPECIAL COLLECTIONS, VPL 802
Middle: Hastings Mill in 1890, with Burrard Inlet and the North Shore in the background. BAILEY BROS. PHOTO, CITY OF VANCOUVER ARCHIVES, MI P11
Bottom: View of "Granville," also known as "Gastown," from Burrard Inlet, c. 1884. WILLIAM NOTMAN PHOTO, VANCOUVER PUBLIC LIBRARY, VPL 12766

Afterwards, a Foreword

Daphne Marlatt

To go back to the beginning, why Strathcona? Immediately, because Carole and I live here, in the midst of houses that speak of another era and people who speak other languages. So there is this curiosity: What was the neighbourhood like before we came here? And, because we are both of white Anglo-Saxon protestant backgrounds, what are other experiences of life in this city where we all live together and yet apart?

Both of these questions, in addition to being personal, are historical, and they both have to do with seeing. "Let me see with your eyes..." The past is as opaque to direct experience as the "otherness" of a foreign language or culture. And Vancouver, like the small town it has so recently been (and some people would say still is), has a history of turning a prejudiced eye on cultural values that are different from WASP values. Two race riots, mob attacks on the Chinese in 1887 and 1907, were symptomatic of a province-wide anti-Asian prejudice that crested in 1942 with the evacuation of the Japanese to camps in the Interior. Black residents we listened to referred to Strathcona as a Black ghetto in the thirties and forties. Powell Street was certainly a Japanese area before the war, just as Chinatown was the city's first racially defined district almost from its incorporation in 1886. So there is this issue of separateness and walls to seeing. How do "we" see "them"? How do "they" see "us"? A district with as many different peoples living in it as Strathcona was bound to have some conflicting viewpoints, and these are evident in what people told us not only about actual experiences of discrimination but also about conceptions of the other groups, as well as conceptions about the rest of the city, the West End as opposed to the East End, mainstream culture as opposed to ethnic minority cultures.

On the steps of Strathcona School, 1890, corner of Jackson Avenue and Princess (now East Pender) Street. CITY OF VANCOUVER ARCHIVES, SCH P142

And yet, what attracted us to the neighbourhood and what we found reiterated in the interviews is a very real sense of community. Family associations are strong, of course, because the experience of immigration does drive a family back on itself. But beyond that is a strong sense of neighbourliness, again intensified by the immigration experience—sympathy aroused by shared difficulties. This neighbourliness transcended ethnic groupings and language barriers, and still does. That was, in part, the answer to our third question, a political one: How did the people of this neighbourhood manage to stand up to City Hall in the 1960s and win their fight against demolition of their homes? Another historical question, and one which goes to the roots of the history of the city.

Because Vancouver is essentially a boomtown built largely on land speculation (beginning with the first rumour that the CPR would terminate here and not at Port Moody), "development" in the name of progress has seemed the natural order of life to its residents. Carved out of the bush and destroyed by a runaway slash fire right after it was incorporated, built largely of wood-frame structures, it has been the ultimate disposable city, its skyline transformed by steel high-rises within the last twenty years. City Hall's plan to "renew" Strathcona—i.e., to raze its homes and build low-income housing projects—was just one more step in the march of progress. After all, the district suffered from "urban blight," the result of a combination of absentee landlords, a penny-pinching municipality, and a population of immigrants who were, by definition, powerless. They lived on subsistence incomes, they couldn't speak the language, and, of course, they didn't "understand" civic politics. Yet it was these people who managed to enlist the support of both federal and provincial governments in their struggle to save what they had, and who were responsible for initiating the first grant and loan scheme in Canada for rehabilitation of their own homes. And, ironically, it was these so-called immigrants (some of whom had been in British Columbia for generations) who declared that their neighbourhood *as it was* had value—if not capital value, certainly cultural and social and, yes, historical value.

First the mill, then the saloon, then the railroad—that was the shaping sequence for Vancouver. The first settlement on the south shore of the inlet was a sawmill established by Edward Stamp in 1865 at the foot of Dunlevy Street, then just a wooded point. This was the beginning of Vancouver and the root of Strathcona. Until Gassy Jack hauled his boat up the shingle of the only accessible beach close to the mill (at the foot of Water and Carrall Streets) and built his saloon

Looking west along East Hastings Street, about 1887. The old Hotel Vancouver is on the horizon. J.A. BROCK PHOTO, CITY OF VANCOUVER ARCHIVES, VAN SC P59.1

there, thirsty mill hands had to trudge fifteen miles through the bush to New Westminster to get a beer. The prospect of that ready clientele attracted other entrepreneurs, and by 1870 "Gastown," the site of a couple of saloons, a general store, and a hotel, had been surveyed as a townsite (known as Granville). By April 1886, Granville was incorporated as Vancouver: four blocks of saloons, hotels, stores, one church, Chinese laundry, jail, and a few houses along Water and Cordova Streets. On the swampy fringe of False Creek (between Carrall and Columbia Streets), a collection of cabins and shacks housed early Chinese settlers, many of them unemployed after the completion of the railroad and most of them unceremoniously run out of town in 1887 during Vancouver's first race riot. This was sparked by contractor McDougall's hiring a Chinese crew from Victoria to clear land around Pender and Burrard Streets. The complaint that Chinese labourers worked for lower wages than whites (and the prejudiced argument that they deserved lower wages because their standard of living was lower) would occasion yet another attack on both Chinatown and Powell Street (Little Tokyo) in 1907.

The disastrous fire of June 1886 wiped out most of the original buildings of the old Granville townsite but stopped short of Hastings Mill, its store, and its school. By 1887 the town was booming: 4,000 people, new buildings, a new business thoroughfare along the plank road of Cordova Street, roads extended through the forest that had stood east of Main Street, clearing fires, houses going up, and a whole new residential neighbourhood mushrooming south of the mill along Powell and Oppenheimer (East Cordova) Streets, Hastings and Princess (East Pender). This district boasted such residents as Mayor Malcolm MacLean, R.H. Alexander (Hastings Mill manager), Dr. Duncan Bell-Irving, Henry Bell-Irving (head of the first fish-packing corporation), Dr. Israel Powell, and the Oppenheimer Brothers (David Oppenheimer became the city's second mayor) and was, in short, "the domain of the political and industrial elite of pre-railway Vancouver."[1] These men had already amassed landholdings in the east end of town—in fact, the Oppenheimer holdings were reputed to be the largest along Burrard Inlet prior to the CPR land grants[2]—and they represented the city's first government, in line with their individual business interests. (Mayor MacLean was a real estate dealer, and City Hall was once synonymous with the Oppenheimer Brothers' grocery.[3]) Consequently, they formed an East End block, which competed with a newly arrived group of eastern Canadians affiliated with that big eastern corporation, the CPR. This new group settled the West End, known as the CPR townsite because it was part of the large parcel of land the provincial government and early settlers on that side of town gave away to the CPR to secure the western terminus of the railroad. Both groups struggled for control in shaping the city, as a rival business district sprang up around the CPR Hotel Vancouver, the CPR-built Opera House, next door, and the Hudson's Bay Company, which was attracted to that same Georgia-Granville corner. The shift of the courthouse, from its original location on Victory Square to a site on Georgia Street in 1911, perhaps best symbolized the waning power of the East End. At any rate, by the turn of the century, most of Strathcona's original inhabitants had moved their residences out to the increasingly prestigious areas to the west.

Their tall frame houses were taken over by newly arrived immigrant families, Italian, Japanese, Yugoslavian, Russian, Scandinavian, who ran them as boarding houses for the many single loggers, miners, and fishermen of their own ethnic groups in what became a largely working-class neighbourhood. Partly it was the area's proximity to the docks, to stores and factories downtown, to Rogers Sugar Refinery, to the many sawmills that sprang up along the harbour and False Creek that was useful to new residents. And partly it was the desire of subsequent immigrants, many of them relatives "called over" by those already here, to settle close to family members and to neighbours who understood their language and their customs. So the district that had once housed the political power-holders of the city became an immigrant basin, catching and holding an influx of newcomers, including Jewish refugees from European pogroms, Chinese or Ukrainian peasants escaping starvation and poverty, Blacks escaping the Depression dustbowl of the prairies, Japanese, Italians, Yugoslavians, all of them with little money and few alternatives in a WASP-dominated town.

Ironic that a district which has become, since the 1950s, largely Chinese should be named after Lord Strathcona of the CPR, which was responsible for bringing over thousands of Chinese labourers in the 1880s and then, once the railroad was finished, setting them adrift in a floating labour pool. Many of them found work in sawmills, and the history of Lord Strathcona School, built on the highest elevation of the district at Jackson and Pender-Keefer Streets, goes directly back to Hastings Mill, where the city's first school was established in 1873. Although that school escaped the fire of 1886, it had to be closed down later that year because it stood on the CPR right-of-way, so Oppenheimer School at 522 Oppenheimer (East Cordova) was opened in 1887 to replace it. Oppenheimer School opened with 93 pupils but two years later had grown to 562 pupils in four rooms, so an eight-room brick building known as East School was erected on the present site of Strathcona School in 1891. Renamed after Lord Strathcona in 1900 (when many of its pupils were still the sons and daughters of Scottish, Irish, and English pioneers, mixed by then with Italians, a handful of Chinese, and a few children of other nationalities), the school stands in a direct line of descent from that first school, and its shifts in location indicate the growth of the neighbourhood southward from those original houses clustered around the mill. Indeed, almost all the houses still standing in the two blocks bordered by Georgia and Union, Jackson and Heatley, were built prior to 1900, East Georgia, with its 1915 streetcar line, becoming a major thoroughfare. Houses dating from that period are scattered throughout the rest of the district, along with many built between 1900 and 1919. Fancy fretwork can still be seen on porches or under steeply sloping peak roofs.

One of our initial difficulties was how to define early Strathcona, what to establish as its boundaries. We found definitions that extended the district eastward as far as Clark Drive or as near as Campbell Avenue. Was Hastings Street or the waterfront its actual northern boundary? Gore or Main its westward boundary? The only fixed border seemed to be its southern one, defined by the old shoreline of False Creek, which Prior Street and Grove Crescent (now Atlantic) once fronted. The RayCam Housing Project on Campbell Avenue now seems to mark the eastern boundary, and this coincides, more or less, with an original ravine running between Campbell and Raymur off a finger of False Creek—at high tide a natural portage to Burrard Inlet. Hastings Viaduct still spans this ravine to the north, but a similar viaduct that once carried Prior-Venables has been replaced with landfill. Strathcona can be seen geographically as a neck of land bordered by water: Burrard Inlet to the north, False Creek to the south, the Raymur-Campbell ravine to the east, and to the west a similar ravine, also once known as a portage, that ran through low-lying swamp around Carrall and Columbia Streets. This subsumes Chinatown into Strathcona, and although Chinatown is historically a separate entity, we soon realized that since the urban renewal crisis of the 1960s, the two areas have become politically merged, and commercial Chinatown itself has extended across Main and up to Gore.

Given these waterways, it's easy to think of the district as a basin, although in fact its terrain is a series of small hills or ridges, fun for sledding but hazardous for horse-drawn carts and Model T Fords. Over the years these hills have been subject to constant grading and the hollows to landfill, so the neighbourhood now seems more uniform than it really was, although some idea of its natural eccentricities can be gained by studying the varying heights and depths of houses relative to roadbed. Perhaps because of the discreteness of these rising and falling landforms, or because of the density of each block—with houses crowded close together, sometimes two to a lot; rows of what are called cabins but are actually tenements built lengthwise down a lot; small apartment blocks; and the larger houses filled with boarders or with extended families—the people we spoke to frequently recalled the distinctive character of blocks and streets. They often discussed the ethnic distribution: Italians on Atlantic, Prior, and Union; Jews on Georgia; Chinese on Pender; Yugoslavians and Japanese on Cordova; Japanese on Powell; Blacks on Prior and Campbell. And none of it quite static, as waves of immigration brought, for instance, a lot of European and Russian Jews in the 1910s, a number of Yugoslavians in the 1920s, a lot of Blacks from the prairies during the Depression, and the great wave of Chinese families who were finally allowed to enter Canada after the repeal of the *Chinese Immigration Act* in 1947. The desire of each of these groups to better themselves, to climb out of the ghetto, increased that sense of waves as first the Jews moved out in the 1920s and early 1930s, the Japanese during the war, and then the Blacks and Italians, with prosperity from wartime jobs, in the 1940s and 1950s as the newly arrived Chinese were coming in.

Although many people remarked on the neighbourliness and tolerance that transcended ethnic groupings, this seemed to characterize friendships among Europeans rather than friendships between Europeans and Asians. A Catholic Italian might form a lifelong friendship with the Polish Jew next door or the Russian down the street, but her friendship

West Hastings and Carrall Streets looking west, c. 1900—early Chinatown. VANCOUVER CITY ARCHIVES, #CVA 677-27

with the Chinese or Japanese family across the way would be less intimate and of a more particular duration. Certainly mixed marriages between Caucasians and Asians were generally regarded as curiosities before World War II. This had a lot to do, perhaps, with the fact that Europeans were assimilated more readily into a society that was prejudiced against Asians. Then too, many European immigrants brought with them some knowledge of other European cultures and languages. Given that, it was easy for the children of Jewish and Italian or Croatian parents to grow up together in groups that had street identities. The Prior Street gang were the kids who recognized "The Sunny Side of the Street" as their song; the Home Apple Pie gang were the kids who hung out around the Home Apple Pie Cafe; the Union Street Princes and the Prior Street Rats came from particular blocks. In such groupings, ethnic divisions were blurred, even if the old Asian-Caucasian division still held. The school they attended was known as a "League of Nations," and, much as it stressed Canadian ways of doing things, it also encouraged the expression of ethnic diversity. At home, many children were urged to retain their "own" language, customs, and religion—at least at home. Finally, no matter how Canadian they might feel themselves to be on the streets of Strathcona, once outside the neighbourhood they ran up against those labels—Chink, Wop, Dago, Sheenie, etc.—used in earnest.

And so, despite their alliances and associations within the neighbourhood, they were not without a painful sense of alienation, the feeling that doors were closed to them because they looked "different" or talked "funny." Italians and eastern Europeans felt this, Jews felt this, Blacks felt this. But for the Chinese and Japanese this feeling was underscored by the outright discrimination of laws preventing Chinese already here from bringing over their wives and children, or Chinese and Japanese, even those born in Canada, from becoming pharmacists and lawyers because they had no franchise. That alienation was twinned by the internal one that occurred within families as Canadian-born and -educated children rejected their parents' old country or old culture values and, longing for assimilation, rejected their own ethnic identity. And yet the majority of Strathcona residents hung on to their ethnic identity and derived support from it emotionally, socially, even economically. The mutual aid societies that flourished among the Italians, the benevolent societies and clan or place-of-origin groupings of the Chinese and Japanese, the Ukrainian Hall, the churches and synagogue and language schools, all these formed an intricate network of support within each community and provided a sense of dignity and worth in the face of external discrimination and indifference. Out of necessity, each group relied on its own resources rather than aid from some large body such as municipal or federal governments. During the Depression, the Chinese looked after their own indigents with a Chinese Benevolent Association soup kitchen, because the city gave them very little aid.[4] Nor was indifference the worst that governments inflicted on various groups. There were also repercussions from such international upheavals as the two world wars when, for the sake of national defence, Yugoslavians in the first and Japanese and Italians in the second were interned in prisoner-of-war and "relocation" camps. The vulnerability of second-class citizens is difficult to imagine for those of us who have no doubts about our rights. Only the lawmakers feel they enjoy the full protection of the law. Our provincial government had stripped the Chinese and Japanese of their right to vote well before the turn of the century, and Vancouver's first civic election was notorious for the way Chinese would-be voters from the mill were chased away from the polling booth. Every story has its other side, and of course the other side to this story is that those fifty to sixty mill hands were sent down by the mill to cast their votes for R.H. Alexander, their boss.[5]

A rather wry recognition that the law serves the interests of those with enough money and power to make the law is common currency among the powerless. Strathcona had the reputation in earlier decades of being Vancouver's square mile of "sin." Yet two of its major illegal activities, bootlegging and prostitution, stemmed directly from a combination of poverty, self-reliance, and minimal social assistance. The clientele for these activities often came from a "better" part of town. Railing against the gambling and opium-smoking prevalent in Chinatown, a Chinese missionary wrote in 1912: "The Chinese segregated districts become...the dumping-ground of those evils which the white man wishes removed from his own door."[6] The same could be said of Hogan's Alley, of the brothels on Alexander and Union and Gore Streets, and of the various bootlegging houses that attracted West Enders out slumming. A strong self-reliance (many immigrants came from countries without social welfare programs), and a certain shame attached to the notion of accepting welfare, led people to find their own solutions to poverty. Bootlegging was one of these. Prostitution was another for girls from families that already had too many mouths to feed at a time when jobs were difficult for men to find, let alone women. Prostitution was regarded as a profession, evident in the reputation many madams had for keeping clean and orderly houses. And "good" bootleggers took care of their clientele, making sure that patrons who had had too much were sent home. Home was not separate from work: most of the small-time bootleggers operated out of their family homes with their children present, if not helping out; and the better-class brothels, particularly those on Alexander Street, tastefully furnished, supplied with cooks and laundresses, were regarded as homes for the women. The moral proprieties of such bootlegging joints and brothels stemmed from a code of ethics that had widespread currency in the early decades of the century when business contracts were sealed with a handshake and one's word, not with a legal document. Consequently, in their daily operation and in the actual experience of both clients and operators and even neighbours, bootlegging joints and brothels did not *feel* criminal, even though, within the framework of Canadian society, they were illegal. Here was another contradiction, one that seemed only to underscore the primary contradiction of feeling oneself to be both Canadian and irrevocably "foreign" in others' eyes.

Contradictions in values ran through every facet of daily life. Obviously there was a value in being self-reliant, in supporting your family by keeping cows whose milk and cheese fed both you and your neighbours, yet the city health inspectors said unpasteurized milk caused TB, cow barns were unhygienic, you couldn't keep animals in the city, etc. More recently, you looked after your own elderly people with collectively financed tong rooms and communal kitchens, yet social workers said you were stupid to pay for it, that the state would do that for you. Because you were "green" and didn't readily understand the transportation system or the currency, let alone the language, you were considered "dumb," yet you might have come to Canada with values or a code of ethics or a political consciousness much more sophisticated than anything you encountered here. At first you came like those others, like the first "Canadians," for adventure or for profit, to make a stake and return home. Always home was there at the back of your mind as a place you could return to with the means, finally, of being someone else—a landowner, a small businessman, a cut above what you were. But you couldn't or didn't get back and you stayed, living Canadian ways, no longer Japanese or Chinese or Italian, but not quite Canadian either. Then later you came wanting to be part of Canada, believing that democracy worked, that this land of opportunity would open doors to your children that would never be opened at home—only to find that the doors remained closed and you were still not Canadian.

Sounding the deepest contradiction of being at once outsider and insider—that is, outside the mainstream of Canadian society but inside the family and groupings of your minority culture—*and yet* Canadian, belonging here and not there, and yet not completely here—sounding this, I begin to hear all of you, the people whose memories we recorded, you who have suddenly entered this introduction as the people I would speak to, I hear all of you in me, in my own experience as an immigrant child in the early 1950s. Which gets this introduction, really a postscript, to the word that has been eluding me since the beginning, "us." Because this is the word that is written on opening doors, doors that allow the two halves of a contradiction to know what they share. It's only as insiders that we can speak of us. And stepping through that door is an individual experience in anyone's life, nothing less than realizing one day that that acute sense of feeling different has gone. But it is also a collective experience that can be measured by the number of generations it takes for a particular people to gain the mobility of education and open employment in our society.

What the history of Strathcona shows is that opening doors is a two-way action. There is the long waiting and struggling for discrimination to cease and that most basic of Canadian rights to be extended, the right to vote, which was finally granted to Chinese and Japanese Canadians after the Second World War. But there is also, once these basic rights

have been acquired, the acting on them, as in the formation of a citizens' action group like the Strathcona Property Owners and Tenants Association (SPOTA), and the long struggle to save the neighbourhood from demolition. The executive of this association, supported by the whole neighbourhood, threw off all the old images of immigrant powerlessness, unconsciousness, ignorance (many of them were second- and third-generation Canadians). They took the mandate to act for their neighbourhood into their own hands and, working *inside* the structure of Canadian politics, approached both federal and provincial governments with a sophisticated political strategy. They formed a working relationship with City Hall in order to govern the rehabilitation of their own neighbourhood, and on the federal level they changed policy about urban renewal throughout the country. Strathcona, as a neighbourhood of immigrants, has tended to conduct its daily life on the basis of collective action (mutual help) and self-reliance in the face of government "aid": this laid the groundwork for SPOTA. But the actual continuity and survival of the neighbourhood through SPOTA represents a leap (that door again) into the mainstream of Canadian society. As such, the history of the neighbourhood is more than a record of assimilation. It bears a political lesson for all of us, here and now.

—1978

Teacher Vernon Wiedrick and a group of boys in the schoolyard of Strathcona School, c. 1935. COURTESY OF VERNON WIEDRICK

R.V. Winch Grocery Store, c. 1888, sold not only fresh fruit and vegetables but also fresh venison. VANCOUVER PUBLIC LIBRARY, SPECIAL COLLECTIONS, VPL 9417

STAYING LOCAL

Carole Itter

From January 1977 until sometime in late 1978, Daphne and I were immersed in the memories of the neighbourhood in which we also lived. It was a privileged position. I have always found it difficult to encompass a political sensibility larger than an area I can walk, so the fact of staying local to a place the scale of this neighbourhood seemed proportionate to my sense of society. Community: what's within it? Picket fences, doors that swing open easily, welcomed greetings on the streets, three generations of one family managing the corner store, the familiar sound of one more apple being knocked from my overhanging apple tree, exuberant children charging in one door and out the other, adults meeting in the evenings to discuss and shape community needs. This is the present—exchange, involvement, concern. The past, as we listened to many people recall it, was not very different—a neighbourhood opening up to new immigrants, people ambitious to make a change in their lives and give their children better educations than they'd known in other countries—ideals held and realized.

This was no utopia. This was the original core of Vancouver's East End—a ghetto, which by definition is "that section of the city in which members of a minority group live because of social, legal or economic pressures." It was, for example, a tough neighbourhood in the 1940s and 1950s for some teenagers who considered themselves a protective force and permitted few outsiders to walk safely through the area. And at times in the 1920s and 1930s, many families were raised and educated on the profits of home-scale bootlegging of wine and liquor, and madams and prostitutes knew their business. There was no money. There were pockets of wealth. There were and still are backyard vegetable gardens feeding households for most months of each year.

So we listened to and then tape-recorded memories of some fifty or more people speaking of immigrating to a new country, or being born here of immigrant parents, learning a new language and customs, trying to make a living, being poor during the Depression, and yet always, always sharing with those poorer *and* having fun. In short, living. People talk in particulars: how her husband lost a job cleaning out washrooms at Hastings and Main because a man of his same race somewhere else in town was charged with shooting a policeman; how a neighbour made a hole in the chicken fence and for the first time ever they smelled the succulent odour of chicken roasting from next door; how a young boy's life was saved after severe concussion by a wise mother with ice packs and people talking to him for three days; how a shootout could *ever* have happened right in this neighbourhood, and how a ten-year-old climbed the fence after it was over and saw the brain matter splattered to the ceiling; what a first job was like at twelve years of age, delivering newspapers to skid row hotel rooms. Those are some particulars, and assembled here, the stories are large and extremely varied and sometimes contradictory.

Those who were students at Strathcona School mention it as a mini-League of Nations, and tallies vary from twenty-three to fifty-seven different nationalities there at any given time. Dichotomies did exist. Language differences were possibly the largest. Who spoke English but the children mixing on the streets? Laundry was hung on clotheslines accompanied by arias from *La Boheme*; songs were heard on Friday nights from the Jewish homes; one Christmas Eve the Yugoslavs danced arm in arm down Union Street singing Croatian ballads; the mandolin lessons at the Ukrainian Hall carried on every Saturday morning, including that black June morning in 1938 when the wounded bodies from the Post Office sit-in of the unemployed were lying all over the hall. Some taught themselves English by reading the newspapers and trying to understand civic, provincial, and federal politics but most didn't. They didn't have the time or energy after sixteen or eighteen hours of each day spent in a hand laundry or on a junk wagon and another three or so hauling and splitting firewood or looking after the household. Parents couldn't talk about their children's education with the teachers because of language differences; but then why did they need to? This was Canada, the land of opportunity, and truly their children were receiving an education they themselves never got. One woman recalled planting beets from dawn to dusk at eight years old in her old country, of being unable to go to church because she had no shoes, and of being warned not to read socialist literature once she came to Canada.

Strathcona School historically attracted excellent and committed teachers, those with a strong interest in teaching language skills to immigrant children. It still has the same reputation, and now, in the 1970s, more and more Cantonese-speaking teachers are being hired and are able to bridge the language barrier between parent, teacher, and child. This couldn't have happened forty years ago, when Chinese-Canadians who were trained to be teachers could not get jobs in British Columbia.

People often asked us how it felt, having moved into a neighbourhood and then meeting with many, many people and recording their memories. The feelings were many and, in retrospect, difficult for me to theorize upon. I returned to my own notebook from that period and found only a few notations, with intervals of weeks or months between them:

A quotation from *Akenfield* by Ronald Blythe: "The old people think deeply. They are great observers. They didn't move far so their eyes are trained to see fine detail of a small place." And I think of my neighbours recalling the mountain ash berries squished to the sidewalk and streets in the fall season, horses slipping on them, walking home from the school in the shade of the huge trees.

Yesterday we met someone who had been carefully educated and had considered the fact of himself growing up in this neighbourhood with a great deal of thought—as he defined it, a "white man's ghetto." And all through his fine articulation, what he said over and over was that this neighbourhood had been *a place to get out of*.

We are offered the best of the house wine in the finest wine cellar yet. Neither of us drink much, especially in mid-afternoon. A good visit and two glasses of wine later, I'm floating over the miniature daisies in MacLean Park on the way home, muttering to myself, "It *is* the nectar of the gods, it *is* the nectar of the gods."

We heard a story last week of a prostitute, old and filthy, how she stood outside her church window to hear the services, prayer book in hand, and how when asked to come inside, she replied, "No, this is my place. I cannot be seen in God's place."

A deeply religious man told stories from within the framework of his religion, stories full of humour and passion. He didn't recount or hold on to the memories of ethnic minority discrimination. Later in the afternoon, he said that he moved out of the neighbourhood when his teenaged daughter couldn't tolerate what she'd seen on the street in the 1940s—a scene that was degrading to humanity, an action that crosscut all racial or religious barriers.

"How do you get rid of the passions of life in history? If you do, then you're distorting it." —Saul Benison.

A musician who spent his life singing and playing the blues told of his wanderings through Vancouver, packing his instrument over his shoulder. One night in a beer parlour he "checked the place out" for good-looking women, spotted one, and sat down beside her. Within minutes he realized he was speaking to his only child, the daughter he had never met.

From W.F. Whyte in *Street Corner Society*: "In my interviewing methods, I have been instructed not to argue with people or pass moral judgment upon them. This fell in with my own inclinations. One has to learn when to question and when not to question, as well as what questions to ask."

From Michael Novak in *The Rise of the Unmeltable Ethnics*: "Ethnic neighbourhoods usually do not like interviewers, consultants, government organizers, sociologists. Usually they resent the media."

Michael Novak: "Whereas the Anglo Saxon model appears to be a system of atomic individuals and high mobility, [the ethnic] model has tended to stress communities to our own attachments to family and relatives, stability and roots. Ethnics tend to have a fierce sense of attachment to their homes, having been homeowners for less than three generations: a home is almost fulfillment enough for one man's life."

Feeling a breakthrough. Let's stop and work with what we've got, kind of wished we'd stopped earlier. Measuring how many more months to go, estimating the hours needed to edit this mountain of transcripts, did our senior editor say 2,000 or 3,000 pages? Relaxing into the desk work, away from the foot and mouth work.

We went for a walk along the eastern "gully," one of the natural borders of this area, once a place canoes could travel at high tide from Burrard Inlet to False Creek, bypassing the peninsula of Stanley Park, Lumberman's Arch, and English Bay. They could paddle by, or stop at another midden, the rise at Grove Crescent on the north shore of the mud flats. Are the shells still under the ground? Leave them there. We follow the railway tracks, the connecting line from the CNR to the CPR, one on the sloping south side, one on the north side of the neighbourhood. This place is on a knoll, centrally mounded, surrounded at one time by sea water, tidal flats, early morning mists, nesting waterfowl. We move through a sweet-smelling marsh, tansy growing brown, bulrushes, frogs—there *is* water still! It's mushy, it's the low spot, where early citizens stood on their back porches shooting ducks for supper, more and more of us.

Overwhelming, the hugeness of this enterprise we have moved into, taken on, collecting the memories of an entire neighbourhood, where hundreds and hundreds of people have moved in and out of over seven decades of living memory, and *we* have the nerve and the energy to try to collect the stories! Seeing boundaries as non-existent, worrying about coherency, can there possibly be any? Collecting what? And all the inherent dangers of inaccuracy possible, the biggest stories overlooked because we "represent government" and the government doesn't hear the human stories because the government isn't human. We knock on a door and we say, "We are putting together a history of the neighbourhood. Can we tape-record your memories?"

I am seeing how important transcribing a tape recording to the page can be, how the person doing the transcribing is truly lifting the voice to print, transferring, and what a huge transfer it is. Lorraine Buchanan, our transcriber, has her master's degree in music and notates silences as well as sounds. The transcription is then looked at by us, as editors, who check it again to the tape recording, delete passages here and there, adjust punctuation more accurately to the aural voice, and it's retyped, and that retyping can sometimes move the voice even further from the print. Essentially the work of an editor is to keep each particular voice alive to the fullest extent as all these transfers take place. *To blow back substance into print through voice.* This is an aural history, meaning a "listened-to" history; and the responsibility of an editor is to keep on listening. Two of us are now, having edited for six months, and one year or more listening, and another person transcribing, and much help and support in the neighbourhood.

For Ines Leland: You speak out, you say it up and out anywhere, in your home, on the corner, at public meetings everywhere, on front porches, in backyards; you give support, you say it, say it, say this is a good neighbourhood and this has always been a good neighbourhood. You say it, that crime is violence. Crime is not bootlegging from a home. Crime is not prostitution from a home. Crime is destruction; destruction of homes, of goods, of people, of community, from outside of it or from inside of it. Crime is lack of care. Crime is irresponsibility to your place, crime is lack of involvement in the issues that are immediate, that are difficult to speak of easily. Crime is power and progress in the form of a bulldozer tearing down family homes and replacing them with cheap concrete housing projects; crime is neighbourhoods lost to super freeways. You speak out, from a love and concern for your parents, your children and grandchildren. And how does it bother you when the others dare not speak up to you? Your temper rises, you shout, you cry out! You continue.

So how did it feel? It felt like being inside and outside simultaneously. Listening by the hour to the stories from the past, involved with the immediate concerns of a household and community. Meeting someone, then tape-recording his memories, returning home to move more firewood up the front steps, arranging to be at the community centre meeting next Wednesday night, listening to a recording and placing the words on paper, going to the corner store for groceries and hearing the same voices there.

—1978

THE INTERVIEWS

BILL ABERCROMBIE

In those days, a youngster didn't go very far from home. You stayed around your home. Now, I was an East Ender, and I just can't remember ever going to the West End on my own initiative. I lived close to the Strathcona School, just a block or so, and I remember coming home from school when Princess Street [now East Pender] wasn't paved and there were ditches running down both sides. We'd find an empty can and we'd kick it all the way down home. We'd play with marbles and we'd work our way down home trying to shoot one another's marbles. There were empty lots in those days, and I remember an empty lot that was in the same block in which I lived, and the kids set down stumps for cricket. We didn't have money enough to buy a cricket ball, so we made the ball out of yarn, or it could have been an old tennis ball, and we'd have a cricket game on this empty lot.

At low tide the eastern end of False Creek would be just mud flats. And at high tide it would be filled with water, and at the far end there was a little ravine, which ran right up to Broadway, and the China Creek ran through that. And as a matter of fact, in the fall of the year, salmon used to go up there to spawn. I heard somebody who'd lived in that area in those early days saying that he'd seen the fish in this stream. The kids used to go in their birthday suits and swim in this False Creek, and there used to be mud slides down there where they used to swim.

I had an uncle who lived in the 900-block Cordova Street and very close by there used to be a biscuit-manufacturing company called Ramsay Brothers. At high tide, the Burrard Inlet would flow into the vacant lot between his place and Ramsay's, and I remember my aunt would shoot the mallards from her back verandah.

There were people by the name of Doig, and they lived down here close to Campbell Avenue. They kept cows, and their cows grazed in sort of a common unoccupied land near Seymour School. Now, there was plenty of wildlife in the area around there. Down on Hastings Street just below Westminster Avenue [now Main Street] there used to be a butcher store, and it used to sell bear, deer, pheasant, duck, all game. In those days it was legal to do that.

A runaway horse was fairly common, particularly around Chinese New Year's when the firecrackers were let off. I remember one incident and it happened on Hastings Street. The P. Burns Co. had a horse and a two-wheeled cart with a balanced body. The wrapped meat would be at the back of it and they'd make deliveries. The driver was making a delivery on Hastings Street and he put the brake on the wagon and then threw this iron weight out. If a horse made a move then, the weight would hold him back and that was enough to check it. But when a horse got frightened and started to run, well the weight was ineffective. This horse ran right down Hastings Street, and at the corner of Hastings and Gore was the Orange Hall, and underneath the

Bill Abercrombie was born in New Westminster in 1897. His father was an Irish immigrant farmer. The family moved to East Pender Street in the Strathcona District in 1898 and lived there until 1916. Abercrombie later taught for many years at Strathcona School.

Orange Hall on the ground floor was a grocery store. And this horse ran right in through a window in this store and right up to the counter.

There were very few automobiles around. Most of the goods were carried on "transfers," which were heavy drays pulled by two horses, and others were light drays and they'd go pretty fast. I had a very good friend whose father owned the Fashion Livery Stable and rented out buggies and horses to gentlemen who wanted to take their girls out for a ride around Stanley Park. My friend and I used to save the licence numbers of cars—there were so few cars in those days and we knew the car numbers. We kept a record and we compared, and if somebody saw a new one, well, he'd add it to his list.

There was rivalry between kids that went to Strathcona School and those who went to Seymour. There was sort of a dividing line and if you went past Hawks Avenue, well, you were getting into a foreign territory, and you'd better watch out. I don't know just to what extent there were fights, but the kids

Chinatown buildings on the west side of Carrall Street, damaged in the 1907 race riot. PHILIP TIMMS PHOTO, VANCOUVER PUBLIC LIBRARY, VPL 939

were not on the best of terms. It wasn't a friendly rivalry, it was a little more intense than that.

There used to be a rifle-shooting competition between the various schools in the city. Strathcona had a team and they were short some marksmen so they came to Miss McKay's class and the principal said, "Now have you got any boys in your class who are well up on their studies?" and my name was mentioned. They didn't give me a test to see how good a marksman I was, this was just the way they picked them. Well, I was chosen to represent Strathcona and shot on the rifle team for several years. We used to go down to the rifle range in the Beatty Street Armouries. Sergeant-Major Bundy was the "in charge," a fine set-up man, a very well set-up man. I think he belonged to the Imperial Army before he came out here. He was in charge of physical education in Vancouver—I don't know whether he knew anything about physical education. In any event, we'd have exercises and drills of one kind or another because he was a military man.

The first jail that I remember was on Powell Street, and there used to be the chain gang. A man would be apprehended for drunkenness or petty crimes and might be sentenced to jail for a week or two weeks. Those were the days before Oakalla, and the local jail took care of the short-term prisoners. And much of the work done on the city streets such as cleaning out ditches—this was before the streets were paved—would be done by the chain gang. Now "chain gang" meant that they were manacled, but I don't think very many of them were manacled. A few of them would be, the ones that they weren't sure of would be manacled, there'd be a light chain so they wouldn't be able to run away.

There was a riot that took place on Powell Street on a Saturday night in 1907.[7] I remember walking down Powell Street on Sunday and seeing the damage that had been done. All the windows in the stores were broken, and I don't think anybody was killed, but there was a lot of damage.

The Chinese New Year was a big event in Vancouver and they went at it in a very big way. They used to spend hundreds and hundreds of dollars. They'd string firecrackers from the second or third storey of the buildings between Columbia and Carrall and when they went off, there was really noise, tremendous noise.

In those days, a lot of the Chinese wore pigtails. We were bad boys sometimes. I used to deliver *The Province* and we'd be waiting for the papers at the building on Hastings Street. We'd go over into a vacant lot and there was a telephone pole and we'd have a big rope attached around the telephone pole. A Chinaman would be walking down, and all of a sudden a kid would run around, and we'd wrap this Chinaman up around the pole. We didn't hurt him at all. But we wouldn't do that with a white man, you see. We'd be afraid to. But we picked on the Chinese.

GORDON (WON) CUMYOW

Gordon (Won) Cumyow was born in Vancouver in the early 1900s. His father was born in Port Douglas about 1861 and was reputed to be the first Chinese person born in Canada.

My grandfather had his business in Port Douglas. He supplied these fellows who went into the gold fields, and they took off from Port Douglas. They tramped and they went by mule, anything they could use. But most of them just tramped it. A lot of them went up to the gold fields by Fort Yale; the sternwheelers used to go up as far as there.

My father was a self-made man, you know. He went to school whenever he had a chance and, as a matter of fact, he went and studied law too. He articled with a lawyer here for years and years but he didn't have the educational background. But he was much more educated than most, because he went to school in New Westminster. After the gold petered out, my grandparents moved into New Westminster because that was the trading centre. When he got old, like all the rest of the Chinese, my grandfather wanted to go back to China to die.

My father talked Chinook. His father, having opened a store in Port Douglas, a lot of Indians patronized him. So that's how my dad learned to speak Chinook. As a matter of fact, back when the Indians couldn't talk English and they talked Chinook, my dad used to interpret for them in Police Court. It must have been strange to see a Chinese talk Chinook. The reporters used to tell me about it, "Your dad knows how to talk Chinook. He talks Indian."

My mother came from China. She came with some missionaries, one of the families brought her here. Of course, they were Chans and she was too. And they gave her an education in Chinese—oh, she could read and write and talk very fluently, but she couldn't speak English. My father was the first court interpreter; he understood English and Chinese. And as the Chinese came back from the gold fields and from the CPR construction, they all landed in New Westminster, and then they got into business, you see. Then when Vancouver started in, why, they moved to Vancouver. The Police Court was involved with the Chinese because they had their difficulties, you know, with white men. They were always the underdog anyhow.

My father sent us to school when we were six, and then made us go to Chinese school after that. That was killing, spending five or six hours in school and then, at half past four, I'd have to come down to Chinatown and go to Chinese school until half past seven, then go home and do my homework. We lived up in Grandview; my father didn't want us to get mixed up with certain elements in Chinatown. In those days, it was more or less of a bad influence down here, when the gaming houses were wide open and the police were raiding them, and opium was being smoked. My dad wanted to keep us away from that.

When I tried to study law, the law society figured that all they had to do was get together and just pass a resolution. It was very simple—if you haven't got a right to vote, you can't study law. Simple as that. And the pharma-ceutical association, same way.[8] But once the Chinese got the vote, that was nothing. I studied law for three years. When they couldn't article me, I quit. My lawyer told me, "Well, fight 'em. Get a writ of mandamus. Force 'em." I said, "What am I spending good money for, fighting the powers that be?" I switched to banking and I worked as a bank clerk for five or six or seven years.

Chinese lottery used to thrive in Vancouver. They had about ten of them running. All these old men that couldn't work sold lottery tickets. It was a big business in Chinatown, three out of every four old men you met were run-ners. Golly, the police had difficulty raiding them. There was a lottery every day on the hour, sometimes every three hours, or sometimes four times a day. They distributed the results. For instance, in the lottery draw at 3:00, by 3:30 the results would be on the street. They used one of the regular lottery tickets and burned holes in the winning numbers, and they marked the time. So anybody, no matter what part of town they were in, when these tickets were distributed, would just look and know whether they had won any money or not. Besides, the runner would tell them because he got a commission on it.

After the war, when Oscar Orr became a magistrate, that's the time he handled all the lottery cases. He killed the lotteries, killed the whole shebang, because he wouldn't fine them; he put them in jail. Sometimes he'd fine them heavy and put them in jail too. And that killed it. The Chinese didn't want to go to jail. It got so he didn't fine anybody; if a man was found guilty, he'd go to jail. Gave him three months in jail, or two months or thirty days. Some-times he gave them ten days—well, that was bad enough, they didn't want to go to jail. The police had a lot of difficulty proving the case, because they had to get a stool pigeon to go out there and gather the evidence. They tried to make me a stool pigeon and I was the official court interpreter and I said, "Nothing doing. I'll interpret for you, but I won't prove anything for you." They said, "Well, you're not one of us."

I used to go to court every morning. Never missed. Always something there, some kind of scrap or something. Or a white man beat a Chinese up or something like that. It was always busy. But since the gambling became legalized in Chinatown, there's no more raids. So there's not so many cases in Police Court now, like there used to be. As time went on, the Chinese became a little more educated and started thinking in the white man's way of think-ing. So he never got into so many scraps and he began to compromise, you know what I mean? For instance, the white man comes in, maybe has had a few drinks. The Chinese learned to compromise with him, to humour him. Not to say, "Get out of here, you're drunk," as that offends the man right away. If a little diplomacy is used, there wouldn't be any fight. I have certainly noticed a decline in these incidents over the years.

The Chinese are great gamblers, they'd stake their own life on a gambling table. The police didn't try to stop it completely, but they tried to control it, so they raided them periodically. In those days, they could gamble any kind

Notary Public Gordon (Won) Cumyow in his Main Street office, 1978. TOD GREENAWAY PHOTO

of gambling they wanted, but they won't allow syndicate gambling now. For example, fan tan is a syndicate organization. You have got to have capital behind it, to play anybody who wants to play. So, if they had a $10,000 capital, they could meet anybody who wanted to play against them. But the bank doesn't rotate; the syndicate is always the banker. For example, in blackjack, if you get blackjack, you get the deck. Well, if you're a banker, you've got a better chance than the man who's playing. Whereas the other way, in syndicate banking, you cannot change the banker. About fifteen, twenty years ago, the city said they would license all the Chinese gaming houses. But they stipulate that you only can play certain games—any game that the bank rotates. But no fan tan and no Chinese lottery.

I never accompanied the police on gambling raids but I've seen them raid. They made it hard for the police to get in, so they could destroy some of the evidence inside. I know one raid there, the cops came back and said, "We had a helluva time down there. We couldn't find the evidence!" You've got to find the dominoes. They said, "You were playing *um gow* or *pai gow*, now where's the dominoes?" You know where they hid it? Chinatown is all built with what's called a "V" joint, the walls are wood where one plank fits into another. And they just slid one of the boards out, threw all the dominoes in there and closed it up. Well, there's a whole wall there, maybe 200, 300 planks which go right up to the ceiling. But finally, the cops spent almost a whole day there, they had the place locked front and back, and that's where they finally found it. The whole thing was to get the evidence. No dominoes? They couldn't prove their case.

The gaming house was set up like this. There was the gambling room and they'd put another partition in front of it. Then you've got to enter through a narrow corridor. And right above this companionway, there's a mezzanine floor, a guy up there watching. There's an electric spring lock on both doors. And if you go in, he pushes a button and this front door opens, and as soon as you get in, he closes it. He presses another button, and then he lets you inside the next door along the corridor. When the police came in, they would give a run or a push or a jump, or bring the battering ram or mallets or a hatchet or axes, anything. But the idea was that they couldn't swing anything in that narrow corridor—there's no space! There would probably be a little store in front selling fruit but the man behind the counter was a watchman too, and he gave the signal. But for an ordinary fellow like myself, when I went there, they let me in. This was the situation there because at that time they were fighting the police.

There weren't many highbinders in Vancouver. I wouldn't even call them highbinders, they weren't that organized. For example, in San Francisco the tongs were organized, everything was what the tong said. They had control of all the gambling, lottery, fan tan, anything—you name it, they controlled it. Nobody could infringe on their territory down there. If there was an infringement, they eliminated him. That's where the hatchet men came in, the *fu tow jai.* There used to be a lot of killings down there [San Francisco], but there were very few killings here.

My dad used to sell opium, told me they used to sell it over the counter, anybody could buy it, it was legal then.[9] This would probably be 1906, 1907. I went up to the county court one day, to the registrar, and this registrar showed me a Xerox copy with my dad's signature on it. He had drawn up the contract that this company was organized to import opium from China and sell it retail.

I used to go down to the cannery at Steveston as a kid, worked with these guys and we called them "hopheads." They smoked opium. You've never seen anybody work like those guys, worked like crazy. As soon as they get up in the morning, they take a shot and in the afternoon, lunchtime, they go in and have another shot. So that'll last them three hours, four hours. That kept them going. When I was working as a kid down in the cannery there, it was illegal. I used to go in the opium joint, and they used to have a small room and they had beds all over the place. It was

Chinatown in 1937, 100 block East Pender. LEONARD FRANK PHOTO, VANCOUVER PUBLIC LIBRARY, VPL 5306

hermetically tight, there were no cracks or anything in it, because opium can be smelled from a long distance—it's a very strong pungent smell. There was about four or five fellows laying in bed there. And when they walked, they would walk very light, sort of semi-floating.

At one time, servant girls were brought over from China as daughters, they got around immigration that way. They used to treat the servant girls very good, except in Victoria—they did abuse them. That's why the Methodist church started that girls' school,[10] to give the Chinese servant girls refuge, who'd been abused by their owners. It could be either one, the man would abuse her sexually or his wife would lick the daylights out of her. [The Methodists] taught them English and they taught them Chinese, gave them an education. And of course, they converted them to Christianity. The Methodists did a wonderful job in Victoria there, just cut slavery right out practically, knocked the bottom out.

In those days, Chinatown was more or less shoddy, there was no neon signs or anything like that. They had boardwalks, wooden sidewalks, and the street wasn't paved, just a hard surface. Mud, you know, when it rained, just plain mud. The Chinatown that I remember when I went to Chinese school after six or seven o'clock at night, they boarded up the windows because there were too many drunks around and they broke the windows. So they put up sheets of boards that screwed into place.

The Depression affected Chinatown. But the Chinese got organized amongst themselves. They said, "Those who have money, will put it up to help the poor fellows who don't have any money." And the Chinese Benevolent Association, which was the spokesman for Chinatown, opened kitchens with the money to feed their own people. Most of them were single men. The merchants got by because they were in business. But the Chinese helped one another, they didn't call upon the white people at all.

The Chinese took over Powell Street after the Japanese were evacuated. The Chinese picked up all their property for nothing; the government just gave it away. A lot of Chinese got rich over it. Buildings that were worth twice the value, the government sold them for half, anything to get rid of them. Of course, when the war was over and everything started booming, the people who bought property down there became millionaires, see? That's what happened. It hasn't caused any bad feeling since the war, no. It was the government's fault, you can't blame the people for it.

George Nitta

George Nitta is a third-generation Canadian citizen, even though he was born in Japan in 1903. His father and grandfather before him were fishermen on the coast of British Columbia.

My mother was visiting in Japan and she went over for a little longer than what she expected, so I was born in Japan in 1903. That meant I was supposed to be Japanese, so when I got to be eighteen or nineteen I was naturalized in order to get my rights as a Canadian. My grandfather had come over here about 100 years ago, and then he called over his son, my father. My grandpa was a naturalized Canadian and so was my father, so my children are fourth-generation Canadian.

Those were the "dog days" then. Discrimination was floating in the air. For example, they wouldn't allow anyone of Oriental descent into the White Lunch Restaurant. And it was the same thing in the public swimming pool. In the movie theatres, upstairs was for coloured people, including us. I was kind of fed up after I found out that I didn't have equal rights, and I thought I'd better go to some other country. But after the war, everybody realized discrimination is real bad for all of us, and now it doesn't matter what colour your skin is, a Canadian is a Canadian. But it wasn't like that before the war.

So, I was helping my father and I didn't even get the chance to go to school. Because those days we worked all year round, we sweated, and no eight- or ten-hour day either. We worked twelve and fifteen hours a day, and maybe we managed to save $300 or $400 a year. The only reason we survived was because everything was cheap then. Once the fishing season was over, then it was another job, eh? And you couldn't choose, you know. You went to work at sawmills, logging, railway, anything you could get. Well, so I had to help my father support the family, and the only time-off he gave me, when I could go to school, was after January 1 to maybe the beginning of May when we'd go back to fishing. So I'd study only a few months a year, and I'd have to keep starting and starting—night school, eh? Even for white Canadians, it wasn't easy then, so I had quite a few white schoolmates at night school. One of them was called Blackie and later he was on staff at the RCMP office in Vancouver.

I was surprised when the war started, and we Japanese Canadians had to be registered and go once a month to the RCMP office to state what we were doing, you know. Because the first time I went up to the RCMP office I met Blackie there. That was almost twenty years after we quit night school. And I was a friend, so he treated me real good. He always gave me a special permit if I had to go to a different town to look for a job.

[In 1941] we had a fish-processing plant on Mayne Island, working seasonally. We'd been doing it year by year for almost fifty years and we depended on it for a small income during the winter months. I also owned three or four boats, and everything was seized. The Coast Guard forced everyone to bring their boats up the Fraser River to Annieville—oh, there were a thousand boats.[11] They didn't give us credit as Canadians. They just took us for "enemy aliens" for the duration of the war. How do you like that? Even if you were a Canadian citizen or Canadian-born, as long you had black hair on your head and a Japanese face you were an enemy alien.

I had my own property and my own business and it took three generations to build up what I lost. That's why I sued the government, and I won the case. Although I won the case, the lawyers took the biggest part. I got maybe 25 percent of the money the government paid us. I felt like suing the lawyer, you know, but we gave up. In the United States, the American government

George Nitta in the coffee room of his fish packing plant, 1978. TOD GREENAWAY PHOTO

Seized Japanese fishing boats being towed up the Fraser River in 1942. PROVINCE NEWSPAPER PHOTO, VANCOUVER PUBLIC LIBRARY, VPL 1352

returned everything owned by Japanese-Americans, they just held and protected all the property and then they returned it.[12]

Anyway, Blackie was with the Security Commission and he told me, "Whether you are my friend or not, you've got to evacuate. So you'd better check around and find out where you could survive the duration of the war without any big income." He gave me permission to take a trip, so I went to Kamloops to see my uncle who was farming there. He said, "Well, I've got enough money to keep us from starvation for five or six years anyway, so you'd better come to Kamloops and stay with me." My wife and children stayed with him while I worked at anything I could get within fifty miles on either side of Kamloops—you needed a permit to go more than fifty miles—farming, logging, sawmill, anything I could get. We went as a self-supporting family and we stayed in the Kamloops district for about seven years because they didn't allow us to come back to the coast until a couple of years after the war was over. Wartime is an entirely different picture, you know. For the duration of the war, there was big propaganda floating in the air *every* day by radio, newspaper. Lots of simple-minded people believed it, and lots of places in the countryside we couldn't even buy a packet of cigarettes. Soon as they knew we were Japanese it was, "No, you get out. No, we have nothing to give you." It was real tough going.

But many groups of people understood our situation. And especially the Chief of Police in Kamloops. I knew him when he was Chief of Police at Prince Rupert. Those days very few Japanese spoke enough English to understand it, so Inspector Barber was always picking me up to act as interpreter for people.

When I first got back, there were very few Japanese in Vancouver, but gradually, slowly, they came back, a few hundred every year. I had taken a little money with me when I went to Kamloops but I spent it all, and when I came back to Vancouver I was very close to coming back bare foot and bare hand. So I had no choice, all I knew was the fishing game, working on water. So I took an opportunity and went to Skeena River fishing and the company rented me a boat. They welcomed us back because they knew we were good fishermen.

Before the war there were 8,000 Japanese in Vancouver. Alexander and Powell and Cordova Streets, from about the 100 to the 700 block, was Japanese. White Canadians used to call it "Little Tokyo." It was said to be the cleanest spot in the whole of the city. They got up early, those old-time Japanese, they'd get up about seven o'clock, and the first thing they'd do is sweep and even wash the street. Talk about clean! After the war, Powell Street was nothing but a ghost town.

War is a bad game, you know. Everybody gets so excited, they can't even think any other way. Near the beginning of the war, this young soldier held up a confectionery store on Commercial Street that was owned by a Japanese young fellow, Canadian-born too, and he shot [the owner] to death.[13] It made me real mad, you know, because everybody talked like he was a hero, said, "Never mind that he killed a Jap, send this soldier to the front." And we believed we were protected by the law, by the justice of the nation. You couldn't even think about this in the common, ordinary way. There is a monument in Stanley Park to the Japanese who sacrificed their lives in the First World War. And people were screaming their heads off, "Move that monument!" I was so sad. Those men only had one life, and they had willingly sacrificed it for Canada's sake.

Discrimination is real bad. We've got to avoid such nonsense in the future. Those things my grandpa, my father, and I myself built up before the war are all gone. I've had to work hard enough for three generations in my time. Fortunately, I've built up inch by inch, and I'm going to continue another few years. Because if you have no hope in the next day, that's bad, you know. So I don't think I'm going to quit completely. If I'm lucky enough to live to be eighty years old, I'll still do something every day.

Gordon Lewis

Gordon Lewis was born about 1905 in Vancouver and worked for many years for the Rogers Sugar Refinery.

Mayor L.D. Taylor, who was famous and maybe I should say "infamous," ran the city into an awful lot of debt, but his motto was "a full dinner pail for all workers," and largely he made work for city projects. One of them was to level out Hastings Street, and it also took in Pender Street and Keefer Street, and Harris [Georgia] Street. Now, on the west side of Strathcona School, there stood a house which was maybe fifteen, twenty feet above the grade of the street, which was the amount that it had been cut down before it was paved and I used to wonder when the house was going to topple down, because it was on such a high piece of land.

Somewhere about that time, 1910–12, the city decided that they would continue with this levelling and paving, and Keefer Street was paved. And it was done in the good old-fashioned way, largely with picks and shovels, and before the cedar-block paving was put down, which of course, was *the* thing

Timbers being loaded on flatcars at the Hastings Sawmill, 1925. LEONARD FRANK PHOTO, VANCOUVER PUBLIC LIBRARY, VPL 3653

in those days, a good heavy base of concrete was poured and then this cedar-block paving and a heavy layer of tar over top of it. Now, Mr. B.T. Rogers of Rogers Sugar Refinery lived in sort of a mansion down on Davie Street. And from then on, he used that street regularly as his route to go home for lunch and come back, and he drove a yellow Pierce-Arrow, which had the two headlights in the fenders. The fenders came up, and then there was a final upsweep for the two headlights, and this car had a runabout top and a cabriolet top, and it was the Rogers' chauffeur's job to swap these tops with the seasons.

The BC Electric, in putting through the tram rail to New Westminster, chose to take the interurban cars down Hastings to Campbell Avenue to Venables. At Venables, they turned east again, and went up from there to Commercial Drive, and then turned south, continuing to Cedar Cottage. There was such a gully at Venables and Campbell Avenue that they had to build a bridge, and the interurban car for years went over that gully by bridge. It was rather a low depression right through to the harbour, and I recall having friends on Hastings Street whose house had been built in the continuation of that gully, and the *whole* house was below the level of the sidewalk. And so, a lot of soil that had been scraped off the high parts on Gore Avenue and Hastings and Pender and Keefer, was dumped in there to fill it up.

The Hastings Mill was started by some real old-timers, and it just gradually grew. The value of wood was entirely different then—they had a glut of wood that they didn't want and people weren't even interested in using it for firewood, and finally it got to a place where you could buy a load of top grade firewood for a dollar. Even what is known as "planer ends," which means that it's finished lumber maybe a foot to three feet long, you could buy that for a song. The Hastings Mill wagons pulled by one horse would deliver anywhere within a reasonable distance of Hastings Mill. Some really wonderful lumber came out of there, some that is almost impossible to get nowadays. If such lumber was stipulated nowadays, you would have to warn the whole crew, right from the woods bosses down through the sawmill bosses to look out for such pieces that would make twelve by twelve, thirty, forty feet long. For example, in the older part of the Rogers Sugar Refinery is one building where in the basement, which wasn't paved in those days, there were great big slabs of stone, about four feet by three feet, and sitting on them a twenty by twenty post and that went up to the first floor. The next floor was eighteen by eighteen, the next one sixteen by sixteen until the top floor was either eight by eight or ten by ten. The floor was made of six by six beams laid just as tight as you could lay them. It's so long ago that a lot of these have now twisted a little bit, but the posts are all there, all solid. And Hastings Mill used to put out that kind of lumber just as a matter of course, there was no question about it. The amount of stock that they had in there was fantastic and for a while, they just about had all the lumber business in Vancouver. They turned out the lumber for all the older places in Vancouver and of course it was shipped out, in the first place by sailing ships and later by steamers.

I walked over the first Georgia Viaduct with my mother the day before it was opened in 1915. There were two big controversies: one, a sort of a scandal about the quality of the concrete, which we've all seen wasn't so good as it should have been, and it wasn't any time at all until cars had gone through that concrete railing, and the other controversy was about whether they should have streetcars on it or not. Anyway, they put rails down and the streetcars never did run over it.

I remember seeing cattle going down East Pender Street, they filled the streets.[14] The men looking after them and the dogs had to watch every intersection and once you got them by the intersection, well then okay, they were free until the next corner. But they certainly had a time.

The Vickers family that lived next to 602 Princess ran a grocery store, and there wasn't near as much canned goods, so they used to sell a lot of fresh vegetables and fresh fruits. There were two companies in competition then, F.R. Stewart and A.P. Slade. Now the successor to those companies, Slade and Stewart, is still down here on Prior Street. They used to call around practically every day, and they did have trucks, and they had hard rubber tires and chain drives on the back wheels. I remember one of their very earliest trucks with pneumatic tires had a flat tire at the corner of Princess and Pender Street. Those two poor fellows on that truck had to jack the thing up, take that wheel off, take the tire off, take out the tube, and vulcanize it. They just about lost the day!

I think the proper name for the Westminster Bridge [where Westminster Avenue crossed False Creek, near the present CNR Station] is a bascule bridge, and it was commonly known as a "jack-knife bridge."[15] On this end, there was a terrific hinge and a counterweight, tons and tons of concrete, so that when the bridge opened, the whole span that moved just hinged to the north side. They drained False Creek by putting great big pumps way outside of Kitsilano, and the twelve-inch pipe was supported on floats all the way through, all the way up. It was pumped as a slurry, and the water ran back of course, and the sand settled. But that last bridge was a really substantial steel bridge. First of all, they put up a smaller station which was called the Union Station, and it was used by both the Great Northern and the Canadian National [actually Canadian Northern Pacific]. Then after some time, the railway business boomed a bit more and the Canadian National decided to put up their own station, and the Union Station was turned over entirely to the Great Northern.

The Salvation Army owned either three or four houses on the north side of Prior Street, and there was nothing on the other side—that was "waterfront property," although it sloped down very gradually to the water's edge. I have ridden over there on a mule that belonged to a man named Marsh who ran a transfer business. He wanted it exercised, so we took the mule and rode it down and it cropped all the way along. The False Creek Flats were not a swimming place because all the sewage emptied into it. This was one of the

Streetcars crossing Main Street bridge, c. 1919, after False Creek was filled in. The Union Station building is on the right. VANCOUVER PUBLIC LIBRARY, SPECIAL COLLECTIONS, VPL 9450

reasons for getting rid of False Creek—oh, it was a smelly place. There wasn't enough outfall from Trout Lake to keep it sweet. If there had been a river flowing into it, well, all right. That's largely the trouble with False Creek now, that there's no outflow to purify it. They've had to eliminate all the water being run in there from surface drainage, and the sewage and so on.

There was a riot on Powell Street Grounds in 1912 and Mayor L.D. Taylor read the *Riot Act*, which meant there was martial law. There was a socialist-inspired organization called the International Workers of the World [actually Industrial Workers of the World], which all the people who *were* working and the more moderates called the "I Won't Works." Included in the martial law was "no public gathering," no large gatherings. So, the Salvation Army, which largely used open-air meetings, found they couldn't hold open-air meetings or marches. This went on for a month or two without any relaxation in the law, and finally, some of the people there [in the Salvation Army] said, "This has gone on long enough. We're going out and hold a meeting," which they did, and from then on, there was never any more trouble. I don't believe any of these gatherings at Powell Street Grounds, and there have been a few, went as far as that one did.[16]

ANGELO BRANCA

Angelo Branca was born on Vancouver Island in 1903, the son of Italian immigrant parents. He rose through the legal profession to become a Justice of the Supreme and Appeal Courts of British Columbia. He retired as a Justice of the Appeal Court in 1978.

People who had good educations, who were well-to-do, didn't come to this country. The people who came here were the people who needed a new life and opportunity. My father really didn't need it, but he was an adventurer. He just wanted to get out to the New World and make his home here, which he did, definitely.

He came from Milano and my mother from the north Adriatic. We learned a lot about Italy by talking about it, you know—artists, painting, and big buildings and architecture. We learned to speak Italian in our home, but both my father and mother were thoroughly Canadianized. Canada was their home. They completely forgot about the old country. That's not too usual with the immigrants at that time.

My father came first to America and my mother joined him. They came up here in about '96 to the coal mines on [Vancouver] Island. He was in the [Klondike] gold rush and made some money up there. In 1903, he decided he was going to leave the mines and he then formed the original Italian food-importing business in Vancouver.

The 400-block Main Street, looking northeast from Pender, in the early 1900s—the building on the right was renovated in the 1970s and became a bank. PHILIP TIMMS PHOTO, VANCOUVER PUBLIC LIBRARY, VPL 3466

His first store was in North Vancouver, just off Lonsdale. Then we came into Vancouver and for a while he was in partnership with a merchant called John Crosetti. That partnership lasted about a year and then he branched out for himself. He was on Main Street for all the thirty-six years he was in business here. He imported a lot of stuff from Italy direct. It was easier to get in wine because in those days we had no liquor control system and Ottawa was where the payment of federal customs duty was and you could bring in good wine. And we had the Italian staples like pasta, cheeses of all kinds, certain kinds of fish, olive oil. Some of the stuff he sold to Woodward's. Woodward's was a small store too in those days. The initial store Woodward had [erected in 1892] is still existing.

When I was four years old I was pulling a little cart with groceries and delivering them down on Prior Street. My father had a horse and a carriage and one of the fellows used to deliver groceries in that, but within a radius of two or three blocks I knew the homes and I'd cross the muddy streets and walk on the wooden sidewalks and carry away the groceries to places that were very close. I remember Main Street was only a mucky old street. They had wooden sidewalks and ditches and trees growing. You had to travel by horse and carriage—there were no taxis as we know them today, taxis were horse and carriage. The same with the funerals.

We were among the first people in the neighbourhood to have a car. A Russell-Knight—that would be 1917—a great big huge thing. You had to crank it and it had a mag and a battery, a canvas covering, huge seats, a huge engine, just a huge car. I was thirteen years old when I drove it. Father couldn't drive it. There was no licensing of the cars in those days. We bought it and somebody showed me how to drive it once and that was all. When anything would go wrong with the car, we'd take it down to a garage and nobody knew how to fix it up, but my younger brother and I could take it to pieces and put it back together and it would go. We used to deliver huge orders of groceries out to a contractor who built the roads to the university. And then eventually we graduated into a Hudson Super Six, and that cost $2,200. That was the early twenties and it was like a Rolls-Royce. There weren't very many cars in Vancouver up until the end of the First World War—see, the major part of the production went into the war effort. It was only after the First World War that people began to buy a lot of cars.

Italian stores on Main—I'm talking now about, say, during the First World War period—there was only my father's store, and Crosetti had one. Tosi didn't move in until, I think, during the period of the First War. But they were not on Main Street until much later, they were up on Union Street then. The Venice Bakery—Battistoni was the man who started the Venice Bakery—that was on Union Street in the 500 block. Beautiful bakery. And immediately across the street was Tosi's store. Used to be an old stable, or the stable was adjoining, I've forgotten which, and they started up there more as a butcher store initially, and then they got into importations and so on, and finally they built that place on Main Street. Minichiello's grocery store was right across the street next to the Venice Bakery. There was another Italian store at the corner of Dunlevy and Union, and that was run by Giuriatti. This area was the centre of the Italian shopping and the Italian community until the mid-1920s.

False Creek then was a body of water that narrowed at Main Street. They had a bridge there, one of these cement-weighted bridges, a cantilever deal that opened up and closed for small little ships like tugs that were going to the other end. And then False Creek went up along where First Avenue is and China Creek and away up to the railway cut over there at Clark Drive and all around Clark Drive down to Prior Street, and came in like a big balloon. Down on Prior Street there were sawmills and there along Park Lane, which is the street behind Main Street to the east, that was called Park Lane—there were a number of sawmills there and an old horse stable. And there was the hotel there, about Main at Central Station, on stilts right in False Creek, and a big creamery near there. The Great Northern used to come in on rails that were set on piles all the way through False Creek down to the corner of Columbia and Pender. That was the terminus of the Great Northern Railway, where the Marco Polo restaurant is today.

When you got down oh, three or four blocks from the bridge area, then you'd get into a shallow part of False Creek and it was shallow all the way along China Creek up to Clark Drive and down Prior Street where, in the old days, there used to be the Restmore Manufacturing Company—furniture, mattresses, beds.[17] When the tide was out all the top shallow area would be dry. The tide ran in there very fast because the neck was a very, very narrow one. But from Main Street almost to Princess Avenue, there was an area where the water was fairly deep. We used to go swimming when the railway was filling it in, and the fill was about eight or nine feet above the level of the water, the high level. We used to go down on the side of the fill, and in some places it dropped off pretty fast, that's why when I was down there one day with three or four boys, one of them drowned.

In the earlier days, there was these travelling opera companies that came to this country. San Carlo, for example, from Chicago. They came here for years and years and put on a repertoire of opera at the Strand Theatre [on Georgia between Granville and Seymour, opened 1920 as the Allen Theatre], even back at the Avenue [Theatre] in the old days. The Avenue was down on Main Street at Georgia, where the electrical substation is now, and it was one of the principal theatres of Vancouver in its early days. Across the street used to be the old Imperial Theatre [on Main between Pender and Keefer], one of the nicest theatres in the city. Then, further up, the old Empress Theatre at the corner of Hastings and Gore. That's where the Charles E. Royal Players played for years. They had a bunch of very talented actors there; he was impresario. We used to get tickets all the time because he'd come around to my father's store and he'd buy Italian goods and then he'd say, "Angelo, how many of you want to come to the show this week?" Well, I'd always say, "'Six, Mr. Royal," that was the whole family. So he'd write out on the slip, "Admit six," and we always took in what they did. They were a magnificent bunch and for that type of theatrical work to go on in a city like Vancouver in the early days, and that successfully, spoke well for the type of stuff they did.

There were some of the old five-cent theatres down on Hastings Street. In the unit block [actually on Carrall Street, 333], and directly across the street from the Woods Hotel used to be what they called the Bijou Theatre. We used to pay a nickel to go in there, and with the nickel you got a ticket to go back next week, so you got in for two and a half cents, really.

My father had a very wonderful circle of friends. There was a Tuscan who came from outside of Florence; he was a longshoreman and it was just a pleasure to hear this man speak Italian. He spoke of Dante, for example, and he could quote Dante from the *Divine Comedy* by the yard. And my father was a great storyteller. We used to sit around the stove in the evenings in the wintertime, eat roast chestnuts and he'd drink some wine and tell us another story. They were all made-up, you know—he was a great storyteller.

And speechmaking. There were many that did it. The Sons of Italy met every month and they would have a banquet maybe a couple of times a year. There would be several speeches made by different people and that was mainly where the talking was done. A little later on, of course, some of the more prominent Italians became lawyers, doctors, and entered all professions. They would have their political meetings and ask the candidates to these meetings and they would make speeches on behalf of the candidates. Marriages, christenings were something after the fashion of a dinner: the usual number of toasts made by people who were there.

One thing that I regret a great deal is that the big banquets that we have, Columbus Day celebrations or the dances, groups don't get together to sing their folksongs anymore. Earlier, you'd probably get five or six groups, amongst three, four, five hundred people, and each one would be singing their own folksongs. And it was nice singing, nice singing. They'd do it in the homes too. For example, you take a marriage in the home of a Calabresi, they'd always do the tarantella, you know. But there's nothing nicer to hear than a bunch of people at an Italian dinner who are drinking and singing. The more they drink, the louder they sing. And it's funny how the harmony comes out.

The Sons of Italy and the Veneta used to sponsor a couple or three picnics every year. They were big events even as they are now. We still sponsor a picnic once a year in midsummer and there are always 3,000 or 4,000 people at it and maybe a thousand turned back because there's just no room for them. Just the idea of getting a big group together so that they could talk to one another and have a few drinks and break bread together. The Sons of Italy was a fraternal organization; that was its main purpose. If some member was injured or got sick or something like that, they would help him. It was one of the oldest associations we had here, dating back to 1905. Then there was the Veneta coming in 1911,[18] the Canadian-Italian in 1935, and a more recent one. We amalgamated them all several years ago under the name of Confratellanza Italo-Canadese.

In the area bounded by Main Street and Campbell Avenue or Clark Drive, and Burrard Inlet and the old China Creek area, the Italian community built in there very thickly and of course the Sacred Heart was the Catholic church in that part of the town.[19] It was the second Catholic church in the city after Holy Rosary Cathedral.

Eventually, when the Italian community grew, the church authorities realized they had to have an Italian priest at Sacred Heart. At the time we had a Father Blackburne there. He had been up at St. Peter and St. Paul's and he came down [1933] from that rich, beautiful church to Sacred Heart, which was at the opposite end of the pole: the people were poor, the church old and decrepit, the priest's residence was worse than a chicken coop. Anyhow, he came down there and took that over and lived there for a while. So, eventually we got the first Italian priest in the Sacred Heart [1936–50]. He was Father Bortignon. He started to build up the parish and built it up quite well. The present incumbent, Father de la Torre, has been there for many years [since 1952] and he's a tremendous priest.

The Italian home was a very, very close-knit home and the respect for the parents has almost been inherent, you know. Today it is disappearing. In fact, it is disappearing from all homes, even the Jewish homes and Chinese homes which also used to be like that. Morally, it was more my mother who trained us. Of course, we were very close to our mother—the Italian families are—but the discipline came from my father and it was very stern discipline and almost inherent and instinctive. My father never had to speak, all he had to do was look. He looked at us sternly and we knew we'd done something that wasn't right. That was enough.

I started school [Strathcona] between 1908 and 1909, when I was a little over five. I remember Bessie Johnston very well. She was sick one time and we sent her some daffodils, and she sent us a little letter back and then she said: "My heart with pleasure fills and dances with the daffodils." Remember that poem, Wordsworth's, entitled "Daffodils"? A dear, lovely old lady. I think she was one of the best-loved of all the teachers that Strathcona ever had. The Cairns sisters were there as well. They were a little more stern, but they too were very well liked. Children who misbehaved were spoken to and if they didn't behave, why, they'd get the strap. The principal, he was the best strapper of all. When he gave you one, you felt it.

We used to play out in the schoolyard. We played soccer there and we played baseball. And in the wintertime we played in the basement. There was always a lot of fighting. We had a large Chinese population there, Japanese, Jewish—and there was a big concentration of the Italian families. So there was always a lot of ethnic wars and the Wops were good fighters. I was one of the best. You know those who weren't of an ethnic group would call the Chinese people "Chinks" and they'd call the Wops "Dagos"—and the Jewish people "Sheenies" and "Bohunks" and things like that and this is what they used to do, the Canadian-born, English, Scots, and so on. They always felt superior. There was a very definite distinct type of racism in those days. As a single group they were the majority, but not if you took all the other ethnic groups. Kids can be terribly cruel and this was the cruelty that made itself felt.

But you build up a resistance to it, and that's why we used to fight. And I think, because we fought, we earned respect for ourselves. We weren't going to let anybody trample on us. You could knock us down maybe but we'd get up. And if the sons of bitches wanted to fight, then we'd fight, that's all. If it was a single fight, then that's what it was. If it was a gang fight then that's what we'd have. This, as I say, over a course of years, I think, is what helped a great deal to get the respect. In the earlier days the Scotch people and the English people over here pretty well controlled everything. If you wanted to get into the police force you had to belong to St. Andrew's Society or the St. George's Society and all this sort of crap. And that went on for years and years and there was always that sense of superiority. It was ill-affected but it took the ethnic groups who came here a long, long time to neutralize it. *They* neutralized it, it wasn't the *others* learning that this type of discrimination was no good. It was the idea that they *had* to forgo it because the ethnic people were no longer going to tolerate it.

George Paris was the boxing tutor for the old Cavalry Club that used to promote boxing matches here. Allen was there in those days, Jack Allen, who subsequently went to Toronto and started to promote boxing there. We had good boxers here in our day. Vic Foley was one of the big men. Jimmy McLarnin was another.[20] I knew Jimmy McLarnin when he went to Strathcona School. He was a very lovely, nice, small Irish boy. He had the most beautiful weave that I ever saw a boxer have and an ability to anticipate a punch. That man was just a dream as a boxer. I took up boxing rather late, about 1927. And by then I was twenty-four years old. Just seems I had a knack for it. I liked all segments of athletics. I never excelled at any but I was up on top in them all—soccer and track and boxing. I never lost a boxing match, and I became middleweight champion of Canada. For eight or ten years I used to go down with George Paris to the police gym and teach some of the police force how to box. Quite a few of the boys that I taught are still around.

I went to the University of British Columbia when it was up at the General Hospital site. I think I went in '21. The main building was the first building that the hospital had used for administration purposes. Then the old buildings on the west side, south of Tenth Avenue, where they housed the infectious diseases later—these were some of the school classes that they had. Of course it was very small, several hundred students. They had the Big Trek in 1924 out to the university site and—that was my class, as a matter of fact, Class of '24. That was the year they went out there. But I left almost a year before.

I'd been going to university for a little over a year and my father told me, "I think you'd make a good lawyer." It was just like a spark caught fire. In two days I'd left the university and I was in law. He had a lawyer whose name was Sutton, he was a solicitor for the City of North Vancouver, and I was in his office two days after. Of course, I've never regretted it. I was there for a year with Sutton, but that was only a single type of practice and that was municipal law, drafting bylaws and that sort of stuff. So at the end of a year I transferred over to another chap whose name was Fleishman. He's the father of Neil Fleishman, the chap who's now a great domestic lawyer. I was with him for four years until I completed my articles and then I went off on my own. I took off immediately after I was called to the bar and established my own office and I was a success right away. Success is a good omen in business. I was at Main and Hastings Streets over the Royal Bank for thirty-seven years, with the exception of five when I was down at the Holden Building.

There was very little crime in the Strathcona area. There were bootlegging joints of course, but no drugs in those days. The Chinese were using opium but that was down along Pender Street. The opium, I think, came from 1910 on, and then generally it was only the Chinese people that used it. They'd almost sit out on the street and you'd see them smoking that stuff, but there was no serious crime at all. There was an Italian detective—that was, yes, about the First War at the time—an Italian detective named Ricci, and he used to work with a fellow named Sinclair, a Scotchman. We used to call the team "Sinclair and Ricci."[21]

People are inclined to speak in a derogatory way about Hogan's Alley. One or two murders took place in Hogan's Alley, but you could go down through there alone at night and no one would ever touch you. There was a bootlegging joint in the middle of that block I used to go to sometimes, run by a friend of mine. And hell, I'd go out down by there and see people at night and, "How are you, Angelo?" and so on and so forth. The one or two murders that I know of that happened down there—one was a fellow who'd killed his wife, an Italian chap as a matter of fact, and then I think there was another after. But there was nothing about Hogan's Alley, Hogan's Alley was a nice place.

Harris Street was the initial name of East Georgia Street and on Harris, in the early days, all the whorehouses of the city were down on this end of Main Street. Later on, the brothels became a little more distributed: there were one or two along Union Street in the 200 and 300 block, there were some along Gore Avenue between Prior Street and Keefer, there were some along Dunlevy, and there were one or two pretentious joints along Railway Avenue and Alexander Street—really beautifully built up.

I used to act for a lot of the madams in the thirties, all of the old-timers. There was one place that's still on Alexander Street: there was a stairway upstairs there, and beautiful drawing room with full mirrors that covered the whole bloody wall, all bevelled up, and beautiful furniture and so on. She was one of the last of the madams. And they were all very interesting characters too. Bawdy houses were always illegal, but the police knew where they were at and they controlled them, they tolerated them, and there was never any problem with them. The madams themselves, the ladies who operated these places, were the sternest disciplinarians that there were with the girls. There wasn't a girl in those days that was a drug user. Today, you don't find the call girl or prostitute that *isn't* a drug user. The problems started to come with the last world war when, for fear that the army personnel would be infected with venereal diseases, they started to bang down on them and the result of that was that we had girls all over the bars and the streets and so on, and no real method of controlling them.

Along Prior Street, if you go down now, you'll see a fire engine place [Fire Hall No. 1] on Heatley. Then going further down you'll see playing grounds. Well, that originally was False Creek where all the sewage used to dump into, and when the railway used to come in the first thing that people saw was this terrible area there. I was the one who, back in 1936, started the movement for the reclamation of that land, and that was a very historic deal too. The dignitaries I got down there were Ian Mackenzie, who was the member for Vancouver Centre and was the Minister of National Defence; Pattullo, the old provincial premier of the Liberal Party; Gerry McGeer, who was the mayor; and three or four of the aldermen, Harry de-Graves, and Gus Seward who used to be with the *Sun* newspaper.[22] You see, the Great Northern owed about $20,000 worth of taxes. It owned all that property. They didn't have the money to pay the taxes—we're talking now about the thirties—and the city couldn't forgo the taxes, and so we got the idea of getting all these people down because we wanted Victoria to pass an enabling act which would give the city the jurisdiction to forgive the taxes in exchange for the property and put the property in the name of the Parks Board. Eventually we wound up getting this enabling act passed, we got the property and the taxes were forgiven, and Ian Mackenzie promised us $75,000 at $15,000 a year to develop it.

Here [Canada] people realize there is the opportunity, you know. And the schooling is easy, and every parent who comes here wants to see that their children wind up in a much better position than life gave to them. I don't know that the opening of doors to the professions is harder over in Italy than it is here. If anything, it should be harder here because you are in a country that is foreign to your ethnic origin, your people, your customs, and so on. But these customs, you know, these traditions, they pass pretty fast if you want to integrate into Canadian life. And the integration on the part of the Italians in Canadian life has been very, very rapid and very successful. I think that ethnic groups should practise their traditions, but they have to be Canadians. If an immigrant comes to this country and he doesn't aspire to become a Canadian citizen, in my judgment he is not a good immigrant. If he aspires to be a citizen, then I think he should respect and retain his traditions, and by traditions I mean the folksongs, the language, the customs—at his own expense, not at the expense of the Canadian taxpayers as we have had during these multicultural programs—because I think a lot of these things might make Canadian life richer.

VIOLET TETI BENEDETTI

Violet Teti Benedetti was born in Vancouver in 1906. Her parents were Italian immigrants.

In the start, when we came down to this neighbourhood, it was all English around here. Then came the Italians. But the English people were really good, I liked them. I was always in their homes 'cause we always had spaghetti, spaghetti, spaghetti, and when we'd go there they had cake, and we thought, "Gee, this is a dream." And they had bearskin rugs and you'd see them laying on the floor, with a big head and we'd sit on that.

In the house on Atlantic Street that I lived in, we had two kitchens. One for the family, and one for the boarders—they were mostly loggers. And they couldn't go to a restaurant to eat, so they put on their little pot of beans in the morning, and they'd say to my mother, "Would you mind looking after the beans?" When they would come home, they'd cook them. Mother had ten boarders. She had to wash their clothes, full of fleas, from a tap. I'd see her take the stick and put them in the boiling water outside. That's the way it was. She had to wash their clothes and clean the house, and every nine months she was pregnant. One day my father said, "You're not going to stand there with a comb in your hand all morning, combing their hair." We girls didn't know what was going to happen. So he just took the scissors, and then afterwards, the razor on our heads. We put our hand on our hair—it was all gone. Beautiful hair, flying all over the yard.

When I was nine, my dad died. He was murdered down here, right in the back, on Main and Union by his best friend. And then my brother joined the army, 'cause none of the girls would look at anybody unless they had a soldier's suit on. He was only twenty-one, you should have seen my mother, it was the only boy she had. She tried to buy him out of the army. Oh, my mother, I'll never forget that. He joined and he went over to Victoria. My mother was sick, she was pretty nearly dying, so they sent him home on leave. When he said goodbye to her, she got out of her bed with a long flannelette nightgown, right out on the sidewalk. I had to read all the letters that came from France, they were all blacked out, couldn't say where you were at. I had to read them because she couldn't read or write. But then when the telegram came that my brother was killed in the Battle of Vimy Ridge, oh, forget it. That was awful. My father had died only the year before.

Well, the children had to work. One had to do the dishes at night, one had to wash floors and clothes after school and iron, and one helped punch the bread—each had a turn. And the one that was best would go to the show with the oldest sister. We always walked. The street car was five cents, but we liked to walk, especially in the summertime. That's all, no dances, no nothing, just go to the show. When the exciting part came, they'd play music and everybody would clap and whistle and stamp their feet. They were happy days, really.

My teachers at school were good. I had two sisters, Mabel Cairns and Kate Cairns. They had the long skirts and the white blouses, with the chain and a watch stuck here. But they were strict. When recess time came, I was always crocheting. I'd never play with the kids. I didn't know anything about sports, not a thing. My mother and I made our living crocheting camisoles and tablecloths and lace for the bedspreads. A camisole was made in a "V," had a little short sleeve and a band. And they had eyelets made for the pink ribbon, and a bow here and a bow there, and a bow on each sleeve. You wore georgette blouses, if you could afford them, and you could see right through, everything.

We lived right across the street from False Creek, where the CN train yards are now. In those days, when the men were courting the girls, they'd go for a rowboat ride. So my mother used to send me along. And I was only about six or seven at the time. Now what could I do in a rowboat? A kid? If the guy was mushing around, we could have been drowned! It was a beautiful moonlight night—sure, for them it was beautiful—but for me, I was afraid, I was afraid of the water! And I was putting my fingers in the water, you know, and my sister would say, "Stop it. Stop it!" I was never so happy to get out of that boat. Then we used to go to Buffalo Park in Cedar Cottage all the time. When they were courting, my sister'd say, "Now, you walk straight ahead and don't you *dare* turn your head around." I was in the dark, walking—I was scared. And my mother would ask me, "What did they do?" I would say "Nothing. I don't know. I was walking all the time. I didn't see nothing."

In 1918 there was the flu time. It took all the big men, the healthy ones, and the little "skinny-marincks," they all lived. My mother had the garlic in the garden, and she made a string of beads for all of us. We wore this raw garlic on our neck to keep the flu away. You can imagine the smell! And we used garlic water for worms. Anything from Mother Nature, from the earth, is good. Like I say, "When the world was made, did God make a drugstore on the corner? He put the herbs for the animals and herbs for us." That flu was terrible. Everybody in the family took sick, and I was about thirteen and I had cleaned the house from top to bottom. Washed and waxed all the floors, the window, everything, like I knew something was going to happen. All of a sudden, I started to get dizzy. Dizzy! I guess a fever was working and I was going up the stairs like a drunk on my hands and knees and I climbed into bed. My brother-in-law came, we left the doors open night and day, he came in, and he had a glass of whisky. I'd never drank in my life, a kid thirteen years old, and he *made* me drink it. He just held my nose and made me swallow it. The Victorian Order of Nurses were good. If it wasn't for them, we would

Mrs. "Benny," 1978, in the garden of the house on Union Street where she grew up. CAROLE ITTER PHOTO, COURTESY OF ROYAL BC MUSEUM, BC ARCHIVES

have been all dead. They used to come with soup and sheets and pillowcases and everything. Once in a while I'd sneak out of bed and I'd look through the blinds. And you'd see the hearse going up and down, taking all these dead people away. Back in where Tosi's store is now was T. Edwards, the undertaking parlour, and the bodies were stacked there like cordwood.

My young brother was the one that was the worst of all, and he had a terrible nosebleed. The doctor said this is what saved his life. But we came out of it, all of us. Every time the doctors went on a call they had a drink of brandy, so they wouldn't get the germ. Not to get drunk, you know what I mean? Just for medicinal purposes.

The big events in the neighbourhood? A City Hall payroll robbery, right in the main street. They never got them to this day. They just went in there and took the payroll that day, the whole works. Well, and then one man shot a girl. She was sitting on the fence, she was one of them floozies. Oh, lots of killings. What about old so-and-so? He knifed her. She wouldn't tell, she wouldn't tell. They said, "Look, you're going to die." Then she told. And they did hang him. News got around by running from one house to another, like the Indians did. There were gabbers. Gossipers. They would knock on the door and say, "Do you know what happened?" and the next woman would relay it all around. In twenty-four hours, the news was all over.

The store [Benny's Ice Cream Parlour, now Benny's Market] was on one side of the street and every day when I was on my way to school, he'd [Benedetti] look at me. But I'd never look at him—I'd always turn my head the other way. So, when it was lunch time and I'd be going back to school up that way, and he'd be coming down this way, he'd say, "Hello, Violet," and I'd turn my head the other way. So I told my mother that every day when I come home from school, he's coming down the same side as I do, and he speaks to me. She said, "Well, *answer* him. Say hello." She said, "It doesn't cost anything." So I'd come home from school, run fast, you know, and change my dress, and he was standing outside on the corner by the pole, white apron on with his hands behind his back, always looking. And I was chopping wood, chopping wood, putting it in the wheelbarrow. I worked like a man—I was the best wood chopper in British Columbia at fourteen years old. So he saw I was a good worker and he came over and said to my mother, "Mrs. Teti, I want to marry your daughter." "Well," she said, "go ahead." And then she said to me, "Well, he's rich, he's got money. He's got a store." What did I know at fourteen? I did what my mother told me, that's all.

When I was going to have my first baby, I thought it was going to come out of my stomach—they took a tape measure and they measured me. I didn't know. They didn't tell me a thing. So I had to go to the doctor and Mother said, "Put all your best clothes on." So in those days, you had all that white embroidery with the pink ribbon and your pantaloons split in the front and the back. So the nurse came in, the nurses all had snowy white hair, elderly women, not like the girls of today. She said to me, "Get on the table and

Two early houses on Barnard (now Union) Street in the 1890s. These houses were originally built by English settlers. TOP: CITY OF VANCOUVER ARCHIVES, SGN 963, BOTTOM: CITY OF VANCOUVER ARCHIVES, BU P182

take your clothes off." I did what she told me and she put a big white sheet over me. I started to cry. But he was a good doctor, really, and he said to me, "Sorry, little girl, if you didn't know the world was made that way, you should never have got married." This is what happened. When I did have the baby, she was four pounds—I thought it was fifty! And I was sick for a long time after, a long time. I wouldn't go back to my husband for six months, I slept at my mother's [across the street]. Finally, my mother said to me, "What are you doing? You're making a mistake. You've got to go back to your husband." I said, "What for?" I said, "No, I don't want to go. I want to sleep here." It was lucky that he was patient.

You never spoke badly of your husband, never. They were the masters. And if you did something wrong, look out. Too bad for you. The father disciplined the kids and the mother got it if she wasn't looking after them. But they all came up pretty good. All the children in this neighbourhood. Some are in big business, some are in New York. Some in opera. Boxers. We did good in the East End.

The West End can't touch us. No way. The West End didn't like the East End. They didn't like us. But when they wanted to eat and drink, they always came to the East End. We'd give them everything we had. When they'd come in, they looked like they never ate for a month. They'd eat up everything. Eat the chairs and the tables. "Oh, this is good tea, this is good tea, this is good…" You'd go and look on the plate, there was nothing left. But you never got asked back to their house. Never.

Where the beginning of the old Georgia Viaduct was, that brick building was the opera house, the Avenue Theatre. All the Italian people went. They had seal coats and they had the bird of paradise in the Roaring Twenties, the feather of the bird. They were the colour of a canary bird and the plumes were fine, fine, fine, and they'd hang at the back of the head. The best long dresses and beads.

Oh, it was so cold in the back of the store. No heat. No basement. And the baby got double pneumonia and bronchitis. The doctor said, "There's not enough heat in here." So I went and bought a stove up at Manitoba Hardware in Grandview. Boy, when I got this stove, it was heaven. Oh, the heat, it was just beautiful. I still have it. When I die, it's going to be my tombstone, and those who want to come and see, can put a quarter in the slot.

In the store, people would stay hours and hours, talking over the counter. We had a high glass counter and there were cigars at fifty cents apiece. Only the big gamblers would buy them, the poor working man couldn't do it. You could buy a sack of potatoes for fifty cents, and feed your family. They'd buy these cigars, and they used to make me sick with the smell. But I had to keep quiet—I couldn't say anything, because the ladies weren't smoking then, just the men. Havana and Marguerita—they had different names. They had cigarettes called Fatima and in every package of cigarettes was a little Persian rug-like carpet. And we made a pillow out of every one of them. They were all ready-made with a fringe and everything on them. And old Bull Durham tobacco came in a white sack with a yellow string. The ladies used the sack for their money, and put it down their bodice. Then they had the stogies, the long black Italian cigars, real black. You'd get drunk on the smell! One time we had a shower down at the old parish hall, great big shower. After the shower was over, they were going to pass the coffee and cake and this lady was old and she came up with a Marco Gallo cigar—it was *long*. We laughed, we died, we fell on the floor from laughing. Even the men couldn't smoke them, they had to cut them in half, they were so strong. And she was smoking it! Well, we had a lot of fun.

YUN HO CHANG

Yun Ho Chang was born in Kwangtung Province, China, in 1887 and immigrated to Canada in 1908. The interview was conducted in the Chungshan dialect with Charles Mow acting as interpreter. Additional translation was provided by Rocky Yang of MOSAIC, Mr. and Mrs. Alexander Wah-Sai Ho, and the West Coast Chinese Canadian Historical Society.

I came from my village of Sha-Tin in the Chung-Shan district of Kwangtung province in 1908. I went to Hong Kong where I paid $500 head tax to the British Embassy and they issued me a paper from the Immigration Office. I came to Canada because that was when China was still ruled by the Manchurians and there were bandits around my village. It was hard to make a living because there were too many people and not enough land and I heard that coming to Canada was good because there was work. I came on the *Queen of India* and it took eighteen days to get to Victoria. When I landed I found many hardships.

I found it difficult to get a job at first but friends helped me and I got my first job at a sawmill near Victoria. There was no Tung-Hsiang-Hui [mutual help organization], although in Victoria people from Chung-Shan organized their own tong. But at that time there were [Chinese] job contractors who would come to town to hire people to work in the sawmills and so on. A contractor would have a camp of his own and the people he recruited would eat and board at his camp and pay him so much. It's sort of mutual benefit: the contractor would get you a job but you had to live at his work camp. If he had a couple of hundred workers he could make quite a bit even if he only deducted a few cents per day from each worker.

Chinatown in Vancouver was ten times bigger than the one in Victoria, even then. In Victoria there were only a few lumberyards where you could find work and there weren't many stores. But over here there were more shingle mills and many more farms where Chinese could work. I came to Vancouver in 1913. I couldn't stand the smell of cedar wood so I started peddling vegetables with a horse and wagon. When I first started you didn't need a licence, but by 1919 I had to buy a licence for fifty dollars and hang it on my wagon. I had a friend out near Windsor Road and Fraser who was also selling vegetables, and at that time there was a white man who was selling coal near there. He was going out of business so we rented his coal shed to put our carts and horses in. It worked out to be cheaper living out there than in town because we shared expenses. I bought a route from a friend. On Mondays and

Thursdays I went to Point Grey, on Wednesdays and Saturdays English Bay, on Tuesdays and Fridays Shaughnessy Heights. It would take the whole day to do English Bay, going down every street and stopping at houses. But in Shaughnessy there would be only one house per block.

At that time two hundred or three hundred farmers would bring in vegetables to the 100–200-block East Pender Street and set them out on both sides of the wooden sidewalk. They were all lined up like parked cars and I would go down and buy my vegetables there and then deliver them. My wagon was six feet long by six feet wide, with forty-inch wheels. It would be about five feet tall, I guess, because I had trouble standing up in it. It had a cotton covering that rolled down to keep the sun and rain off the vegetables. My horse was tall, his backbone was higher than my shoulder, and he took a lot of care. Morning and night I washed the dung off him and then, because the streets were just dirt roads, the mud clung to his hair, so I washed that off. His hair grew quite long so I had to trim it once a month. Every week I scrubbed him down with soap, gave him a good clean-up. And then of course he had to be fed and watered every day. And I covered him with a blanket at night or in winter when it snowed. It was important to keep him clean all the

Mr. and Mrs. Yun Ho Chang in their home on Keefer Street, 1978. TOD GREENAWAY PHOTO

Chinese vendors on Dupont (now East Pender) Street in 1904. PHILIP TIMMS PHOTO, VANCOUVER PUBLIC LIBRARY, VPL 6729

time so he wouldn't get sick. He cost me more than $300. But he was a tame horse and very smart. After one week on my route he knew where to stop of his own accord. I peddled vegetables for fourteen years and I used that horse all the time.

After I quit vegetable peddling I bought a farm, about three acres on Knight Road around 28th Street, and I started growing vegetables. In 1923 they had brought in restrictions so that Chinese couldn't bring their families into Canada and of course there were regulations against Chinese buying land or houses. I bought that farm in 1926 and I bought it from a judge who wanted to sell it to me [under the equal rights principle]. I didn't know he was a judge but I understood that he had some power because the sale went through. He put a notice of it in the newspaper and nobody objected. I was the only Chinese in Vancouver who was able to buy property then. I lived on it with my nephew and another man. They paid me $200 a year for rent, and we split the rest of the profit from the farm three ways. I couldn't have handled the farm work otherwise. Most of the land around there was just forest, not even many roads through.

In those days Clark Drive was mostly bush, and the water [False Creek] went all the way up to it. That's where they dumped all the garbage and there

The W.K. Chop Suey at Pender and Columbia in 1920. DOMINION PHOTO CO. PHOTO, VANCOUVER PUBLIC LIBRARY, VPL 20832

were a lot of rats down there, it was teeming with rats. Whenever I drove by, I would stop for a few minutes and watch because these rats were all running around, dragging each other along by the tail. Some of them were as big as cats. Lots of other people watched too, it was a sort of rat theatre.

I learned English on the job from white workers. I asked them about things I didn't understand and gradually I picked it up. The missionaries were teaching English then. There was a Fook Yum Tong [church], Presbyterian, two or three streets away from Woodward's. It wasn't a big church, about the same size as the Good Shepherd on Keefer Street is now. They gave me an English book and they taught in the daytime so I went whenever I was free. On Sunday nights they taught the Bible. They provided tea, bread, snacks, and they asked you to donate a dime every week. People wouldn't go at first because they thought they were being charged a dime to hear Bible teaching, but then we learned the dime was used to pay for the food. Every Sunday people would joke with me: "Chang, it's a good chance tonight to eat out at the Fook Yum Tong!" I read several different English books and I learned to read and write, though I've mostly forgotten it now because I don't use it. When I was working at a plywood mill, I learned to pick up the right boards just reading out the order. So when I was building a barn for my horse and wagon I went to a lumberyard—there used to be a lumberyard where King Edward School was—and I had written out what I wanted, so many two-by-fours and so on. The fellow asked me if I was the person who'd written it out and I said yes. Then he talked to me and offered me a job, but I was young and afraid to accept. I said I had a business of my own already, selling vegetables.

In those days Chinese people went to their herbalist doctors, they didn't see white physicians, except for maybe two or three—Dr. Monroe, Dr. Fox, I remember. But everyone went to Chan Oy-Mo, the herbalist doctor whose house was on Pender Street near Gore. He was very good. He was killed before the war, murdered by some white people who were trying to rob him after he'd won money at a gambling house. And there was another doctor named Tong who was the only one who could visit in the hospital. But often if a person got flu or something like that, they simply prepared soups from herbs like Ma-Tse-On and Wu-Bo-Cheung, and they worked, the herbal remedies all worked.

I went back to China in 1911, just before the revolution, and I was still wearing a pigtail. This was in September, and when the revolt spread to Shek-ki we cut off our pigtails. I spent six months in my home village and during that time I got married and spent three months with my wife. Then I came back to Canada. She didn't come until 1949. I went back several times after that, but I couldn't bring her over without paying the $500 head tax which all Chinese had to pay. And then after 1923 she wasn't allowed to come at all.[23]

Dr. Sun Yat-sen came to Victoria and spoke to the Chinese Benevolent Association there, and then he came to Vancouver and spoke at the Chinese

Benevolent Association here. He spoke the same dialect I do, and so he spoke Cantonese with Shek-ki accent. Most people here were from Sze-Yup (Four Counties) and they didn't understand him. They said if Dr. Sun couldn't make *them* understand his speech, how was he going to get China back from the Manchus. They were swearing in the background, while he was talking. His talk lasted for two or three hours, and then he asked for suggestions and people asked him questions about his plans. He would answer in a very calm confident tone. Some people contributed money on the spot, I did too, and Dr. Sun wrote out a receipt to each person who contributed. After the overthrow, if you went back to China with the receipt, he would refund your money. When I went back that was just before the revolution, and there was a regulation that anybody caught with this sort of receipt would be executed immediately so I burned mine. But some of my friends were given their money back. And one man who donated $100 was later given a life pension. But there was a difference of opinion among people here. Those people from Chung-Shan were very enthusiastic about supporting him, but the Sze-Yup people were doubtful, and they would ask embarrassing questions like, "You don't even have a ship or a gun, how are you going to overthrow a whole dynasty?" And "You don't have any money, all you have is talk." They nicknamed him Bullshit Sun, but he said support would come from the people if the overseas Chinese worked hard, and when the time came plans and cannons would be available. The people that were against him, many of them were for the Chinese Empire Reform Association. And there were skirmishes between the two groups.[24]

In the old days, Chinatown was located more towards the west side,[25] around the 100 block—around Carrall Street and Shanghai Alley, which ran behind it. The area around the Trans-Nation Emporium [89 East Pender] was the hub of Chinatown. That's where most of the Chinese lived. But the site of today's Yuen Fong Company [242 East Pender] was outside the Chinatown limit, although today it's a prosperous spot. Most of the laundries were situated on Shanghai Alley and Pender Street, although I remember one on Pender near Gore, and one on Union. Laundries weren't big business at all then, because everything was done by hand, and the hours were long. People worked in them when they couldn't find other jobs or when they had some free time. Their customers were all white people. I remember they delivered by wagon and they'd go from place to place collecting the laundry in baskets.

The places where Chinese people lived were small and overcrowded. They'd cram four bunk beds into a small room. All the cooking was done on a wood-burner and there were never enough pots and pans.

The theatres in Chinatown started a long, long time ago because they were already well established by the time I got here. There was one on Columbia Street called the Chunking, right behind where the Ho-Ho is now [corner of Pender and Columbia]. And there was another one, the Gold Sing, on Pender Street next to the Freemasons. They're both torn down now, but I remember going to them and watching operas from Hong Kong. They always came in the fall and winter. You paid twenty-five cents to go in at seven o'clock, but if you went in after the show started, you paid fifteen cents or ten depending on how late you were. They were big theatres, bigger than the Shaw Theatre now, and they were comfortable. No benches, it was all single seats.

In those days, everyone gambled and there were gambling houses all over Chinatown, on Carrall Street, Pender Street, and in practically every alley. The games were different then. Now it's more mah-jong and poker, things like that. But then it was mostly the Italians who played cards. The Chinese games were things like guessing a word, guessing buttons from one to four, Chinese bingo, this sort of thing. The gambling houses were illegal so they were usually behind storefronts which sold cigarettes and pop or fruit as a cover. And the owners must have had connections, because they usually knew ahead of time when the police were going to raid. A lot of Chinese got so heavily into debt from gambling that they couldn't go back to China, or bring their family over.

During the Depression, a lot of the lumberyards, shingle mills and so on closed down, and there were no jobs anywhere. The Chinese Benevolent Association set up a soup kitchen in a building that stood next to the garage at the corner of Pender and Gore. If you had no money and no job, you could go to the CBA and register with them. Then you got a ticket and you could go for two meals a day. You got thin rice soup once in the morning at nine, and once in the afternoon around four. And that was it, whether you were full or not. The CBA raised their own funds for this relief. There was no government help at all. I was still working, because I was selling vegetables and they're a daily food necessity. The people I sold to were rich people and white people, because most of the white people had social assistance to help them.

Before the war, Chinatown was very quiet, almost a no-man's land, because the Chinese could seldom bring their families over. Most men came by themselves. They lived together in tongs and they started working each day as the sun rose and they stopped working when the sun set. You hardly ever found a man who had a day of leisure. But nowadays Chinatown is crowded with women all out shopping. It's at least ten times more prosperous now. In the old days, the grocery stores used to sell just some stock provisions and a few odds and ends. Now they sell a whole variety of fruits and vegetables, and they're not limited to season. Yes, there's been a big change in Chinatown, a very big change.

MARINO CULOS

It was about two years after arriving here that I went to Strathcona School. The boys and girls seemed older than we find them in elementary schools now. One of the boys who was the leader of the school, Bill Brown, was pretty tall, he was almost a man. But he wore these pants called bloomers, and the

Marino Culos was born in Italy in 1904 and came to Canada with his family in 1910. He was president of the Sons of Italy for nine years.

Mr. and Mrs. Marino Culos at home, 1977.

TOD GREENAWAY PHOTO

others had also that sort of stovepipe tight pant going up to the knee and practically cut across. The Chinese were really a section on their own, they kept to themselves. The Italians had difficulties—I know I had fights frequently. We were the foreigners and we wanted to be a part of them, though I don't think we realized what we really did fight for, because we also fought Seymour School. I recall taking tops of garbage cans and going down to False Creek and groups from Strathcona and groups from Seymour School would throw rocks, sticks, and fight each other. Our song was, "Seymour Seymour, run, run, run. We can beat the Seymour bums!" The "Dago" part, I suppose, was quite common in those days—we had to fight for an existence, it seemed.

In the home most of the women had boarders, in some cases as many as eighteen boarders, and the men received room and board and washing—clothes and so forth—for just about fifteen dollars per month. A woman had to supplement the few dollars that the husband brought in. The men were hard-working men and enjoyed their beer and they used to get together and play cards. They would make a fund out of so much savings and then buy a keg of beer and they would bottle it. I recall the men delivering the beer on a sort of wagon with a tailgate, it was set up so that the keg would hit and then bounce to the road and they would roll it in. When they played cards, the winners would drink and the losers would have to pay, and that would establish a fund for the next barrel.

They also played a game called "la Mora" and that was a game played across the table with four or six men or even two men, and they used their fingers. Some of them were so fast, you know, that they even got down low on the table, and they used to go, "Pshaw! Grr!" and all this. It was an exciting sort of a game, and it would finish off with quite a few arguments afterwards, "You did!" "I didn't!" because they used to do it so fast.

There was no radio then and they would principally get together and do a lot of singing. My parents weren't too bad with their voices and being from northern Italy they had a song they sang called "The Castle of Udine," meaning that the young men were the tallest and the strongest and the bravest of all. I think that most Europeans seem to be bold and proud, and you wonder just what made them like that, what was the background. Perhaps within them and within their own small sphere there was nothing there, but it was something to build as a mental outlook towards the hardships they had to face here, to feel strong and important. Things could be done, and they were done.

The Italian was a worker and he wanted to work and he wanted what money he could get. In a sense, he was a money collector and that's the way he thought of it: he was going to make enough money to buy himself a little farm in his home town in Italy. But instead, he decided that it was easier to bring the family to Canada and so the wives came in and the homes were in this section of the city. Things were very difficult for that group, who were mostly from the northern provinces, Venetia, Friuli, Tuscany, and Piedmont.

The Piedmontesi were more inclined to get into business, they seemed to be better prepared that way. The others worked in construction, they worked railroads, they worked on the streets, and on the buildings. It was handwork. I've seen where men had their hands so tough from handling shovels, their *whole* hand, that it was just like leather.

In 1904, a number of businessmen of Italian origin got together to discuss the needs of their countrymen. They found that so many men had come from different parts of Italy and found customs entirely different and a language barrier. There was no *easy* means to learn the English language and they were lost. They badly wanted to work, almost anywhere, and they did not know how to go about getting this work. These men thought that their countrymen needed help, and so they called a general meeting and then on December 1, 1904, they had an official public meeting. They thought that they would create this organization which they called Sons of Italy. It was established on January 1, 1905. From then on, this organization did very much for the needs of their countrymen.

Just to show the interest of these men, there was one particular case where my father was helped very much. He came to Vancouver in 1907 and finally got work with one of the railways, and on the third day, while working, some big rock dislodged and before he could get out of the way it hit him and broke his leg. He was taken to the hospital and there he could not even answer to "What is your name?" because he knew nothing of the language. Fortunately another person took up from there and helped him and he then became acquainted with several members of the Sons of Italy, who were always glad to help and also, the first president, Mr. Giovanni Carrelli of the Klondike Hotel. So when my father became well, he was asked to work for this hotel owner and he worked there until 1917.

When Vancouver was suffering a depression, my dad loaned his faithful boss some money to get him out of some difficult debt situation. Mr. Carrelli owned a cafe [in the Klondike Hotel] and he and my father discussed it, and Carrelli said, "I haven't any money but I'll tell you what you do. You take a hold of that cafe and do what you can, and if you earn you can accept it as money paid on account." My brother, my two sisters, and I worked there as kids, so we did our part. Before school hours I helped Dad. I used to wash the glasses that were used in the saloon. The saloon opened about 6:30 and we were there about three, four o'clock in the morning to clean up. We used to stack the glasses up in front of the mirror and they were the kind with the handle, pretty heavy. In the mornings, if you were there from the night before, they'd toss you a whisky for nothing and start you out again.

The Sons of Italy helped members who wanted to bring their families over, with the general documents. We had Giovanni Carrelli as court interpreter, and we had Giovanni Galetti, a notary public. The families were assisted in every way. They had to have persons to speak for them, they had to have people who knew other people so they could get homes, and then,

Entrants in Sons of Italy six-mile race, 1927: third from left, Marino Culos; fourth from left, Angelo Branca; on far right, Peter Battistoni. MARINO CULOS COLLECTION, COURTESY OF ROYAL BC MUSEUM, BC ARCHIVES

finally, helping them in any way where documents were necessary. In 1926, they decided they wanted to be within the rules of the country and they decided to incorporate under the Societies Act.

I ran a race organized by the Sons of Italy in 1927, a six-mile marathon, and I took the winner's side and Mayor Taylor presented me with a trophy. The marathon was a first in the Italian community, under the leadership of W.G. Ruocco, who was a brilliant, forceful man. As a matter of fact, we called him "the dictator," but he was a fourth-degree Knights of Columbus, which was tops in that organization, and he was a good businessman. He organized this sports day and it was held at MacLean Park, and Angelo Branca was one of the runners. We had girls running as well—one was Tosca Trasolini [aviator and sportswoman]—and you may have heard of Norman Trasolini, he was also in that race. He was quite a sportsman, quite a ball player, and in some ways a comedian—they nicknamed him "Bananas Trasolini." And then Peter Battistoni, he came second and he was only a little skinny fellow.

One day we read where Chamberlain had come back and said, "There'll be no war," and he showed the paper, but then Hitler went through Poland and the rest, and England declared war in 1939. And of course, in Italy, we had a Fascist—same idea, Nazis, and that was the Axis, Mussolini and Hitler, they worked together. And when England went to war, we knew the dangers of the repercussions in Italy because of the same type of government. And so here in Vancouver, Angelo Branca and a few others called a meeting—that was the early part of 1940—and that same morning we heard Mussolini say, "Sometimes history grabs us by the throat. There's nothing we can do, and we're now with Germany, with Hitler." And so we began hearing that, in such and such a home, was a sad eruption, you might say, of feelings when the RCMP went in at five, six o'clock in the morning and said, "You are so-and-so?"[26] He wouldn't have time to have a cup of coffee, no time to say something to his wife. They were taken, quite a number of them, and placed in the Immigration Hall at the foot of Burrard Street. And no one, their wives or anyone else, could get near them at all, they couldn't talk. "Incommunicado" they called it. And then there was sadness, sure a cloud then, boy—some of the best men were taken.

If you talked about Italy and Italy being good in those days, you were a "Fascist." I recall telling a friend, I said, "Look"—this was before they started to gather them and place them in the shed there for internment—"don't *talk* that way!" But he had to go too. Then his wife got sick. He had a little business, she tried to run it, she couldn't do it, she lost her senses. And I went to Angelo and I said, "He's a good man. I *know*. He wouldn't hurt anyone. He's not the underground"—the fifth column in those days. And Angelo and I had much to do to get him out of Petawawa, the internment camp. Mind you, by this time even the Allies were thinking a little differently about these things. They had a commission that went from city to city to hear if there were any wrong dealings, and we finally got where they heard this story and he did come out. They let him out before the end of the war. His wife, by this time, had been in the hospital and so on.

The Japanese got treated worse than we did. We didn't lose property, we were just taken away. But the Japanese, they lost their property. Some got little or nothing back.

However, there came a time when I too was called. I was waiting for it, and I don't mind saying that we didn't have a phone and they traced me to my wife's people. They asked them to get me to report. So the mother was afraid, because of this knocking at doors and taking away, to even tell me, but she had to. And I said, "Don't worry. If they called you instead of coming to our house and saying, 'mister, come out,' we can't have much to worry about." So I presented myself before the RCMP inspector in the Federal Building on Granville and Hastings, and of course he had the briefcase there with the records of the Sons of Italy marked. And it seemed that the Sons of Italy was not the type of organization that was playing heavy Italian or Fascist organization, that we were properly organized and were not of the fifth column type. So they said, "Now look, the society can stay if you want, but our suggestion is that you don't group together, don't have meetings together." So I had to report once a month and, as the policeman said then, "Well," he said, "if you've never had your fingerprints, you've got 'em now."

I had occasion to go and see my sister in the States and I had to get permission from the government in Ottawa to be able to go to the State of

Washington. We couldn't move, you see. Many families were affected and quite a number of people were hurt. Many of us got thrown around, abused, and we can only forgive them because, while we had nothing to do with it, there was little else we could do without hurting more people. And it was the Sons of Italy decision that we'd go along with the authorities. This was no time to rave and those men who *were* members, good members of the community and of the Sons of Italy, were disappointed that we did not make a stronger stand for them. But we were told, in no easy terms, what we had to do. Angelo Branca and I and others of the groups that were organized in 1940 to help the Italians even gave an ambulance to the Red Cross, provided with the funds of the members of that group. However, the war got to the point where it was ending, and the men began to come home, but very few took active part in the community again. We lost the best men.

CHOW YIN WONG

Chow Yin Wong was born in Hoishan, China, in 1896. He immigrated to Canada in 1911, paying the head tax of $500. The interview was conducted in English and Chinese (Hoishan dialect), with Mr. Wong's secretary at the Keefer Laundry acting as interpreter. Translation was by Kwok Chiu of the Strathcona Property Owners and Tenants Association.

I lived with my brother on Keefer Street [after coming to Canada in 1911]. He ran a laundry in the house. In 1919 I went back to China and came back in 1921. Then we tore down the old laundry and built a new laundry on Keefer Street [where the Mandarin Centre is now]. I built up the laundry with my own hands. Everything in the laundry was done by hand. We had one mangle, a small one, to press the sheets, and then we had to fold by hand. We just used the metal iron for the shirts, put it on the stove and then pressed, like that, all by hand. We hung the stuff upstairs to dry—kept the stove so hot, in two hours it was dry. In 1911, people were making only thirty-five to forty dollars a month. By 1921, everybody was working eighteen hours a day for only fifty dollars a month. Morning at seven till night at seven, twelve hours a day from 1927 to 1941, same thing. A lot of Chinese laundries were built before 1911: the Cascade, the Pioneer, the Star, Mission Laundry—oh, I think over eight. Every family got their laundry done, you see. Pioneer Laundry was a very big laundry, and Dominion. Horse wagon was used [for delivery], over a hundred wagons to all the city.

When I came from China in 1911, all restaurants were five cents for a big bowl of rice or a big bowl of soup, and fish and fried chicken, fried pork, five cents each. For ten cents you got a very good meal. I worked for a family half-days and got ten dollars a month. Washed floors and did everything but cook. Lots of Chinese young men worked for families—about 40 percent. About 50 percent worked in the laundries. And Chinese people worked in the work camps, worked for the railroads, in the summertime. In wintertime they all came to Vancouver, couldn't work in winter. And every year from May to September, they worked for the fish canneries, maybe made $100, $200—that's not very much for one year. In the winters, they lived at the Wong Society, the Lee Society, the Cheung Society, living upstairs. Everybody cooked up there, all went to the farmers, got their 500 pounds of vegetables, cabbage, 500 pounds of potatoes. Everybody went fishing. That was how they lived during those months. The society lent them some money for living for those months and after, when they got a job, they paid it back.

ELDA BATTISTONI VENTURATO

We arrived in Vancouver in 1910, in October. My dad had arrived the previous year. We had an uncle that was here and he was a shoemaker. He made plans to have my dad come over here and then us—the two boys, myself and Mother. My mother said that when she left Italy her father said to her, "You're leaving and you're going to Canada. All the world is the same and you have to make a living and you have to keep up." He meant that everywhere you go you have to work and you have to eat and nothing comes for nothing. There were poor families in the old country. My grandmother would go out and pick up wood and bundle it and she'd bring that home or maybe sell some of it. Her kids were left quite young alone in the home all day while she went out to pick up this wood and sell it to go and buy something to eat. There were very poor families, yes. I remember my mother saying if people are well-to-do in the old country, they have no reason to come out here.

During World War I, soldiers came around to the houses to see if you had anybody hiding [from conscription]. I never forgot this one time, they came to our place and one was quite severe and I remember my mother getting kind of frightened. And I guess knowing that we had all these boys in the family, well, they came around to see if somebody was evading to go to the war. I remember my brother having received a paper that came over from Italy saying he was of age to attend military service in Italy because he was born there, but he never went back to Italy.

When we went to Strathcona School, I remember Mabel Cairns and her sister, and a Miss Bolton, from which I received a book, *The Lady of the Lake*, for being a very good speller. I had a teacher that was fond of me and things were so tough at home. I remember it was a terrible rainy day, just coming down in buckets and the shoes that I had on my feet were full of holes and I went to school in them and naturally my feet were quite wet. My teacher told me to let my mother know that she would be taking me downtown—it must have been Woodward's, when they were down here on Georgia at Main—and she bought me a pair of shoes and a pair of rubbers. Now when my mother came from Italy, this house must have been rented by English people and they had left cutlery and china. There was a particular butter dish and it was beautiful—cheap crystal I guess, but it had all fluted edges in gold and the cover was beautiful and it had a gold knob on the top. So my poor mother wondered how she could repay the teacher, and she said, "Look, I have never used this, it was here when we came. Take it to the teacher and tell her to take it from me, that I would appreciate it if she did."

My brothers used to deliver the bread with a bicycle to a few spots and

Elda Battistoni Venturato was born in Italy in 1907.

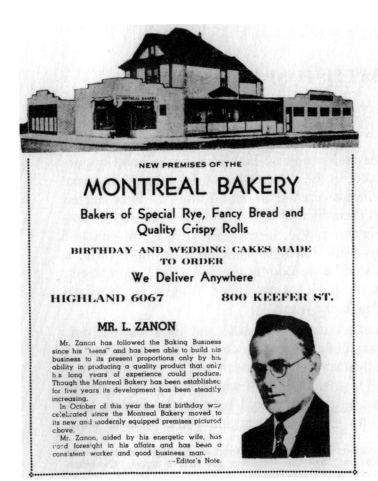

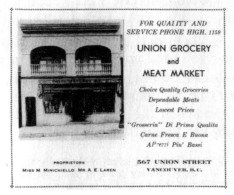

my dad with his horse and wagon would deliver bread to the houses. Then he would pick up his flour, bake those two sacks and then go and sell that and then go and buy another two sacks of flour. That's the way we started out. The bakery was in the back and we had the kitchen and we had a dining room and one other room downstairs and we had bedrooms upstairs and it was an old house and it was very damp and cold. My mother scrubbed the floors with a broom and then buckets of water, rinsing it like that. All the people around here did their floors that way,[27] washed them and rinsed them good and then they just dried on their own. Maybe that brought the dampness also. We had a kitchen stove and we had one of those wood and coal heaters and, I'm telling you, there was plenty of times that we about froze to death because the heat from the dining room could never reach upstairs and the walls at times were full of mould from the dampness. My mother would bring the sheets downstairs and would stand in front of this heater to warm them up thinking they would be warm when we brought them upstairs, but when you crawled into bed it was just like crawling into a bath of water.

There was a store down here on Prior and Jackson, Mr. Omae, the Jap, and he did quite a business with the Italian people, in fact he was learning to speak Italian. After the Japanese evacuation in 1942 I never heard from them anymore. They were good people, very good people. Really, these people that were here were fishermen, they were working hard, they didn't bother anybody. It was pitiful down on Powell Street to see them taking their fridges and all their belongings.

We didn't think the evacuation of the Japanese was right, but we couldn't say too much because it pretty nearly happened to us too. I remember having to go up and report to the Mounties because I had married my husband who had come from Italy in 1922.[28] It was nothing, you just had to go up there and report every month. But the evacuation could have happened to us. Yes, some Italians *were* interned too, at that time. I think a lot of people were kind of afraid that maybe the same thing was going to happen to us that happened to the Japanese here. And then you couldn't get any news from Italy at all. The only news I remember is that my husband lost his father and the news came through the priest.

This neighbourhood is a good place to live. I'm seventy years old now and I can't say that I've ever been bothered by anyone on the street. In fact a lot of my friends say, "My, you're still living down there?" "Well, certainly," I say. "It's my own home and I've been living here all my life and quite a few of my friends are still here." I never did have any idea to move out, I'm quite happy here.

Peter Battistoni

I had an uncle here by the name of Joe and I suppose he said it was a good opportunity here for a bakery. My dad was a baker in the old country so he decided to come. They first started the [Venice] bakery on Princess Avenue, in the 900 block. They started a real small bakery with a metal oven. And then my dad discovered the oven wasn't very good, it didn't turn out the product that he wanted. So, fortunately, through my uncle I suppose, he met this Tony Cianci. He was well known in Vancouver in those days, a man that could speak English fluently. He said he would rent the house on Union Street, 565 Union, and he would build a bakery in the back for my father. Vaglio, on Hastings East, was a bricklayer and they got him to build the oven.

They built a big oven, the one you had to put a fire inside and then wash it out. First you fired your oven and then, after it was hot enough, you could bake three or four batches of bread before you had to fire it again. Basically all European ovens were like that, just one big chamber like an arch. You had a small little wall where you put your wood in, and then the rest of the oven'd be open and the fire would burn in the firebox, and then the flames would shoot over this arch up to the chimney and you'd have to wash out the fine ash dust that would settle on the brick. You used this long paddle that would go right to the end of the oven, and you would put your loaves all in a row. And then you would flip it, and they'd all lay on the brick. It would hold about 240 ordinary square loaves.

Peter Battistoni was born in Vancouver in 1912 of Italian immigrant parents. His father started the Venice Bakery in 1909.

We never used sponge doughs, like most bakeries use. We used a straight dough, like they do in the house, and let it rise a couple of times. A straight dough will give you more flavour and crust, and less keeping qualities. All my dad's working life it was mixed by hand, with his arms. That's where he got the asthma from, inhaling the flour. And if you think that's not hard work—I did it when I was six, seven years old, just helping my dad. I used to have marks on my stomach from trying to lift that stuff, it was just like lifting cement. That's how this baker that worked for us worked and how my dad worked. Always by hand. Everything. The weighing of the bread with a scale, and the shaping—it's quite a procedure, you know. I don't know how my dad did it. And you know he used to bake *and* deliver before he got this man working for him.

I finished public school at twelve years old and I said to my dad, "I'll do the delivery and you stay home," and he said, "You're too small." I weighed fifty-five pounds and when I was delivering bread, the truant officer would give me the devil, ask me why I wasn't in school. So I started delivering [by horse and wagon] and my dad would walk with a basket in the neighbourhood close by and do those customers, but I did the ones a little further.

The first thing I drove was the horse, because I couldn't drive a car. I had so many close shaves with that horse! In fact I used to get heck from the police because I was going faster than the cars. That's true! This horse was a real good horse. She was one of them small Arabian horses that run with their heads down. She wasn't big, but could she go! You didn't have to abuse her, no way, she was always ready to go.

I nearly lost my life three times with that horse. And I felt sorry for her, because she got injured too, you know. Believe it or not, this is true: right in that alley between Union and Georgia, on Heatley there, this fellow had a Model T truck and he was loading manure, and I came down this hill from the opposite side of Heatley where the alley comes down sharp, and then up. I went down full speed and I seen this Ford sticking out of there and I couldn't do nothing, and she knew, she knew she couldn't do nothing either. So she took one big leap and we went right over—the whole thing, with the wagon. Oh boy, you want to see the mess! There was harness and bits of wire, and I don't know how I got out of it alive. Because I could feel the roof of the wagon just pressed down on me on the floorboard, I went down like an accordion. She stopped right by Princess Avenue and she had a bunch of cuts on her, and the guy said, "Look at your wagon!" My two wheels were *this* way [splayed]. She did go right over, the wagon and all. She took one big leap. And the very next day. I came down the same alley and I run into another Model T, but this time I run headfirst into it, and she got a big gash on the side of her face, and that's when I said to my dad, "I'm not going to drive that thing another day."

When our own kids started Strathcona School, they had some of the same teachers that we had. Actually, my favourite teacher, Miss Farrington, was there for forty-three years. When I went to school, she was real young, just out of first year's teaching. We had a party, and I don't know how old we were, but I remember I was trying to make my hair go pompadour and it wouldn't go, it stayed straight up, and they were sure teasing me about that. We had the party at her house, down in the West End, and one of my chums, when they brought the sandwiches—she brought these little teeny sandwiches—so he puts the plate in front of him, that's *his* plate. See, being from the East End we had big meals, you know. And I said, "Those are not all for you. That's for everybody." He said, "What do you mean? I can eat all those."

Bessie Johnston was old when *I* was going to school. She had a very good vision of children that she'd think would make something out of themselves, and she would talk to them and tell them to carry on and that she would be proud of them if they went further in their education. But the teachers were really dedicated, they didn't fool around. They really meant business when they went there. They would take an interest in your home life. If they thought there was something should be investigated, like if a kid played hooky, or there was poverty, or maybe some kid might have thought that he was getting a beating, they would visit the parents. They took an interest in the children in everything, not just the teaching. And when a teacher went to a home, people thought that was really something. She wasn't just an old busybody. They *listened* to her when she asked questions, because she was interested in their children too. And in those days, if you got a strap and you went home, they would say you deserved it and maybe you got another one. I got a good one for no reason at all. They used to chew Picanninny Gum in them days and this kid, he put a whole packet in his mouth. And this Japanese boy was getting up, so he took it out of his mouth and put it on his seat and let him sit down on it. And I burst out laughing, and the teacher said, "What's going on?" and I couldn't stop laughing. I just *couldn't*. She told me to go into the cloakroom and I went, and then, after school, she took out the strap and she gave me fifty of them. She hit me here on my wrist, and boy, it just felt like two lead gloves. And she was only a substitute for the day. But I was more afraid of my teacher, when she come back the next day, because I didn't have my work done. That scared me more than the strap.

When my dad came and all them that came in the area, they stayed and they lived like a community. They were mostly Italians, but there was other nationalities. You come home from school and you could tell what they were cooking, their big pots of borscht, or spaghetti, or gefilte fish, or whatever it was. Everybody seemed to know what they were having for dinner before they got home.

And there was one thing about the community: at nine o'clock you'd hear all the neighbours whistle. Everybody knew their parents' whistle, and then by five after nine there wasn't a kid on the street, they were all home. And the ones that stuck around till ten o'clock, they took them to jail and gave them a good talking-to. It was a curfew, but it was a curfew that was natural. They were all working people, went to bed early, so the kids had to be in. Mind you, there was still kids who got into trouble. Hallowe'en, they used to do a lot of damage. When I had my horse, we had her in a big barn on Prior at Jackson—you could put fifty horses in there. And they would let all the horses go, take all the wagons and throw them over the cliff on Atlantic Street. And the poor Jews'd come the next day for the junk wagons and they're all broken down there.

It's amazing how many junkmen there were. One we called Barba, he had a big beard. And another guy's name was Sam. He used to call the guy with the beard Yeedle, and he used to live up in that apartment where the Omaes' store was. This old cripple would come in the morning and he'd get his leg and turn it and call, "YEE-ee-dle!" They always went together junking. They were always together, and when one of them died he had something like $80,000. And they used to eat stale bread and water and go junking! I couldn't understand a lot of things.

All the kids used to play and get along fine. We used to play "badlam," "shipmen sailors," and "peggy"—that's where you cut a piece of a broom handle and put a point on it and put it in the little hole in the ground. And "mungo sungo," where we used to cut papers, orange wrappers or apple wrappers, cut them in little strips and put them all together like a rose, pull it through these Chinese cents which got a square hole in them. You kick it, you just see how many times you can do that, and you keep going. Kids would be going to school all the way like that.

False Creek Flats would be all slime, sludge, and sewerage. We went skating when it froze over, though. Every year you could count on it. Oh, what a skating area, boy it was *big*! The tide went close to Clark Drive then. And do you know that we used to go swimming down there where the sewer outlet was? We used to call it "Chocolate Pool." And we never got sick. On Prior, where the Fire Department is now, that was the city dump, all tin cans. And just a little ways down the hill there was a cavity there and it was always rust red. I don't know where it came from, maybe the iron of old beds. A girl who lived on Prior fell in that, and my brother tried to save her, and they both drank that stuff. That was enough to kill anybody, and they didn't get sick. And then below was this pond that we used to go on with a raft, two big boards nailed together, and we'd go from one end to the other, chasing these ducks with a slingshot. We never could catch them. And rats, oh hundreds and hundreds of them.

After the war, everybody made wine. And they used to make a wine that was made from raisins, they used to call it "baccaro." These old veterans used to buy that, ten cents a quart or two bits a quart, and go and sit down there by False Creek. You'd see half a dozen rings, and they'd pass this bottle around. I knew about two hundred vets, and the years I was delivering bread, there was none left. They all died, from old injuries, ptomaine poisoning. And canned heat in them days was rampant. The viaduct on Georgia and Main, that's where most of the canned heaters used to go. There was canned heat tins the height of this room packed underneath the viaduct. All the vets, they used to put that through a sock and drink it. That's what killed them, dying from wood alcohol and canned heat and shaving lotion. A man'd fall asleep in the snow, the snow would melt a yard away like a big silhouette around him, you know, and I could see him steaming when I went out to peddle bread. There were a lot of things that were pathetic in a way, and enjoyable in another, you know. There was always two sides to every story.

Every house would have wine, and some Italians had stills. But they didn't make the hard stuff to sell, they made it for their own purpose. That's the way they used to preserve their cherries and grapes. And the best tonic there is: they used to take a herb, "ruda," and put it in this "graspa." Boy, if you had stomach trouble you'd take one little teaspoon of that and it's gone. The grapes came from San Mateo in boxcars, right down on the flats there. That's where we used to pick them up. But the bootlegging was a friendly kind of bootlegging. If you go in a house, they got wine, right? Well, if a stranger comes in, you give him a glass, but you ain't going to give him a gallon every time he comes, so you sell it to him for two bits a glass. And people made extra money that way. Tell you the truth, from Christmas, or two days before, to New Year, some of the loggers would go through $3,000, just throw it away. They'd say, "Give everybody a drink," and they'd have all this money crumpled up like newspaper, hundred-dollar bills, you know. And they'd put a handful on the table and leave it there. This woman I know, she made a fortune. They used to catch her once in a while bootlegging, but she was a widow, she had to make a living. So these loggers would go there and then when it would be New Year they were broke. So they would ask her to lend them the money for the fare, and on their first paycheque they'd send the money down, to pay for getting back to work.

And Hogan's Alley. A shingler lived there for years and years. I always stopped my wagon there and put a loaf of bread up there on a shelf. I think he was English. He always wanted the burnedest loaf you could have in the wagon. But I was delivering there every Monday and almost every Monday you'd find a body. I seen two women dead one day under a barn. One in a garbage can with her feet sticking out. And you'd always find somebody. Now that was a big thing for anybody that lives out of the district. They thought they would drive through there fast with a car, like rich people go to a slums, slumming, yeah. They'd go through there about sixty miles an hour—they're so scared to go through Hogan's Alley. And I used to wonder, "What's wrong with them? There's nothing wrong with this alley." Sure, you find people who are dead, but that's an everyday thing. There was every kind of people there, Hindus and Negroes and white people. And, funny you know, they're all good in a way. They wouldn't steal from you, and if they could give you something, they would. Most of the evil would come from the outside, actually, into this alley looking for something different. Oh, most of the women there

Hogan's Alley, 1939–40, with inset portrait of Carl Marchi, referred to locally as "mayor" of the district.
CITY OF VANCOUVER ARCHIVES, JSMS-NEWSPAPER CLIPPING COLLECTION DOCKET 4206—HOGAN'S ALLEY

were...Gee, there were some women that belonged to society too, because you could tell how they walked, you know, stately. And they would wind up with a coloured fellow or drinking down there. That was, like, "the lowest you can get" is move into Hogan's Alley. And yet people were raising their children there and going to Strathcona School.

Carl Marchi, he lived there. Made his money selling wine. He had a big funeral when he died, because he was quite well known. Me and Carl Marchi were good friends. In fact, he lent me $300 to buy my first car. I couldn't get a nickel from my relatives, not from the bank, nobody, and I go and ask him and he says okay.

Me and my brother, on our bread routes, we had 130 sporting houses. And all around Union Street, there was about seventy. The white slave traffic was really rampant then. They would get young girls that come in from the prairies, or anywhere, to go in for prostitution. That was in Joe Celona's time. Oh, they would bust them, you know. And if they had VD, they would get six months' jail. They had to have a certificate that they were free from disease. But they knew when they were going to get busted, somebody would tip them off, and they'd close up for a week when there was a little bit of a stink about it. When we were kids, we'd go down a street, and we *knew*, because when you're born in the East End, you learn everything.

In the old days, my dad and his friends would get on an old truck, four or five of them, and play music down Granville Street and Hastings Street on Sunday evening, just for a lark. And they used to sound good. They'd play all the Italian songs. There was lots of pep to it, maybe with a guitar, a mandolin, an accordion, and Dad's clarinet and a trumpet.

And I remember it did something for people when they were walking down the streets. For many years after, they would gather, one week at one neighbour, and one week at another neighbour, and just enjoy their Saturday and Sunday like that. There was quite a few musicians in the neighbourhood. And the women, they sure could sing. I don't know where they learned, but they sure could sing in harmony. I remember once on Georgia Street they were singing, and it seemed to come and go just like the wind.

Easter was the biggest celebration. You'd colour eggs, visit each other, and go to church, and everybody seemed to be in a festive mood, I think even more so than Christmas. You could feel it in the air, it was really something to look forward to. Everybody would make those "focaccia," the Easter bread like the Russians and Ukrainians make. Some would put those little coloured candies on. The youngsters would put a hard-boiled egg, a coloured egg against the wall, stand it up and try to throw a penny into it. If it stuck there you took all the eggs that were laying against the wall. And they used to make a kind of twisted little bread out of butter, a kind of bread stick called "grissini"—boy, were they good! You could feel the holiday in the air. Everybody would be walking and smiling and laughing and singing. It just made you feel good inside, you know, something like it wasn't even true, like a dream.

At Easter, people dressed in the best they had. My uncle, he was a dresser—oh man, that guy had white pants with stripes, and a black jacket, carnation. He used to be the Adolphe Menjou of Vancouver, he was always known for his clothing. He had a tailor shop on Main Street, next to London Drugs at Union, and he used to keep all the loggers' and miners' clothes in his store. When they come down, they'd just go to the store and pick up their suits. He had about two hundred suits in there at one time. They wouldn't know where to keep their suits, it would be no good to keep them in a suitcase, because they would ruin them, you know. So they'd be all hung up in the covered glass case against the wall.

Then the Depression came, that was really bad. You see, my dad was making bread but he couldn't collect enough to buy flour. So what are you going to do? Go on? He had to, he couldn't quit. Fortunately, next door was a grocery store, and this Minichiello, he would let my dad have a sack of flour. My dad would use that, maybe make 130 loaves of bread and go out and sell it. And then one Christmas, just on Christmas Eve, my dad didn't have a dime, and they didn't know what to do. So in walks this fellow who had a store on Georgia and Main, where Woodward's used to be—his name was Crosetti, paid my dad ninety dollars. Boy, what a bonanza! So my mother went out shopping till three o'clock in the morning, the stores were open, you know, and bought some satin candies, coconut candies, and oranges and apples and candy canes. And you know, that was the biggest Christmas present I ever got.

Christmas Day 1929, my mother was run over by a big milk truck and she lost one leg and the other one was all skin grafts. She was in the hospital for nine months and when she came home my dad died shortly after. He had become quite sickly with asthma several years before. He was only forty-eight when he died, and I was quite heartbroken. My neighbour next door, by the name of Sam Minichiello, seeing our circumstances, came to me and says, "Well, you'll just have to knuckle up. You're the man of the house now." So I carried on for a short time with the old oven, and then he moved from Princess Street to Union Street, right across from where we had our old bakery. Well, I talked it over with my mother. We didn't have no collateral, no money, and all we ever had was the horse and wagon. But we said, "We'd like to have that house, you know, but we can't move because we haven't got a bakery." He says, "Well, I'll put up a bakery for you in the back of the house and I'll pay for it and you can pay as rent." I thought that was really good. And this baker that had worked for my dad, Enoch Benson, he used to do everything, right from the beginning to the end, all by himself, same as my dad. So he stayed with me.

In the meantime we were building this other shop. I designed it. I never knew a blueprint but I knew what I wanted. It was only a twenty-five-foot lot by about sixty and I had to find room for the dough table, for the oven, and where to mix the dough. Steam boiler went in the middle of the oven, there was no other place to put it, and I figured where I was going to put my truck. I took the plans to my neighbour who knew how to do blueprints and he put it to the measurements. The contractor was a good man. He built that place, not counting the oven, the oven was separate, for $1,500. And when my baker moved in there, he thought he was a king. But we never made no money, you know. The only reason we stayed in business was because we didn't have to pay our labour. We'd all pull together.

After we quit delivering house to house, and I think we were the first of the bakers to quit the retail trade and go wholesale—we got our army call, the four of us at once. I wanted my mother to say, "Let's close her down. When it's all over, we'll start up again." And she wouldn't do that. The army didn't take me and they didn't take my other brother, but they took the two young ones. So we

Peter Battistoni at work in the Venice Bakery. PETER BATTISTONI COLLECTION, COURTESY OF ROYAL BC MUSEUM, BC ARCHIVES

carried on. It was getting difficult: we couldn't get bakers and we couldn't get tires or nothing, so we were left with one truck, we were using all the parts from the other one. Finally, I did close her down for a while. But even when we went wholesale, from all over, every Sunday, people would come down and pick up a few loaves. They'd just walk into the back alley and holler, "I'm here, give me two loaves of bread." There were hotel owners and businessmen and old friends, and they'd drive for twenty miles for a loaf of that bread.[29]

JOHN CROSETTI

Our store was up on Main Street where Tosi's is now. Later, we moved in the corner where Woodward's store used to be, at Georgia and Main. Tosi moved to where we used to be before and of course he was wholesale *and* retail, and we used to buy wholesale from him but we couldn't compete with him.

I was about thirteen, fourteen years old when I first started delivering [groceries] with the horse and wagon. We stabled the horse on Georgia Street,

John Crosetti was born on Vancouver Island in 1903 of Italian immigrant parents. His father worked as a coal miner. After he was in a serious mining accident, the family moved to Vancouver and started the Europe Grocery store on Main Street.

the stable is there yet, just before you get to Gore Avenue there. Another big stable used to be on Keefer Street, just down from the Stratford Hotel, about four storeys—that used to be wagons and horses. It's still there but it's a Chinese vegetable place now.

MacLean Park, where the tenement housing is now,[30] had a bandstand in the middle and we used to play cricket, baseball, and things like that. Of course it used to be a ball park years before, and then they made it MacLean Park. Used to have a track to run around, like on Columbus Day we'd have sports and the big race around the city, down Main, up to Twelfth Avenue, around Grandview, a marathon race. It was a very entertaining thing, and then the big dance at night.

Oh, we used to have wonderful dances. We used to go to the O'Brien Hall, at the corner of Homer and Hastings. Used to be O'Brien, then we took it over, the Italians, and we renamed it the Majestic Hall. We had banquets in a great big room in the back and after the dance we'd go to our banquet. We always had somebody there, the mayor or something, or Hon. H.H. Stevens—he used to be there too.

We did Charleston dancing and all that. My sister and I would get up and we used to do the Charleston, the two of us. We used to be crazy for that in those days!

The Empress Theatre was right on Hastings at Gore, right on the corner. Used to be a stock company with wonderful shows, oh wonderful shows they used to have. There were three floors, we used to go up to the gods, it was twenty-five cents to go on up there way at the top. The Avenue Theatre was across from the Cobalt Hotel on Main, and across from that was the Imperial Theatre. I was on the stage one time, a circus thing, and they gave me a costume and I walked on my hands with my feet sticking up in the air. That was the Imperial, it's still there yet. But the Avenue, they tore that down.

When we had our store for a while right behind the Imperial on the lane, we used to play there as kids in the alley. We lived right behind the store, you see. All the kids used to play lacrosse. There were some big players from around here, Mario Crema, Durante, Jack Green, they were good players. It was played right in the alleys, they had the end of a bedstead and they would shoot at it. Then they had their club and they had a field they used to practise on.

Down on False Creek it used to be all water there and we used to skate there. Ponds, you know. And we had rafts when we were kids—there was always some logs sitting around. We used poles, just poles, pushed ourselves up and down. Oh yes, it was a great place to play in because when you went further, there was a lot of water. That was all dredged in there. Do you know where the Ivanhoe Hotel is on Main Street? Used to be a bridge there. The tidal water would come around from English Bay and down round Prior Street. The north side was sawmills. The tidal water used to go way down past Clark Drive and way over to the other side, up against China Creek there.

John Crosetti in the kitchen of his home on Heatley Avenue, 1977. TOD GREENAWAY PHOTO

Used to be a big bank there and it looked like coal, near China Creek Park. We'd walk all the way around. There was a big orchard over there and we'd go with bags and steal the apples when we were kids.

This side, the water would come right to Union Street [in a low area near the foot of Hawks]. It was a swamp there, that's where they put the trestle in [on Venables] for the interurban cars. False Creek was all dirty water, mud-like, black, muddy. [Where Vancouver's No. 1 Firehall is] used to be the city dump, then they started filling it in. The place was infested with rats. We used to go down and try to kill them but we never got them. Then after a while, the mushrooms came up and all the people round here, in the morning you could see them down there picking mushrooms, those nice little white ones, they'd bring them home and cook them. There were two kinds I picked—one was the cluster ones, flat-like, but kind of hard. Some were big plants, eight to ten inches high, but pretty hard to find. The ones that came in clusters, you used to dream about at night when you went to bed, that you'd step on them.

The Imperial Theatre, 724 Main Street, about 1915. After some time as an auto salvage company and eventually reopening as a theatre, a residential apartment building stands here today. STUART THOMSON PHOTO, VANCOUVER PUBLIC LIBRARY, VPL 11032

I watched them building the Canadian National train station. It was built on piles, I guess rock bottom was too far down. False Creek was drained then, they had sewers, great big sewer pipes the size of a whole room. That was sand around the station that was built there—and the Great Northern station too. The water came right to Keefer Street near Columbia, like a little inlet.[31] Well, the trestle was just the other side, and we used to go swimming down the other side of the trestle there, even though the water was dirty.

There used to be coloured places around then—and Sid Beech's over on Robson Street, he used to make wonderful tamales. And there was Old Man Price, he used to make tamales and he used to have a wagon and go around the beer parlours and sell them. He was just the same kind of character as old Joe Fortes at English Bay, oh a very nice gentleman. Oh there was different coloured people around—they used to call one Brown Bread, and when the BC Electric's observation car came around, old Ted Lyons used to wait for the coloured people to come around, and Brown Bread would get up and she'd dance. Everybody'd get up there and laugh. There was some good characters around. One used to beg all the time. She didn't have to go and beg, she was an old lady, and she always used to say, "Oh I'm going to faint, I'm going to faint!" Always somebody would grab her and she'd say, "Have you got two bits?" The kids would go and look at her and say, "Oh look, she's fainting again."

Before the old Georgia Viaduct was built [opened July 1, 1915], there used to be the red-light district behind the Main Hotel there. And on Alexander Street, some of the big buildings are still there yet, that was the red-light district that was in the high class. And Hogan's Alley was down this alley here [between Prior and Union], right off Main Street. Oh, they were all drunks. As kids we played around there, we didn't worry about it.

The only [killing] I remember was up here on Georgia Street. The house is still there yet. A boy was shot to death, this coloured man committed suicide, and the detective lost his eye. I can remember because we were hiding behind a post down by MacLean Park, and the police were all around. He took a shot and killed this young boy, his name was Rob I think. He just lived right close and he was across the street. The coloured man—I think he was staying with a white woman. The landlord went up for rent or something and she said to get the dickens out, so they went back with this detective. And he wouldn't come out. He shot at Detective Cameron—he lost his eye—and he killed the boy, and he committed suicide himself.[32] We went up and looked in the room after, you could see everything was all blood all over the place. This was when we were kids going to school.

The circus used to come in at the Great Northern down along the side here and we used to wait in the morning, you know kids, stay up at night and wait to see them unload. You'd see all the elephants coming off, and the horses and all. They used to have a parade first, parading down Hastings, Main Street. They had all their wagons with the animals in and the men on top playing bands. Ringling Brothers, Clyde Beatty, Barnum and Bailey, all the circuses used to come here. It was a great big tent, and there was all these coloured people, they would just put the pegs up and push them into the ground—they used the sledgehammers and down they would go, then they'd raise the thing up with the poles in the middle. There used to be three rings and you brought your own seats. When they were leaving town, you'd stay up at night time to watch them reload again.

All you'd see around this neighbourhood then was the grapes. Everybody would be making wine. I used to make it myself, I used to make about forty gallons, then my mother would get after me, you know. My brother and I used to go and chop wood in the garage and we'd take a couple of bottles of wine and we'd get in there drinking—used to be we couldn't carry the wood up the steps!

During the Depression, our store was on Georgia Street. Mother and Father had a lot of money out, couldn't pay their bills, my father used to give

Reverend Andrew Roddan of First United Church with makeshift cookhouse, offering relief to unemployed men in the "jungle" at the city dump on False Creek Flats, 1931. W. J. MOORE PHOTO, CITY OF VANCOUVER ARCHIVES, RE N7

credit, credit, credit, so then he went bankrupt. Those were bad days then. Kelly Douglas started him up in business again and then we moved over to Woodward's old place. Later it was my mother and I—you see, my father had died then and we couldn't manage it all, so I said, "Oh close up the darn store and I'll go out to work."

Reverend Roddan's church [First United] at the corner of Hastings and Gore helped the poor people all the time. He used to give speeches, like on a Sunday after the church service. They had a big auditorium there and then his office used to be in the back. He helped the poor a lot, helped them with food and all that.[33] He was a very good man, good speaker too, and every Sunday he used to have his program on the radio. He stuck up for the poor all the time, like when they had the jungle, he used to come over to see the boys there. They weren't being ignored, people were helping them all along. But gee, it was an awful-looking place down there. Oh it was terrible in those days. But they conducted themselves pretty good. People seemed to get along, you know. I used to see people on relief come into my parents' store and sometimes my father would say, "Well, you haven't got enough, so wait till your next relief ticket comes in."

NORA HENDRIX

Nora Hendrix was born in Knoxville, Tennessee, in 1883. She came to Vancouver in 1911 via Chicago and Seattle. One of her grandchildren, Jimi Hendrix, became a noted musician in the 1960s.

When I came there was no church. What few coloured people were here had some kind of little club, you know, that they used to gather and have a little affair, like, meeting and singing and whatever they did. They used to have it down on Homer Street, was a hall there, they had that going when I came here. Them fine years different people was coming from Alberta. There wasn't very many come direct from the States like I come, right just crow-flying like that. Of course, there used to be different little people, missionaries, come through, but they'd always get some little store place or something, you know, rent it, and have a little church or something like that. But nobody had ventured out to try and get a church for their own. They commence getting together, say, "Well, we should get a church of our own." Yeah. "Ain't got any other business of our own, so got to get a church anyway, if nothing else."

So, let me see, it could be back in 1918, as far as I can think back, when we first taken that church over on Jackson Avenue. I don't know who had it before,[34] but when we saw that we could be able to get this church, well everyone then started in, working together. All the families and everybody that wanted a church, we all got together, and commence working for it to get this church started. And some of the men, they intercede and got ahold to the high-ups in the States, and they always from the States, we got all our preachers and residing elders all come from over in the States. That's where the head office of that church was, the A.M.E. [American Methodist Episcopal Church] it was called. So then we got together and so they said, "Well, if you raise $500, we'll raise $500." So all of the sisters and brothers and everyone, we commence getting busy then, to start to having entertainments and bazaars and suppers and everything we could have, to raise the money to buy this church. So when we worked around and got our share of money together, well, they let the residing elder know that we was ready, and so they came over and then set up our church, so then we had our own church then. So it was $1,000 we had to pay down. Getting dollars together them days was hard. When you went out to work, all you got was a dollar and a half for your day's work. And your carfare. That's what you got in them days. So, you see it taken us a little while to raise up $500.

Nora Hendrix, 1977. TOD GREENAWAY PHOTO

I think Reverend [Ulysses S.] Robinson come from the east of the States, the first reverend we had here to work in our church. Then after six years we commenced getting different preachers every year pretty well, after he was here. And we had a Reverend [J.W.] Wright. He was here for quite a while, he was a kind of settled man. He was a good preacher. Well I finally, after a while, after years going by, well, I kind of pulled myself out and of course, a lot of my old friends had gone. After the younger bunch came in the church and commence working, well I said, "I'll let these young people take it over now, and I'll just get on out and kind of rest myself. Let *them* run it."

Of course, you see, we was supposed to *pay* the preacher, he isn't supposed to do any work at all, he don't have to. But most of the preachers we had that come here, they all were pretty handy, they'd do things around the church, you know, if they see something to be done. Sweep up, if it happened to be we didn't have no regular janitor or nothing. So we always was kind of lucky to have good preachers, that would do anything that was around.

We used to go around and sing. There was one musical man come here, named Bartley. He came here and got about fifty of us and got a big choir, and we used to go around and sing in all different theatres or churches. I guess that was in the twenties, all in the twenties where we put on all these singsongs. And the old Avenue Theatre, I think we sang in that with our choir.

On American Thanksgiving the church used to always have a big turkey dinner on that day and then other nights we used to have the chitlin dinners. Them chitlin suppers—we'd sell out so fast, why, they wouldn't last no time. You see, 'most all those sporting people, they like that kind of food. We often wished we could have got more, you know, but you couldn't always get the amount you wanted, and when they cooked down, you see, they cooked down so small. There were chitlins and corn bread—that had to go along with it—and with the cabbage slaw and whatever other things we'd put with it. But we'd sell it so fast, oh, make your head spin. Just put the word out. Somebody'd just go around down in the district where all the sporting fellows and what not, and tell them the sisters going to have chitlin dinner over at such and such a place. Why they'd be there setting in the hall. If they didn't come eat it, they'd send plates and buckets and things to take it out, and then you'd turn around in a little while they're all gone, just like that. Ah! You can't buy no chitlins now. No, they run out of chitlins, I don't know how many years back.

Well, we used to have a minstrel show around here that this club put on every year, for about five or six years there in the thirties. I didn't belong to it, but I used to be in the minstrel show every year with them. Mrs. Pryor was the head of that and this girl Chaney-belle. It was only fifteen belonged to this club, but one year, Mrs. Pryor said to me, she says, "Next year, Mrs. Hendrix, I want you to be in our minstrel show." I said, "All right, I'll be in it." So the next year come and when they got ready to do the rehearsing and the piano, well, she let me know. So I went to the rehearsal and get lined out what I was going to do, because I was going to be one of the end men. You would crack jokes to the interlocutor—he's the interlocutor that's sitting in the middle there, you know, the dressed-up guy. And of course, we the funny guys on the end and we ask all kinds of funny questions, you know, and say, "What made the chicken cross the street?" Well, any old funny something, any old thing. 'Course, we had it all lined up. We done practised it, you know, when we went to rehearsal, we done rehearsed and had all of them. Then we had to sing songs, too, in between, and then the whole bunch would sing. Oh, all the people used to enjoy that, and they'd fill up that hall. I kind of missed it myself, when they give up.

Down in the 200- and 300-block Prior and Union and Keefer is where most all these chicken places were. Mrs. Pryor had a eating place on Keefer [Chicken Inn] and then there was a Mrs. Alexander had one on Union Street [Mother's Tamale and Chili Parlour] and there was Mr. Soldier Williams [Martin Luther Williams], he had one that used to be a funeral parlour. Well, there used to be different fellows around down on Prior Street and Keefer Street that had little clubhouses and things like that, years back in the twenties and the thirties. George Paris used to teach the policemen to box, and of course, he used to be around Mrs. Pryor's place a good deal. He'd be around there for any disturbance, or anything that come up, he could be around there, you know, to look after, like, bouncing a fellow, I guess. He's pretty good size, yeah, and he didn't wear no hair on his head, and his head was skinny. Yeah, kept his head bald. That's the first place I saw him was around Mrs. Pryor's. And as I say, Dode Jones, he had some kind of club. And this Mr. Holman, I think he had a club, too. And Buddy White. They was all around down in that category, close to Main Street. The railroad fellows'd go down them places you know, play their games and gamble and whatever, like men like to. And 'course, oh yeah, the city and the mayor and them know a lot where all the different places was. That's why they could keep things so straight, like, 'cause if the railroad men come in, they know just where to go if they want to play their games, and gamble, go right to these places, as though they were right there for them. So that's why I say, that they could keep all the different things in the spots where they supposed to be. And they wasn't a whole lot of carryings on, nor a whole lot of fighting going on.

Everybody liked Mayor [L.D.] Taylor [mayor of Vancouver, 1910–11, 1915, 1925–28, 1931–34], 'cause he was one of those kind of plain man, he looked like he was for everybody. And he had the town fixed so that the sporting people lived in one part of the town and the other class of people live in another. He had them all separated. And they had a red-light district, you see? That was what a lot of people liked about Taylor, having this red-light district, because it did help to keep the people, you know, the what-you-m'a-call women was all in this one category. And when the boats come in, when those fellows want to go somewhere for a good time, well they knew where to go. See, they'd go to this street in this neighbourhood, 'cause it was all set for them. And the women had these houses and they had these girls in there and they had doctors that looked after them and all that, you see. All that was when Taylor was in.

Then the Chinese used to have their gambling, playing their lottery, and everybody'd want to play it. A lot of people—it was a dime—and sometime they get eighteen dollars, just all according to the way they marked the ticket. Well a lot of guys that didn't work or didn't want to work, why they just spend ten or twenty cents and they'd have something to live on again, then they'd always keep a ticket in there, so they didn't have to beg, you see. Sometimes a law used to come around and pinch them, because the law would get money out of them, because they'd take them in and fine them so much. If you happened to be caught in this place when they come get the head man, and you happened to be in and the law grab them and grab you, and take you downtown or wherever they take you, well, the Chinaman, he paid the fines for everybody and they go. And he's home, he gone and go on back to his little place and start all over again. Yeah! Got right back and the people would be *waiting* there to come in!

Chinatown was just a real dull place then. It wasn't built up and lights all around like it is now. I used to go down there lots to buy different things, especially when I want to get some black-eyed peas. Oh yes, I used to go down there and trade, sure. But sometimes, some of the Chinese would look at you so funny, you feel kind of funny when they look at you. 'Course, I couldn't blame them for looking. That's what their eyes was for.

The people, they didn't bother you on the streets like they do now. You could walk all around and didn't nobody bother you. Men wasn't grabbing women and all that stuff. 'Cause a man coming out of the woods or something, well he'd know where to go. He didn't have to bother you or any other lady walking up and down the street. No. It was a good thing to have that red-light district. I know a lady and her daughter used to do the washing for the girls that worked in them houses, and they made all kinds of money washing them women's clothes. Them girls didn't have to do nothing. They had people, maids, to come clean up the house and all that. There was a lot of coloured girls that used to love to go there to work, 'cause it was good money. Sure. Go there and cook. I know a lady who cooked there and she made a thousand dollars, in a little while, and she sent back to the States and brought her family here. Yeah. A woman that's looking for a job, to cook or to clean up, that's where you could make your money. And nobody'd bother you. 'Cause the men that come in there, they wouldn't bother *you*, you were just a working woman around there.

Most of the men worked on the railroad. Except only those that worked in the buildings downtown, down in the big buildings, they had coloured men janitors down in there. I know one man, Mr. Wallace, he was a kind of overseer. Well, he was a little bit richer than the rest of us, and 'course he had a job of overseeing, getting men to go around and do the janitor work, you know. Like they give him the job to go to get the help for these different buildings, you see, and he'd get the men to do the janitor work and the cleaning up. He worked some, but he didn't have to, because he'd have all these men that, work under him like.

It was hard for coloured men to get just the ordinary jobs. One year my husband was supposed to get a job working in a gents' restroom but when that policeman got shot, there's a lot of stuff come up, and he didn't get the job. There were this coloured fellow and this sporting woman who was a friend. Marjorie Earl, her name was. And all the policemens liked this woman too. 'Course, she run around with anybody, and this sporting fellow, this coloured boy, she was friends with him. And this policeman, he jumped on the car when they come in from the racetrack and raised the devil, and one of these policemen got shot. Well, they blamed this coloured fellow, and they send him to jail. But they said that they didn't find no gun on him.[35] Everybody was all mad about this coloured boy shooting a policeman. Well, you know, that put a damper on where the coloured boys were working in different places, it made it hard for them, they want to bar them out. So then my husband didn't get this job. There was some excuse.

The few families that lived here, they had certain kind of jobs. There wasn't a whole lot of shoeshining stands, because the Italians had a lot of those. Oh the Italians, leave it to them, brother. They come in here and they commence to getting rich, I'm telling you. 'Cause they had all the streetcars running and the streets had to be fixed, and the Italians would do all that work. They had a night shift, day shift work on them streets, and keep men all night working. They'd be out there, working like sixty. Oh yeah. I think the Italians had the taxis, too. 'Cause they was pretty smart, when they arrived here. They got busy and commence building up their part. Yeah. Like I used to tease a friend of mine when we'd go into the bootlegger's. I says, "You see all them nice carpets and things we're walking over? You helped to buy them," I said. "You helped to buy them a good solid carpet that you go way down in you can't hear you walk. You helped to buy it. And don't say a word," I says.

MYER FREEDMAN

My father and my family came here because of the terrible pogroms that took place in Europe, and they just felt there was no future there, and thank God they did or I wouldn't be alive. In our village where I was born, on the border between Poland and Russia, there are no Jews left, period. They've all been killed off because the succeeding wars just travelled all over that area.

Dad came here in 1910, and brought my mother and me here in 1914. He never did really learn to speak English well, 'cause he immediately had to make a living and try and get enough money to bring his family over. And the only means that he could was by being a peddler. So my two uncles who preceded him here, two uncles and an aunt, pooled their resources and bought him a horse and a wagon for something like forty dollars and he went out peddling and meagrely put together enough money so that he could bring us out here four years later. Then he opened a second-hand store, after I had been here about three years—I remember distinctly the time 'cause I went out on his horse and wagon with him.

Some of the early Jewish pioneers lived near Georgia and Keefer, in the 5, 6, and 700 blocks. The neighbourhood was an orthodox community. The Schara Tzedeck Synagogue had not been built yet.[36] We used to hold services, to my earliest recollection, in a rented store on Union Street. Then a movement was made to buy a building of our own, and it still exists, on Heatley and Pender, and that served as a synagogue for quite a while.

You can see the original ark today in the synagogue at 19th and Oak. It was moved from the older place and placed in an encasing. It was made of a very precious wood, seems to me it was kind of a hardwood, and built in traditional European style with lions engraved into it. The altar was all turned wood and of course, they placed some emphasis on it, but even more, they use a hanging curtain over the ark shielding off the holy Torahs. And all the women of the congregation used to make those by hand and they were kind of ornately done. The synagogue itself had hard pews, there were no cushions on the seats, and the acoustics weren't that great. The poor cantor used to have to shout his lungs out to be heard, there were no microphones. The first building, the small one, couldn't have seated more than ninety people. But then the second one seated something like three hundred and that was with the balcony, that was really supposed to be big and super.

We had our Hebrew School, an after-hours type of a school for extra-curricular learning of language. I went to Strathcona School in the daytime, then always put in two hours in the late afternoon, five days a week and Sunday, in that particular building. The first building is the one that's on the lane and it faces Heatley Avenue. That was the original synagogue which later became our school. When we were using the [store as a] synagogue on Union Street, we had a Hebrew school in an old store at the corner of Jackson

Myer Freedman was born in Poland in 1910. He came to Canada in 1914.

Avenue and Georgia, and the kosher butcher shop was just about three or four doors away from that particular spot. My first Hebrew schoolteacher was Dr. Narod, the chiropodist, who became a dear friend of mine.

Rabbi Pastinsky was just a gem.[37] One in a million. And a very dedicated person who came here from the east, and he just fell in love with our community and they fell in love with him. When Rabbi Pastinsky passed away of diabetes at about the real age of sixty-one, he was an old man—he was eighty years old—because he had worked day and night for the community. He was everything. He was our spiritual adviser, he was a cantor of a synagogue, he was our immigration officer. If Jews arrived here without passports, as sometimes they had to do to escape, or if they had any problems at all, he would go down and personally guarantee to the Immigration Department that this person would be a good citizen and would seek citizenship within two years, and he always followed it up. When Jewish folks had trouble with the courts and they did, we had our miscreants—not too many, thank goodness, but we had them—but if Rabbi Pastinsky appeared in court on behalf of anybody and said, "You can probate them in my hands," the judge never refused it. And he attended to all circumcisions, Bar Mitzvahs, and things of this nature. He was just a one-man everything in our community. Of all the people who I was brought up with, he was just Mister Jewish Community.

I used to help out a couple of my uncles in their stores sometimes in my time off. I had a favourite one because he was such a fine character and he *was* a character of the early city of Vancouver. His name was Maurice Goldberg. He opened his establishment around 1898 on the corner of Cordova and Carrall Streets and it was called the White House Clothing Company. It was a double-fronted store, it must have been seventy-five feet in width. It was an old-fashioned type of store designed to provide clothing for miners, loggers, fishermen—strictly that kind of a trade. He heated it with a big, round cast-iron stove, and in the winter, you couldn't stand near the stove but you froze if you were twenty-five feet away. A large part of his merchandise was hanging from the ceiling. He would get suspenders in, or handkerchiefs, or whatever it might be, and one of the things I got paid for was to take a needle and thread and run it through all these in such a fashion that it was all tied together and strung from the ceiling. If a man came along and picked out a couple of these big red or blue handkerchiefs, white spotted, that the train men used to like, he would reach up and yank one down and the thread would break.

People helped each other out without signing notes and interest and covenants. My dad's main business was a very large store at 625 Main. It was about 50 feet and went back to the lane, 120 feet, and had a lot of space. So he started to deal largely in supplies for logging camps. In those days, there were a lot of gyppo loggers who were working shows up and down the coastline. They would go to the government and lease an area to be logged. Individuals would do it, with maybe ten men and a cook. They'd come in and see my dad in the springtime and say, "I want an outfit for ten men," or twenty

Myer Freedman in his shoe salon on Granville Street, 1978. TOD GREENAWAY PHOTO

men, or whatever it might be. Dad would have big cast-iron cookstoves and dishes that were such heavy crockery you could throw them on the floor and they wouldn't break, and cutlery, silverware, blankets and camp-cot beds—this sort of thing. He would gather it all up and they would look at it and they would make deals to the value of it, and *never* sign a piece of paper. He would say to Dad, "Well, get it down to the ferry dock, such and such a day." Dad would have a hired hand working for him who crated it all, made a list of it, put the list in the crates—I used to help him do this—and they would ship it up to this logging camp. Sure enough, in September or October, this all would be shipped back to us, badly wrecked up, some dishes and cutlery missing. Poor Mother would go through and count it all, and Dad would look at the stove, figure out what it would cost to repair it and put it back into good shape, and note whatever was missing. A week later, the logger would walk in with a pocketful of money and the two of them would fight and argue for all of maybe fifteen minutes about how much he was going to pay for the damage done and for the use of it and how much Dad was to pay for taking it all back. You'd think that they were mortal enemies at the time that they were arguing about all this. And then he would peel off this money, pay Dad in cash, shake hands and, "I'll see you again in March" and walk out. And sure enough, March he'd come back.

I think that the most trustworthy people then were Chinese. They would come in, they would be very cautious—tough buyers, you know, you'd have to work with them. But just the same, their word was the greatest. I had an admiration for them. They had a great respect for my father. My father was an extremely religious man—in our religion and tradition, he would not open his business on Saturdays, as many Jewish folks didn't. Yet Saturday was the busiest day on the street, really. His Chinese clients were the most faithful, they knew that he was closed on Saturday so they'd come in Monday or Tuesday, and they would never deal anywhere else.

Family life was very close, and all the Italian kids had closeness to their families, the Jewish folks were extremely close to their parents, and Japanese were a very close-knit group, and I think that the Chinese community was absolutely exemplary. I made close friends with them, I used to go out to the store and help my dad, and most of his clients were this group of people when he had the second-hand store. The Yip family, the Louies, the Wongs, lived in some of the rooming houses, that was their homes in those days. I helped Dad deliver furniture and they patted me on the head, the seniors—they were just wonderful people.

You didn't have the automobile traffic that you have now. It was mostly horse and wagon. The sounds I could hear would be the beautiful Percheron horses that would deliver milk and dairy products. The drivers took great pride in those animals, and they used to just go around the city. So you'd hear these horses clip-clopping down the street, and the streets were then paved with wooden blocks to accommodate the hooves of those beautiful animals.

And later, an automobile was a noisy contraption—the motors really chug-chugged along. If they went twenty-five miles an hour, that was an enormous speed. They were noisy, and milk bottles were lifted on heavy crates and you'd hear them jangling along.

Just below Keefer and Main was a very famous blacksmith shop. And horses, of course, had to have shoes put on, and carts and wagons and everything else had to have repairs done to their springs and wheels. But he would park his work outside on the street—all the gigs and the wagons and whatnot. The doors were wide open because the men couldn't work in the intense heat that they had fired up in these kilns. People wouldn't bare themselves in those days, but they had light shirts on and they sweated profusely as they worked there.

Liquor was a big crime then. I can't remember what years the Prohibition days were on [1917–21] but it was quite a going deal and part of the crime that went on was from that particular area. There was quite a bit of prostitution. For a while I delivered for a drugstore and the red-light district then was down on Alexander Street, and of course I took some of their supplies in my deliveries to that area. The police condoned it because of all the sailors off the waterfront—it was a home for them. And I use that word kindly, in a way. They'd go in and they'd say, "Hi, Dorothy," or "Hi, Mary," or whatever it is, "I'm back in town." And they'd get a cup of coffee and something and have a chat, and it was a place to meet and talk to their buddies, and it was a different atmosphere entirely.

There was a lot of opium being smoked in Chinatown. Dad and I would deliver furniture and the minute you opened the door you could smell the sweet smell of opium. And there was some cocaine being sniffed, if you want to use that term, among the fast crowd. I don't think, from my pharmacy background and from what I saw in those days, that those two drugs were greatly harmful. The old Chinese fellows used to sit around, drowsy-like, in a sunny sleep, and you would see them quite often. When they were told by the leaders of their community and by the police that this was illegal and they were going to go to jail for it—and some were jailed for it—then the community gave up that particular drug action almost en masse. And I think the gang that were sniffing cocaine, or "snow" as they call it in their vernacular, were not addicted to it the way we know modern narcotic addiction. So I think it was no different in their minds than drinking liquor. In fact, I think alcohol was worse because there were a lot of alcoholics.

Chickens were killed by the rabbi and my mother would go down and pick up her own live chickens in Chinatown. All our neighbours bought chickens live. Nobody trusted anybody else to give you the animal dead. It had to be fresh in those days. I can remember Mother blowing the feathers and having a look to see whether there was enough fat on the chicken because they would use everything they could from the animal. Then she would take it to the *shochet* and have the chicken killed and she would take it home and open the entrails. The women were trained that, if anything didn't look right in the entrails of the chicken, they were to take it to the rabbi who was trained in discerning whether a chicken was edible under Jewish law. Inedible being if there were spots on the liver or entrails or if there were things showing up where the chicken may have been diseased. I can remember plucking chickens in the early days, then Mother would open it up and render the fat and that was used as part of the cooking, the chicken fat itself. And the legs and other portions, gizzards, neck, would be used to make soups with. Nothing was left unused.

We always had at least three barrels on our back porch, one of which would have cabbage in it maturing to sauerkraut, and the other would have pickles going and as the fresh batches of pickles came around, we'd get rid of the old ones and put fresh batches in. And some kind of a wine percolating in the third one. The Jewish women, at certain times of the year, instead of making sauerkraut, would make cabbage for borsht, and this was part of home. Back porches were big then. They would have the old washing machines and I can remember even helping Mother heat the water on a coal and wood stove and pouring it into the washing machine so that she could wash the daily clothes on a scrub board, wring them out and string them on the lines.

We never locked our doors. I'd come home from school and I can't remember ever using a key to get in. You know, the house was open and if a woman wanted some flour or something or other, she would walk in and get it, and tell my mother that night, "I borrowed this from you," and return it. I just wish those days would come back, when people had trust and there was honesty all around us. We were poor as hell but we enjoyed life.

MARY TROCELL VELJACIC

For most emigrants, it was their economic situation that led them to leave, but I don't think it was for my parents. My father's people were landowners, and my mother's people also had a lot of property. My mother and her sisters went through business college—in those days already. But you see, Croatia and Slovenia were under Austrian rule and that's what they would talk about when they would discuss why they left the old country.

My father came to the United States, then to Canada in 1906, with friends. In those days, usually three or four up to a group of ten would leave. You see, in our part of the country, especially the coastline, they always talk about British Columbia being closest to the climate, and the fishing, which is their way of life. He came from Croatia, and he went back in 1912, and married my mother—they were neighbours in the old country—and then they came back to Vancouver in 1912.

When he first arrived, the men were working in mines. He got a job in the Britannia Mine so that he would be close to home, you see, and he worked at that for a number of years. In the old country he worked on the land and

Mary Trocell Veljacic was born in Vancouver in 1913 of Croatian parents.

he fished. The ones from the mountains went in mines and logging—we were not from the mountains, so that was unusual. Then he got a form of arthritis, so he was in bed for ten years. But he still did all the interpreting because his mind and everything was okay.

As an interpreter, he helped to find jobs for the people, or if they had to go to the doctor, or for any little thing. There was this here man, he was from the mountains, and he got hurt in a blast in a mine, he said he was totally deaf. I remember, I was just a child, and my dad would take me with him whenever he went to these things for interpreter, or to be a sponsor for citizenship papers, or anything like that. And this here man said he was totally deaf. Now he was dickering with a man from the Compensation Board, who knew my dad, naturally, because my dad was in there quite often for these cases. The Compensation Board was saying that he was not totally deaf, but my father said, "Well he says he is, and he doesn't hear anything." And so okay, now they're going to come in for this here big final meeting, and I'm with my father, and this official, you see, is talking in an ordinary tone of voice, then he asks this here man to sit over in the corner, and the official's talking to my dad, and he says, "You know, I was in your country when I was on a trip at one time," and my father said, "Oh, isn't that nice. How did you like it?" He said, "Beautiful country," and he made some remarks on it. He says, "And you know, I also was in the part of the country where this gentleman is from." Now this was all in an ordinary tone of voice, he didn't point anywhere, he just said, "You know, they grow grain, and it grows three feet high." And this man who said he was deaf says, "No, no, six feet." I'll never forget it.

Mary Veljacic in her home, 1979. TOD GREENAWAY PHOTO

My mother, if we were out, downtown somewhere, I would speak in our own language, Croatian, to her, and she wouldn't answer me. She said that we were in—now I was *born* here—she said we were in Canada. At home, I was to speak Croatian, but not when we were out. And I used to resent that, I'd wonder why I couldn't speak my own language, you see.

We had boarders there in the beginning for many years and that's why, when we built the house at 423 Prior Street, we just moved the small house in the back and that's what they used. A lot of the boarders were boarders, but I mean, not paying. *All* our people that I remember at the time, they thought nothing of feeding people who came to the door. Or someone who came from Italy or someone who came from the old country to our house, or to the Kalanj house. My parents and the parents of Milke Kalanj, my girlfriend, because they were the ones who were here first, were asked for advice. If they had to go to the hospital, the doctor, the Compensation, a lawyer, or the employment office. Or advice about even getting married. And how many girls were married from our home who were nothing to us! Even mail came to our house, lots of mail, 'cause they knew that this was a stationary address, it wasn't anybody moving or anything like that. Even after the Second World

War, I got letters for my father, who had passed away a long time before, from people looking for relatives of theirs.

When I was growing up, Sundays was our day when everyone got together. Usually they'd come to our home, or the Kalanj family. When the men were working in the mines, it would be when they'd have their holidays. And fishing in those days was different than it is now. They would go out for a long time, you know. But we got together quite often. A lot of times it would be just talking. People would get mail and they would say what someone from this city had written, the other one would say what from his city, and exchange news. Later, the ones that came in 1926 and '27, they were playing the bocce. The Italians had that, but our people nearly always spoke Italian. Who would win would pay for a bottle of wine. It would be just for fun. But when I was a child, it was mostly cards. We played "briškula" and the other one, "trešete."

We had our own music, and our own musical instruments, the "tamburitza." Some of them look like a guitar, but they have more strings, and some of them look like a flat small mandolin. And we sang a lot. That's a thing that I think we're missing now. Because, you see, we sang, even we that were born here sang all the old songs. I mean, at the drop of a hat you sang, and everybody sang. Mostly they were love songs, folksongs from the old country. But we who were born here, naturally, we all sang the songs that they even sing now, when they get together, "On the Sunny Side of the Street," and "By the Light of the Silvery Moon," and all those old standards. But it was mostly ballads from the old country we sang.

And the old stories, they were mostly ghost stories. A lot of people believed in, let's say, in strange happenings, or seeing someone who had died at a certain place. As a child I remember listening to so many of them, and no matter what part of the country they came from it was mostly all ghostly appearances, or a strange happening. We had company nearly every night of the week and it was the men, the older men that had their wives in the old country, who told the stories. I'm speaking about one in particular. He looked like an army major. And, goodness, his tales were endless, he knew hundreds of them. And we could hardly wait for this Tomo Boroevic to come, you see. Of course, after he left we'd never get to sleep.

In those days, there were so many family hours where you would sit and talk with your parents. I remember when I was still young my dad would say, "Look at how the Woodwards have money and position and yet, look at how he opens the store every morning.[38] And so does Mr. Spencer and the family,"[39] meaning that if you become prominent in something, you're not supposed to forget to do your job properly. This would be the story of the evening, you see.

Just to show how my father taught us respect for other people, there was this lady who was a madam and lived on Union Street. Had a beautiful home, the curtains were absolutely snow-white all the time. And as I was growing up, I would hear the men that would come into the house, not talk in derogatory tones or anything, they would just mention they heard this or that. In this way, growing up, I *knew* what kind of a house it was, and what was going on there, although I never mentioned it. And on my fifteenth birthday, my father said, "I'm going to open up a bank account for you, so get dressed and we'll go down to Main and Hastings." So I got dressed, and we were walking down Union Street, and I see from a distance this lady who was the madam taking, I guess, her usual walk during the day. And as we came abreast of each other, I heard her say, "Hello, Mary," and I didn't reply. A few steps onward, my father said to me, "Are you deaf?" I said, "No." I was surprised. And he said, "Didn't that lady say hello to you?" I said, "Yes, she did." And he said, "Why didn't you answer?" And I was embarrassed, of course, so I said the truth, I said, "Well, you know what she is." And he said, "Is she using *your* body?" By this time, of course, I was absolutely embarrassed. He said, "Now you are to go back there, and I know you'll have to lie," he said, "but go back there and apologize and say that you didn't hear her." I had to go back, run back, I remember running back, and I touched her shoulder, and I said, "I'm sorry. My dad said that you said hello, and I'm sorry I didn't hear you." Now she knew I was lying, but she said, "That's all right, Mary." And I went back to my dad. He didn't say a word, by the way, ever again, about that. But when my father passed away, she was in a black limousine, driven by a chauffeur, and everyone was looking, because everyone in the area knew, and they said, "Look, she's at this funeral." But she was there to show respect to my father because he wanted me to respect people, it didn't matter who.

When they say "bootlegging," I think of someone of the Capone era, with the barrels and bottles and the trucks and all that. And I resented that word, even when I was younger, even when the Italian people themselves would use it. I resented it, because, to me, that was not bootlegging where people who were lonely would come to the house and have a glass of wine, or two glasses, or three glasses, whatever, in their own environment, with their own people. A lot of men had to leave their families back home and were here by themselves. They wanted to hear their own people talking, and of their own lives, and it was a way, I think, that they were made to feel happy, without actually having their family with them. That's one reason the Italians call some of the Italian ladies "vecchia"—that's the same as "stara" in our language. That means "old one." It was a form of addressing them as if they belonged to that person who's calling them that, you see.

It was mostly Italians on Prior Street. Then there were a number of our families in the 500 to 800 blocks on Union. But on Prior itself it was mostly Italians, and it was just like one family. If anyone needed any kind of help in anything—gosh, I remember my parents in the Girones' garden, the Girones coming to us, or the Piovesans. And if anyone was sick, they thought nothing of coming over and we thought nothing of going right into the house and getting to work, if there was anything to do, or fixing up the babies if they were small. And of course, amongst our own people, my mother was in nearly every house, because, you see, they didn't speak the language, they were newcomers and we did anything that we could, taking them to the doctor, or being there when the doctors made house calls.

Dr. Tompsett had a gruff way of talking, which then put you at ease, you see, enough that you weren't thinking of any pain that you were going to have if he looked at a boil, or an ingrown toenail.[40] He would come by even if it wasn't for a house call. It would be a lovely day and if it was too early for him to go in the office he would come by Prior Street or Union and walk right into the garden, look at the tomato plants and ask what you used, or what you had on your lettuce. His office was in the Vancouver Block, on the first floor, for all those years. People would ask, "Goodness, if he's such a well-known doctor, how come he's got his office in the first floor of the Vancouver Block?" And my dad would say, "If he moved to a better location, you'd finally get a bill."

There was Service Cab [Co.] on Main Street. That's where the young boys, my brother was one, played cards. All the Italian boys who grew up with my brother, they used to always tell how my mother would go where they'd be playing the cards, you see, and knock on the doors, when it was dark already and say, "Get home." She never thought it was a chore for her to go and find them where they were and send them running. Everyone took care of everyone. And it didn't matter how much younger someone was, or how much older, it was a kind of a different rapport with people then.

I can't even recall how it started, but we called Prior Street the "sunny side of the street," because it *is* the sunny side of the street, because there wasn't anything on the other side. And like, if the boys, when they were out somewhere and if they got into a little bit of whatever when there was another bunch coming in from the West End or from Grandview or whatever, and if they needed any help, then they would just have to whistle the song. Whenever there was an affair, that was the song, we sang that first. And whenever we went anywhere—in those days it was a big thing if you went to Seattle, you know, or Bellingham, and Portland was "Hmm-hmm!" If it happened to be a holiday where more people would go down, and if you saw a table of someone from Prior Street, we'd just hum or whistle the song, you see. That was our song.

On Prior Street at Jackson, there were two Japanese brothers, the Omaes. One was shyer than the other, and he was the taller one, and it was the shorter one who was quicker on the languages. But there were two, oh yes, and the store was called Omae Brothers'. During World War II, they were both evacuated at the same time. I don't know of anyone important that had such a send-off as they had. We were crying, I don't think anyone was there that wasn't crying. The Japanese, they were predominant in Strathcona at that time. And because my dad and mother knew the Japanese—they were boat builders, they were fishing company officials—if someone passed away, we went to their Buddhist temple, you know. Any affairs that the Italians had, we went to. Any affairs we had, the Italians went to. I had Jewish girlfriends. We went to their synagogue the days that you could go. We were just like all one family. Some of the words that I hear today, the ethnic names that they call people, I had never in my life heard. Never. And yet, what could be more ethnic than where I grew up?

But in the First World War, it was our men who were not married they sent to a camp, mostly to a place in Ontario called Kapuskasing. I didn't understand why, because I was only a child then. One of the men that we took care of afterwards told us that to earn money [in the internment camp] they made walking sticks [decorated] with snakes and boxes to hold jewellery. But our people are not the kind to carry a grudge or think that someone discriminated against them. Another thing, the only case that I ever heard: the day war was declared, at a small butcher shop on the south side of Union Street, my mother came in to be served. That's where she bought her meat and he had a man who worked for him who was very, very nice. She was walking over to him, for him to serve her, and the butcher said in Italian—but of course, my mother understood—he said, "Don't serve the Austrian." And then my mother never bought from him, nor did we ever, although he was

Croation funeral in front of the original Sacred Heart Church, Keefer Street and Campbell Avenue.

right there. And when I got married and then that wave of wives came over, I would take them to various stores but I never took them there.

Our Croatian lodge first met in my parents' home. That's where the meetings were for a long time, so that we didn't have to pay anything for a hall. Later there was the Croatian Hall. The lodge probably gave some money to help build it, but it had nothing to do with our lodge. That was mostly the ones that were slightly "pink," and it couldn't survive, that's why it's now the Russian People's Home. The main body of the Croatian Fraternal Union and our main lodge offices are in Pittsburgh, Pennsylvania, and always have been. Ours in Vancouver, I believe, was formed in 1929. That was for sick benefits, death benefits, if you wanted, you know. Well, people joined it mostly so that we would have something together. As a matter of fact, I was the secretary and treasurer and whatever, gosh, I think, for ten or eleven years. But there was no pay. You did it to keep alive your nationality and because you loved doing it. Also, any of our people who wanted to become citizens had to know English, naturally, so they would come to the house and I would teach them basic English.

Our three children speak Croatian and our daughter reads and writes, not very well, and our youngest understands everything, loves anything—our language, our leather-work, our musical instruments. They all love our music. And when we go to *pure* Croatian affairs, a lot of the younger children who have come from the old country don't go, but my children love going to them, and they ask, "When is this going to be?" You see, the girls that I grew up with, that were our language, we all of us loved our own country—not "our own country," our country's Canada—but from where our parents came from. And we wanted to know about it.

BENNY PASTINSKY

My father [Nathan Mayer Pastinsky] was a rabbi in Winnipeg, in a small synagogue, and he got tired, I believe, of the snow, and he came here roughly around Easter, in 1919. When he got off at the CPR Station in Vancouver, flowers were growing in the little garden they had in front of the station, and he was wearing a coon hat and a big muskrat coat, and he said, "If this is Vancouver, I'm going to stay here," and he remained in Vancouver until he died in 1948. He was a gentleman of the old school, with a red, flowing beard. And for the many years that we resided in the East End of Vancouver, he was known and beloved among all ethnic groups as Father Pat, or the Padre, or whatever the equivalent name would be.

He was Yiddish interpreter at the police station and in the courts. Plus, if they needed a pinch hitter in the Slav languages, they would call him in too. He knew everyone, practically. People of all religions and nationalities came to him for advice or help or solace, whatever. Apart from his religious functions, he was very heavily involved with the immigration problem of the

Benny Pastinsky was born in Russia in 1908 and immigrated to Canada in 1914. He was a police reporter for several Vancouver newspapers.

time, people who came here who had escaped from White Russia and got across the borders, got to a port where they could sail to Vancouver. And then he was very much involved with people who were coming from the Atlantic across Canada to settle here, or they had friends here who brought them out, or family—compassionate grounds, and so on. He was never too tired to help others who needed that help. It's easy for *me* to say those things, as his son, but I think you will find, in our community, as few that are left now, many who were helped because of his doings in his early years.

We were living at one time, on Kitchener Street, right across from Seymour School, and on the Sabbath my father would walk to the synagogue for services and then return home for lunch by Sacred Heart Church. And the priest would come out and say, "Good morning, Father," and my father would respect him too, "Good morning, Father" or "Good afternoon, Father." And the priest would say, "You're having your troubles in your people, like I have them in my parish?" and they would stand and chatter, and it was a picture to behold, of two men far apart yet very close. It was a kinship—maybe because it wasn't the richest parish in the world. They all had to look for somebody who needed a ton of coal. They had to look for somebody who needed a bed in the hospital. All the things of human life. Living.

We were the only family on East Georgia Street, in the days that I can remember as a youngster, that had a telephone for quite some years. You must remember that in those days, East Georgia was practically a Jewish ghetto. Union Street was "Little Italy," and Prior Street the same. Keefer Street was more of a Jewish settlement. East Pender was, of course, Oriental. I went to school at Strathcona School, which was a conglomeration of everybody and everyone, and we knew each other's swear words very, very well. That's the first thing you learn in a foreign language.

I was too much involved with growing up to accompany my father much, but in latter years I did. Went to visit prisons, visit hospitals and that sort of thing. But he didn't need me, he got on very well alone. And, though he may not have spoken fluent English, he spoke well enough that you understood what he was driving at. If his heart told him that he was dealing with a human being, he would "stick his neck out," as we say today, to speak for the man so that doors could open a little further for him.

The compassion between peoples, for *other* people, was far greater then than it is today. Canada was born because of immigrants, and the same with the United States, and many people still had not forgotten, if they came from Scotland or Ireland or even Great Britain, there was somebody else who came from other parts of the world who had the same problems that *they* had. And after World War I, the immigrants who came from the Chinese part of the world, because they got to Shanghai, they got to Harbin, they found a kindred spirit who had gone through some suffering himself. Anti-Semitism, per se, was rampant then in Russia. My father reminded the children of his family for many years that when he came to Canada in 1913—we followed him a year later—he always told us that when he got off the boat he kissed the ground of the new country that he had found.

The first thing we must do, he said, is to learn English—immigrants I'm speaking about, from various parts of the world. And he instigated a woman's organization [which became the National Council of Jewish Women] to see that they got their schooling. That was a must. Whether it was night school or whether you went to day school, you had to go to school to learn the language, and you had to obey the law. Because when people came from everywhere, they thought the law was as they found it in their own country. But that was one thing he insisted on: "This is the way of the country that you're living in, and that's the way you've got to be."

Our synagogue was just in a home or a small house where we had services, until we built that building on the corner of Heatley and Pender.[41] I think at that time [1911] our community was under two hundred Jewish families,[42] and that became a big building. It was built by a construction firm, I think by the name of George Snider and Company. Originally there was a small, wooden building on the lot and it was pushed a little back, to make room for the main house of worship. It was the original Hebrew School, and they just put it together you might say, and it lasted for a long, long time.

My father was the only rabbi in Vancouver for many years. He did

Schara Tzedeck Synagogue, Vancouver's first synagogue building, on the corner of East Pender Street and Heatley Avenue. DOMINION PHOTO CO. PHOTO, VANCOUVER PUBLIC LIBRARY, VPL 21011

everything. Certain meat has got to be killed in a certain manner. He did all that. For years he was up about five to five-thirty, to be at the slaughterhouse at six, or before. All that was his department. But I think more than taking care of the synagogue per se, he was interested in taking care of his people, in seeing that his people were well, physically, financially. Interested that their children went to school. Interested in the hospitals. He went to visit the sick, to visit the prisons, the asylums. To keep in touch with people who were lost to the world. The rabbinate to him consisted not to the letter of the book so much as to what he could do to help the people who lived by the book. I remember the community had given him a car, an old Ford car, so he could travel around to where he had to go and visit his people. Every policeman knew him and knew that he broke more traffic laws than any other driver in Canada, never mind Vancouver.

During the thirties there were many, many people who were rich one day and broke the next. I would never mention names, but I do know how many people came to sit at the same table as I, my sisters, to get something to eat. It was not meant in that way—they were guests. But we knew why. And we survived. How good, how bad, my mother would have answered much better than I can. If we had two apples, then we had to share a half, or a quarter, but we had an apple. Or bread: instead of having two slices, we may have had a quarter of a slice. You took things the way they came.

The women at home lived in a world all their own, and I lived in a world all my own, because I was working away from home. I joined the *Province* newspaper in 1924, and I worked on the *Province* till 1929, and then I went to work on the morning paper until 1934, when I was married and went east. During that time, my sisters were going to school, I was working on the morning paper, I'm working on the night beats, I was never home at night. Our family life, per se, was centred upon the Sabbath evening, when we all gathered. It was a must. You had to be with Mother and Dad. And the holidays—on the Passover, my father would be through with the services at that synagogue and he would stand up and say, "For those who are strangers and have no place to go for the celebration tonight, if you will remain after the services, and follow me home, come home with me." Mother never knew if it was going to be one extra for dinner on those nights, or twelve, or twenty, but somehow or other, we all got fed.

Well getting a job then, I'll tell you, I had a double [disadvantage]—like all of our people, first because I was East End and secondly because of my faith. I got a job on the *Vancouver Daily Province* for two reasons: because the man who introduced me to the city editor of our day—a man who was *the* city editor for all times, a man I worshipped named Lou Gordon, gone many years now—the man who introduced me to him was at that time a big advertiser in the *Province*, the door had to open. He was a merchant prince of his day, and he introduced me to the advertising department, they took me upstairs. And the city editor asked me, the first question he asked me, "What education you got?" I didn't have very much, and I said, "High school." "University?" No, I said, I hadn't got to university yet. "You start work tomorrow morning at nine o'clock." That was a different attitude entirely.

When I was police reporter, and still living at home, I got home late one night—police used to drive me home on a motorcycle, whoever was on shift. And my father woke me up next morning, he said to me, "I want to speak to you before you get away." And I said, "What for?" And he said, "I got a call last night from the Police Department." "Yeah?" I said. "A 'Mr. McGillicutty' called me and he said he wants to see me. He's in great problem." I said, "You mean George 'McGillicutty'?" and he said, "Yes, do you know him?" "Dad," I said, "what are you doing with a character of that nature? He's the worst pimp in Vancouver, and you name it—he's got a record from here to China and back and upside down." He said, "So?" I said, "There must be a time you've got to stop somewhere, Dad." He said, "Do you know him?" I said, "I've known him too many years, unfortunately. I've seen him going down, down, down." He said, "Well, my boy, he came from a good family, and they've got troubles, and they've asked me to look into it." I said, "Do me one favour, please. Don't go to the magistrate. They'll laugh me out of court, the guys. Say 'What the hell is your dad doing?' They're trying to put him away for twenty years." "There's a little bit of good in everybody," he said. I couldn't talk him out of it; he came to court next morning. I never brought it up to my father except one occasion. I was sitting in court, and this same man had abused a couple of women in the most degrading work in the world, living off the avails of prostitution. I mean a guy like that should cut his throat. And I never brought it up until my father said, "Do you ever hear from him?" And I said, "Dad, I had the sad experience of seeing in court..." what I just told you. "Well," he said, "somebody got to him before somebody *else* could have got to him." That was his reasoning.

In those days nobody from this corner [West End] who lived here, would ever *think* of going down to the East End—wouldn't dare, in his mind. I was a great guy when people used to come from out of town, "Hey get ahold of Benny Pastinsky. He'll show you the town like nobody knows it." I wasn't proud. But you know, you show off, like everybody else. There wasn't a corner...all right, Union, just off Main Street. Used to be a drugstore in an apartment block there. We used to go in there, the Police Department, I don't know how many times. The Main Hotel. The London Hotel. *Full* of troubles. But mostly different troubles than we know today. Different entirely. One of the biggest crimes, was when a kid was picked up in one of these joints. The police would "*kill*" the guy or the woman who were playing around with youngsters. That was a no, no, no. Nowadays, you hear it at this end of the city [West End]. You don't hear of male prostitutes in the East End, or youngsters. Mind you, there were gambling joints in the West End, 'cause there's more money. East End, you know was different work—bootlegging. Every home on Prior and every home on Union would sell wine. When I used to take people to Hogan's Alley I opened up a world they never knew existed, never *dreamed* it existed. And there's nothing to Hogan's Alley. They should live in the East End of New York.

There were a lot of stables [around Hogan's Alley], people kept their horses there, junk dealers and so on and so forth. And the people who kept their horses were straight. But certain areas, like honey to bees, you know—because it's so low, that's where a lot of people congregate. I don't speak about "people" people. I speak of an element. And there were several murders in there. People getting drunk, drinking wine. And somebody take out a knife and stick him. I'd come by—they would have picked up one or two. You know where the Georgia Viaduct was? As you're going east, there used to be a club, gambling joint. Anything else you wanted. But who the hell went there except the people who were looking for it? It wouldn't interest you. It didn't interest me, except the fact that, "Hell, I might get a story out of it." That's why I knew them. There were four or five coloured people in that locale and they drowned out a thousand beautiful coloured people who are here, now, because people won't forget. And if they took and revived all the stories that ever happened in the City of Vancouver, nobody would know what's left out. Including the Police Department's records. I'm sure they wouldn't have all of it. I don't know. The story is for the moment. Now. You know what I mean? It lives just as long as you do this. And when it goes out, it's forgotten. So. All those stories.

TED HOVI WITH GIL TIVERON

Ted Hovi was born in Aberdeen, Washington, in 1909 of Finnish parents. Gil Tiveron was born in Italy in 1909 and immigrated in 1911.

TED HOVI: My dad got properly settled and he got on the waterfront as a longshoreman, so he made very good money. I think they were getting about seventy, eighty cents an hour in the mid-twenties. Anyway, my mother was a kind of a businesswoman and being of Finnish extraction, we had a lot of these Scandinavian single men who worked in sawmills, mostly logging camps, and whenever they'd come in town they'd stay at our place. They were quite a rough bunch, you know. They'd go out in the woods and probably stay three, four months, maybe some would stay longer, and as soon as they'd come in town—liquor store. And they'd drink sometimes for two, three weeks, possibly a month. Straight! Without proper eating or anything like that, and then be broke. When they'd go broke, they'd go back in the woods. I remember one particular incident, a lot of these Scandinavians were great snoose chewers. And this guy, he had that snoose in his mouth all the time. You could see the wad, his lips would be bulging with this snoose, and he'd be drinking and raising hell and all this stuff, and next morning he'd get up and his favourite expression was, "It isn't the whisky that makes me sick, it's the goddamned Copenhagen stuff I chew." I'll never forget that.

GIL TIVERON: I went to Strathcona School. And there was quite a bunch of Chinese, just about all of the yellow race was there. I remember one time,

Gil Tiveron, Ted Hovi and David deCamillis in the latter's apartment office, 1978. TOD GREENAWAY PHOTO

we were having a snowball fight and we used to gang up. And they used to gang up. And of course, we used to chase 'em down towards Pender Street, down Chinatown. And one instance, one Chinese turned around and he stabbed one of us. And we could never find out who it was, you know. We always used to go after the Chinese then. Remember when they used to have the big, long pigtail, on the back of the head? And we used to call him "Chink, Chink, Chinaman," and chop off this tail. Oh, we used to run after them Chinamen all the time. There was all kinds of different nationalities. I think that that was the only school in town that had so many different languages in there. There was quite a bunch of Japanese there, too, but they didn't side up with either of us. They'd very seldom get in with a fight. They kept by themselves.

TED HOVI: And then that tough Mr. Brown, principal. Oh boy, he was tough. Oh, my goodness. He used to favour those Japanese there a lot. I remember, he'd come in there and we'd all freeze, not a pin would drop in the room—about thirty, thirty-five kids. And he'd find anything, least little thing. His favourite was, he'd pull you by your ear and pretty near take your bloody ear off. There was some number of minor incidents and the kids were expelled. They just wouldn't take his vicious treatment, you know. He didn't show no tact at all, that old...

GIL TIVERON: He used to come out with this big strap, it was about two feet long, and thick, you know. *Whang!*

TED HOVI: But the majority of the teachers, they were very good. I often wondered in my later age how some of them had the patience to stand us kids. Sometimes we'd get unruly, you know. Couldn't do much with us.

GIL TIVERON: I went to school with Jimmy McLarnin. He was very nice. I remember one time when he used to sell papers, and he came home one day, and we were in the sand, playing in this MacLean Park, and he lost his money. It was two dollars, and he was just crying to beat the band, you know. Later, he used to go away from the gang. We'd wonder where in the world he was going all the time. We found out after, he was going and practising boxing. What was very unusual was, he was a good boxer, he was a very good boxer amongst ourselves, you know. 'Course as far as wrestling, he wasn't so much, because I used to get him down all the time. But boxing—I didn't want to tackle him in boxing!

TED HOVI: Did you see him box that Chinaman there for three hours after school one day? It was in the early twenties. He fought a Chinaman there for three hours and they were so all in, they just collapsed. Both of them. But that was before he actually earnestly took up boxing. You know. Scrapes between kids.

GIL TIVERON: He was a square shooter, though. He'd go home and whatever money he'd made, whatever money it was, he would give it to his parents.

TED HOVI: He made money, too. And he kept his money. And he had a wonderful manager, Pop Foster. He had the first dime he ever made, and he looked after Jimmy, and oh, he must have looked after him *good*. And Jimmy must have done exactly like Pop told him to do and I guess that's how he got up to where he was, welterweight champion there of the world. And his brother, Sammy, was a prominent boxer too, locally. I remember correctly, Jimmy quoting once there that "Sammy would have made a better boxer than *I* was." But poor Sammy couldn't keep his weight down. In 1923 and '24, they used to live on the 700-block East Hastings, big grey house there. Well, it had to be big. It was a big family, you know—five boys, and there was two or three girls.

Ninety percent of the buildings are standing up that were here sixty years ago. The synagogue's the same today as it was built about fifty years ago—1920. They used to have their prayers or ceremonies there quite often, and the place was *full, absolutely full*. And they must have had some sort of religious trait there, because they wouldn't turn their lights on, and if there was any kid outside, we'd have to put their lights on, and when they'd want them turned off, they'd call for another kid to turn the lights out.[43] And whoever turned the lights on got ten cents and whoever turned the lights off got another dime.

GIL TIVERON: Old Spencer used to have a big building on Prior and Jackson, great big building. And they used to keep the horses there. We used to live a block away, and it sounded just like thunder. Because every time the horses would go up and down these big floor boards, they'd be making an awful big noise. Spencer's had them for their department store, horses and wagons for their deliveries.

TED HOVI: In wintertime, the coalmen came selling individual sacks of coal. And they were mostly, if I remember correctly, Italians, you know. Jews, they wouldn't go for that heavy work—that's heavy manual work, carrying a hundred-pound coal sack. They used to sell for about seventy-five cents a sack. They called quite loud, so that you could hear them, "Anybody want coallllll? Coallll." You know, drawl like that. And the Jewish, with their junk wagons, they'd do the "Yonk, Yonk, Yonk."

GIL TIVERON: "Any bottles and rags?" And the Chinese used to have a cart with a horse, and they used to come around with vegetables, and as young kids, we used to go on the back of the wagon, pull all their sacks away, and boy, they would be ki-yi-ing after us for blocks!

TED HOVI: Apparently, you guys there on Union Street were much tougher than we were. We were in gangs around Heatley and Pender there, gangs of sometimes eight, ten, or twelve. We never done anything wilfully destructive. Never! If someone had a dime and we wanted to go to a show, we'd all go into the show on a dime. The guy that had the dime, he'd get in there and he'd open the side doors, we'd all go in. Of course, some of us would get caught, you know, but most of us would get in free. But we never dreamed of doing anything that would be destructive, not even to those Chinese carts—we'd never do anything like that.

GIL TIVERON: You wouldn't, eh?

TED HOVI: You guys were pretty tough joes around there, just a few blocks away from us!

GIL TIVERON: One theatre they used to have was the old National, where Wosk's is today. We used to go in, walk in backwards, and we thought we'd make them believe that we were going out.

Charlie Chaplin was really the one that we went after. Charlie Chaplin there. Walking around. Just a piano, that's all there was.

TED HOVI: The piano player would be hired by the theatre. And they'd have the music for the tempos too, like for instance, if a horse was running, there would be some type of a march, and if it would be a love scene, well you'd hear excerpts from "Desert Song" or something like that, you know. But for dancing, the Silver Slipper used to be quite a place. I think it had its popularity during the thirties.

GIL TIVERON: Yeah, I used to go up there. I put in $200 to build that place up. The Italian Society built that, the Società Veneta.

TED HOVI: It's still there, Hastings Auditorium it's known as, 800-block East Hastings. Oh, it used to be very, very popular in those days. It was mostly patronized by people around this district, Hastings East. And a lot of loggers used to go there, and miners, and sometimes it used to get very rowdy, particularly when they'd start drinking and someone trying to get someone else's girlfriend—you'd get fights there.

But that's something that can be expected in a dance hall. But, oh, I would say I had some of my best fun in my life there, at the Silver Slipper. They had regular dances, they used to be about twice a week there. Music—I think it was saxophone, violin, drum, and piano. Loggers mostly those days were Scandinavians, and they used to play the hambo, it's a dance between a waltz and a schottische. But I know, before that, the guy that ran the dances at the Parish Hall, he was a Scandinavian. And he rented a hall for the occasions, that's going back around early twenties. He run there for years and years. And that's where you'd see a lot of the rough stuff there. The Scandinavians, they were in the logging business and sawmills and such, if they got drunk, they really wrecked a joint, those days. I could offhand say there was half a dozen Finnish families, about half a dozen, within a radius of a block around here. And there was the Norwegians, and there was some Swedish people that lived around here, but we were a minority, not too many. The bulk were Italians, Chinese and Japanese, and God knows what, Ukrainians, Polish people, you know. It was a regular League of Nations, those days.

GIL TIVERON: Very few English. It was us that they might have called riff-raffs, but, actually we weren't riffraffs, we weren't troublesome. Now Hogan's Alley was a pretty rough place there, that was. Really all the "bubs" in there, bootleggers and everything else, all together. Gambling, and slitting each other's throats down there. You could walk through all right during the day. We were kids, we used to go down through it just like nothing, you know. And we used to hate it. I remember one time, there was a big crowd right in the middle of the alley, and everybody was laughing. We were kids, well, we pushed the guys around to get in to see. Here was an *old lady*, with her pants sticking up and pulling her dress way up like this, showing everybody. What a place that was! Everything was open, you know. Nobody cared what they said or what they did or nothing.

TED HOVI: Those were hard times, very hard times then, going into the thirties. My dad kept on working, but myself, being a young man, why, there was just no work for a young fellow. The only work I used to get was three, four months painting. Been a painter now for about fifty years, retired, of course. And most all springs and summers, I used to get employment, anywhere from three, maybe sometimes if I was lucky, six months. And wintertimes, they were pretty grim, you know. Naturally, we were all on relief—everybody that lived around here. No one had work. I think my dad was about the only one. Being a longshoreman, he did work steady and made big money. But those days, the single men could get relief and we all had small, white cards. They were maybe about four inches by four inches and on top of this white card there would be a "transient," big "T" marked on the face of this white relief card. Later on in the thirties they started building these relief camps, and they used to send *tens of thousands* of the single men to relief camps. Those days we used to get $1.05 a week for bed, and then we'd get $2 a week for, like, board. If we brought it into a Chinese restaurant, we'd get $2.25, so the Chinese all got our business. After they got those relief camps organized, and if you happened to go to the City Relief Office and you happened to have a "T" there, it was about a 75 percent chance that they'd send you off in a relief camp. And we all dreaded that sight there. There'd be lineups about thirty, forty, maybe fifty, a hundred men there, *hundreds* of men, going there weekly to pick up their dole. And then we'd ask the guy that came out, "Well, did you get your relief or did they send you out in the camps?"

The worst strike, I think, was possibly the one when they had that big longshoreman's strike there at the mid-thirties [June 4 to December 9, 1935]. They organized this march [on June 18] and of course, they got us single unemployed in with them. Oh, I guess there was a couple of thousand of us. In the meantime, the waterfront was wide open, imported scabs and local scabs working the boats those days. So we got as far as the foot of Heatley Avenue, right up to the CPR's tracks, and there was the Mounties, there was provincial policemen on horseback, I think there was about thirty, forty of them there, ready to pounce on us. But I give 100 percent credit to the Chief of Police. He was on the waterfront side of the tracks and we were about to cross the tracks to go on these boats and try to get these scabs off the boats. He came by himself, singly, and spoke to the executive officers—one of them was Oscar Salonen, he was a business agent for the longshoremen. And he told Oscar, in a very nice way, he says, "Please, don't bring your men over these tracks," and he pointed up there, up on top of Ballantyne Pier—there were Mounties poised out there with bloody machine guns. That's the God's truth. And they were pointing at us. He says, "Look." About forty provincial police out there with their bloody old billies, with another twenty city policemen on horseback, maybe another fifty policemen on foot. He says, "You can't possibly make it, Oscar, don't come beyond these tracks." But apparently Oscar Salonen said, "This strike has been going long enough, and we're going in there and we're going to take those scabs off the boats." As soon as he crossed those tracks, out come the police. That was about the biggest riot I've ever seen out here. There was lots of people got hurt, some even in the hospital. And I saw some police that got hurt pretty bad too, with us unemployed. Of course, we've had scrapes with the police too, the unemployed, but that was the worst one. When I seen those machine guns, I wasn't going to go beyond those tracks, but there were a lot of those fellows that were going to go through. The police were situated on horseback, and they were, I would say, anywhere from seven to nine feet higher than we were and they were on trained horses and they had billies—I think they were about three feet long. They'd hit you over the head, they'd hit you anywhere. The people ran all over, sure, to get away from them. From the CPR tracks to Hastings Street was approximately two and a half blocks. Well, that riot extended right up to Hastings Street. When there's a riot like that, you know, you're going to go and hide anywhere. There were small businesses there, such as a steam bath, a bakery, a bicycle shop and there was a couple of small grocery stores. They had motorcycle policemen throwing tear gas into those small business outlets. They had no business doing that. That's my personal belief, you know. Of course, there's always two sides to a riot. There's bosses and labourers—they clash. Which we did. But when it got two and a half blocks away from there, they had no bloody business whatever of throwing those tear gas bombs into those small businesses. That was about the worst I've ever seen.

GIL TIVERON: A policeman had this great big whip and he was just giving it left and right and I could see him coming straight for me, so I took a big dive in the bush, you know, and that saved me, right there. Oh, it was terrific, that day.

TED HOVI: I think it extended from about the 200-block East Hastings, right up to the 800-block East Hastings. That's how big of an area it took, right from the waterfront. The longshoremen lost it, sure. They lost it.

DAVID deCAMILLIS

David deCamillis was born in Vancouver in 1913 of Italian immigrant parents. His father immigrated to Boston in 1902 and his mother to Vancouver in 1910.

My father was a labourer. He was a little smarter than the rest, 'cause when he landed in Vancouver the first thing he did was to see where he could learn to read and write English, which he did. Consequently he became a foreman on these road gangs because he could interpret, so he always got a little bit more money. He thought it was a great country, all this vacant land, couldn't understand nobody on it.

My parents bought this place [Kirby Block at Hawks and Keefer Streets] in '29. Then the Depression set in, and my mother raised the four of us here, and the average net rent we'd collect from twelve units here would be from two dollars to thirty-nine dollars a month. To look after *five* people. That was the days before supermarkets, so, in the store we had all kinds of groceries, two or three employees. Back of the store was a bookie joint for horse races. Then in one section of the store, there was a shoemaker's shop, but he went broke, then a butcher came in and he went broke. So it continued with that, between groceries and renting part of the store out and horse racing, he was able to pay thirty-five dollars a month rent. But there was good Italian people ran the store, because in this area, it was predominantly Italians and [immigrants from] the Balkan states, and a lot of Finns. That would have been the early thirties. Most of the Jews had left by then.

As kids, we went to the Princess Theatre once in a while, and you took a chance going in if there was a seat there—they were wooden seats, or you'd have to sit on the floor. We always tried to sit in front. It was silent movies, and this girl with long red hair was playing the piano, and when she was playing the real cowboys-goin'-shooting, we'd sneak up behind and we'd pull her hair, and kind of put her fingers off the notes. And then we used to go to the Royal Theatre that had vaudeville—later called "City Nights." And there were a fantastic group of dancers there. They were all "has-beens," and our favourite trick, we'd go into the loges and throw rolls of toilet paper on them when they were dancing and we'd laugh at them, and popcorn all over the place. And they'd keep dancing. We had the Pantages Theatre—*there* was your loges. There was two floors, then you had your big pit down there, and the orchestra was there all the time. Say at 2:30 in the afternoon—it wasn't a continuous thing—first you had some news and then you'd have a serial or a cowboy picture. While you were waiting, they got this big screen with everybody's advertisement, the coal company, this and that, then cowboys, then you'd come next week to see the rest. *Then* comes this mighty stage. They used to have about six acts. And a fellow would walk across the stage with a big card, "what's coming up," you'd be able to see that, and it was real good vaudeville. Juggling, dancing, music.

I was about fourteen, on a delivery truck, and our run was down on Alexander Street and the stores downtown. The driver told me after we'd gone in these alleys and seen these beautiful rooms—looked like a warehouse, all these drugs and liquor and laundry in the basement, and being a kid I didn't understand. These were prostitute houses, you see, he told me, "You know, a lot of the women that are in here, their husbands go out to sea for two, three years, and they come here and make a buck." But they had all the nicest brick buildings. If you go there and walk up, the tile is still there on the verandah, and you can see the name of the madam, and she would run that house.

The couple that I managed to see inside when we did early morning deliveries were absolutely deluxe. Posh. The best. Beautiful wallpaper and a lot of the beds had big curtains behind them, right on the wall, to give the warmth feeling. And beautiful big soft chesterfields. Now these would be the high-class places and you'd go in there with a feeling of extreme wealth. Beautiful glassware, like, for liquor. According to this driver I was with, he said that they'd be checked over by a doctor every week, and they were run by a madam. No pimps at all. The girls would come from the prairies, the innocent type, they'd come here because there's a city that's growing, there's money to be made here. They'd come from the States. They would come from eastern Canada, where they had the experience. And then you'd have the odd runaway from home. "Well, I want this type of life." The odd one may be forced into it. One madam was a *fantastic* person. She had her own daughters prostituting too. Wonderful clothes. There was no smuttiness in their talking, they were real ladies. And they had the highest class of clientele. Besides prostituting, they did their bootlegging, and it was unreal—this was in the Hungry Thirties, the early part—the *amount* of money they made. They'd never bother with their own car, always the best of taxis. Those days, there was the Avenue Taxi and Service Taxi on Main Street, and they'd have Packards, and Dominique DeSoto used to have a big Stutz Bearcat. Well, you go in one of them, you were really class. The smart ones saved money and they'd go into some business or the smart ones, they'd get married. They weren't regarded as a base person in the community, because the prostitute of those days had certain morals. A lot of them had illegitimate kids. Sure, you get the odd tramp, you have to in this sort of a profession. But there was nothing dirty or cheap about 'em. They didn't care who knew they were a prostitute, they were in there for that business.

When I was in the taxi business, I was only a young fellow, I used to pick them up from Empress Hotel and take them down to Gore Avenue. There would be about six of them pile into this taxi, and only have to go about four or five blocks. And all they'd do is argue about how much their expenses were—the towels, this and that, and one said, "You know, yesterday, I had to turn a trick for twenty-five cents. That's all I had all day." And they had a pimp and they'd have to pay him. That's what the argument was about—how much it cost them. And then another taxi driver said, "You're going to take a different trip today. You're going to take three Chinese prostitutes down to Chinatown." I'd never heard of this before—Chinese prostitutes. They were the most *gorgeous*-looking girls you ever seen in your life. And I just couldn't get over it. And they stayed in the Empress too. If a man wanted the services of Chinese prostitutes in those days, it was ten dollars as against two dollars for the white prostitute. But to reverse that, a Chinese who would go for a white prostitute, would cost him ten dollars.

My father rented the basement of the Lotus Hotel and called it the Lotus Cabaret, with a partner who used to own a taxi company here. I was about eighteen [1931] and I went down to see my father. He says, "Would you like a job?" I said, "Sure." He said, "Well, you be bartender." It was fixed up real nice with these booths on the side with curtains, and we had a five-piece orchestra up on a stage that was all built-in. It had an Italian effect; the cooking was all Italian, that's for sure. I was pouring drinks and we had waiters there and we had what they called hostesses. These would be seven girls. They were supposed to drink tea while the guy was paying for rum or scotch, they were to make everybody welcome anyhow. And then you paid off so much in those days, that was no secret—everybody was paying off. We had a full house every night and Sunday night there'd be a lineup. Now Sunday, everything was closed but *they* were open—bootleggers and like that. And there was a policeman there looking after the lineup waiting to get in! Always skulduggery. "Why give these here guys a straight drink for twenty-five cents?" I'd take a drink of Scotch out to sell it, and then I'd replace that with hot water. Until one guy that wasn't drunk, he said, "You know, we're only drinking hot water every night we come here." I said, "I don't put no water in there. I don't know nothing about this business." So my father said, "Don't do that no more. You overdid it." We would clean the beer bottles off the tables and there'd always be a little bit of beer. Well, we'd make full bottles out of that and then put a rubber cap over it, and then they'd be really loggy by four or five in the morning—"We'll give you a good bottle of beer, that'll straighten you up a bit." Well, we'd bring them all these drippings, take the cap off, pour it, and that was *fifty* cents! And boy, they'd drink that—it was so flat, they'd *have* to sober up. We had like a peek hole, and one friend would bring another. If we didn't know 'em, they wouldn't come in, no way. And no drunks whatsoever. If they got drunk on the premises, that was fine. In fact, the hostesses weren't allowed to take anybody out. They had to stay on the premises. And they were getting pretty mad, 'cause we got these loggers coming in and they'd want to go out with these dames, and they'd like to go—they could pick up maybe ten dollars for a whole night. But they weren't allowed, so they made their money on these cold drinks and a lot of tips. They'd serve as a waitress and they'd sit with the client. And it worked out good.

We always did make wine. And like my mother says, "As long as you've got wine in your cellar and a crust of hard bread, you're rich. You don't need nothing else." Because you've got all your vitamins out of your wine, and you've got your bread, and even if you're poor, well, you could sustain yourself. And she'd make her own bread, of course. We'd come home for dinner, and she put the hard, dried homemade bread on the platter, then put homemade wine over to top. Well, we would go to school and we'd go to sleep. And the principal came down to see my mother, said, "You know, your two children came to school, but they're either drunk or sleeping. What do you give 'em for lunch?" She told him and said, "See, they're strong children." He said, "No, no, they're drunk." So she had to cut out giving us wine and hard bread for lunch. Those days it was not so much grapes, because of transportation from California to here—it was mostly dandelion wine, and raisin wine. You could buy raisins in cases, quite easy and cheap. But everybody was out picking off dandelions because there was all kinds of vacant lots, and all kinds of wild blackberries any place you went, so it was quite simple. And you picked gunnysacks full of the stuff.

My mother said, "When a baby's born, you should dip it right away into a little tub of good wine or good brandy," that's to clean it off. And they used it for medicine if you got a bad cold. Before you go to bed at night, you heat a cup of wine hot as you can stand, and drink it. Then go to bed, and boy, the sweat's fierce. And then, if you've got to have energy in a hurry, you get wine in a big glass or a tumbler with hard bread and soak it and eat it. Boy, talk about energy! I don't think they used wine here the way they did in Italy. Here, the average husband took advantage of it, used it as an excuse to drink. And he was half-tanked most of the time, you know, with a stomach like this. A bootlegger here, well he never did manual work. And he thought this drinking plenty of wine was still good for him. Whereas when they came from Italy, they had to work like *slaves* to survive, so this wine was a benefit to them then. But some of these guys were drinking it by the gallons every day. They thought they were getting healthy, and they were killing themselves. And then they would distil the pulp from the grape, and make this grappa—it's pure alcohol. Well, that'll blind you, it's so powerful. And a lot would make this, it's very illegal to make. They'd set up their own little still and they would just come out and draw off the steam, they'd use it for coffee. Well, they became addicted to it, and they'd drink it straight. It would peel the skin off your mouth, it was so powerful. *And they'd go wild.* They thought they were healthy; they all died. It just burns you right out, if you ever become addicted to the pure alcohol like that. They were powerful men, all right, they worked on garbage trucks and worked in the yard, you know, but not *that* powerful. Nobody's that powerful.

Some of the men riding the freights in the thirties were sure *diversified*— lawyers, doctors, engineers, anything at all. Coming into Vancouver, they'd try and jump off before they got in the yards, and run like heck. That's when a lot of them got killed. They used to call it the "bull horrors." If you go down the ladder and it's moving too fast, that train, and you've got a foot on the ground, it's pretty hard to get back up and you get dragged underneath. I've seen more than one like that, and a lot of them had heavy packs. Well, they'd be frightened to get arrested or chased by a dog or get clubbed by the police or yard workers. And that's why everybody would try to jump off before it got into the yards. The only way, I found out, was to wait till it slowed right down, then jump! When there was a lot, the police were there, "You go right down in there," and they'd show us. It wasn't too far from the tracks, and there's where you stayed. "Don't go into the town or city at all." Most of these jungles were located where there was some sort of supply of water for these people. Like in Calgary, it was near the Bow River, you could have a bath and everything. Some of these jungles were well-organized. You'd have to take turns to go out panhandling for vegetables, meat, or anything you could bring back. And you'd have a big clean garbage can. Well, there'd be two or three guys do the cooking. Great big mulligan, fill that whole thing right up, feed the whole works. There were soapbox orators, people standing up and giving speeches, how rotten the country is and how rotten the government is. Oh, a lot of good speakers. Most of the time you'd sleep on woodpiles, coal piles, any place you could sleep, that's all. Some of the train crews were good, and some weren't. For instance, when we were going through those tunnels, going up so slow, they sent the word back, "Get off and walk," because you could suffocate from the smoke from the engine. That was an experience. Coming back, it was cold, so the engineer, he only filled his locomotive half full of water, then he'd stack us like cordwood on there so we'd get more heat. We'd be piled on the engine, well those who couldn't get into inside the box-cars, and you'd be burning on your back and your sweater would be frozen to your nose, it was that bad.

About 1937, '38 there seemed to be a different feeling through the whole area. You know, Mussolini was great, Hitler was great. Look at those countries there, everybody's working and everybody eating and we're starving here. And I remember very distinctly one day I went to the Rex Theatre and the editor of the *Province* who was just up the street there, came on the stage and he made a speech about the Depression. He said, "The only thing wrong with BC is we need Mussolini over here for *six months*, and *everybody* would be working and *everybody* would have a lot of money." He said, "Look at Italy: everybody working. Look at BC: we got all this natural resource, and we're all starving." Which was right, in those days. And then Hitler came along, and he did the same thing—everybody's working. So that funny feeling started to come over everybody. And then, we had the Fascist parties here, Fascist party, Nazi party. Before you could start a party or club, you had to have the sanction of the government to have a club licence—this is what I found out. And they *welcomed* the Nazi and the Fascist club here 'cause Communism was coming up and they wanted somebody to combat this. And boy, they had a big following here, the Fascist party.

They didn't play very fair with the Japanese here during the war. They just *wiped them out*. Blackmailed them and everything. Very unfair treatment, and they all had to get out. These here idiots set fire to their apartments. "Japanese

The "jungle" at the city dump on False Creek Flats where unemployed men lived in makeshift shelters during the Depression. W.J. MOORE PHOTO, CITY OF VANCOUVER ARCHIVES, RE N3.1

are no good," and they'd get a rag full of gas and throw it in an apartment block. But the Japanese community here was the finest and the cleanest there was. They had open-air markets, fish, vegetables. It was a glorious thing to go down Powell Street when the Japanese were there, it was really something. They had their doctors,[44] their dentists, and everything. And certainly, no violence. So many people went down to shop at these open markets, it was busy all the time, Powell Street.

And I know none of them deserved the treatment that they got, 'cause they were darn good citizens. The Japanese here was a very polite person, extremely polite. And you know, the war made people think different, unknowingly. And *that* was an *awful shame*.

Mary Lee Chan & Shirley Chan

Mary Lee Chan was born in Vancouver in 1915. Her daughter, Shirley Chan, was born in Vancouver in 1947. The interview was conducted in both English and Cantonese, with Shirley acting as interpreter for her mother. Further translation was done by Kwok Chiu of Strathcona Property Owners and Tenants Association.

Mary Chan: My grandfather came over from Kwangtung in 1879 on a sailing ship. It took him several months to get here and he came right to Vancouver. He was coming to look for gold. You had to walk a long way along the river and then all you got was a little bit of gold dust. He made just enough to eat. So then he went to work on the railroad. Many people died during the construction of that railroad. They lived in tents along the track and it was cold. Some people got arthritis. They were attacked by mosquitoes and blackflies, and some people eventually went blind. And then, after it was finished, there was no other work. So he settled where the old Immigration Building used to be, and he raised pigs and chickens. He used white cloth to partition off his land.

After he'd been there for a time and managed to save some money, he brought over his son, my father. After my father started working, he brought over fifteen or twenty of his relatives, half-brothers and village "brothers" [men from the same village, therefore with the same last name]. There was no other kind of work, so they were sawing wood for a lumber company for twenty-five cents a cord. They'd each cut maybe two cords a day, three if they were fast, so they made fifty to seventy-five cents a day and that was good money.

Then the government expropriated my grandfather's land because he didn't know how to pay taxes. It was at the time when they were looking for ways to develop the harbour and they found that the water was deepest at the foot of this street, so it would make good facilities for big ships.[45] So then they came and asked him if he had paid his taxes and his question was, "Taxes? What's taxes?" They said, "Old man, that land's worth lots of money. If you build a house on it you've got to make lots of money to pay the taxes. That's too bad." They bought him out for $200. So he killed off all his pigs and chickens and sold them and went back to China. My father stayed here cutting wood, and then later on he became a gardener working for a different household each day of the week. That's how he met his wife, because she was working for one of them.

SHIRLEY CHAN: My grandmother had come over in 1907 when she was twelve or thirteen. She came as a housekeeper and babysitter for a business family who lived in Chinatown. That was the year of the Chinatown riot and she remembered being very frightened and hiding in the back of the store. At that time there were very few women in Chinatown. She wasn't allowed to go out, she wasn't allowed to even go downstairs to the store, because girls, as soon as they became mature, were not supposed to be in the company of men.

MARY CHAN: She married my father in 1913 when she was nineteen. By that time she was working in a house on Slocan Street which that same family owned. They gave it to my parents as a place to live in and that's where I was born three years later. Chinatown then was very dilapidated. There was a knitting mill and a Chinese bakery, I remember. The streets were unpaved and it got very muddy when it rained. My brother and I would go and play on boards in the street, one of us would stand at one end and the other would get on the other end and the water would be flying and the mud would be flying—we had a great time. But I got my dress dirty up to my neck and my mother spanked me afterwards. Up on Slocan Street, it was all trees, all forest. I was afraid to go to school because the kids would beat me up. There were very few Chinese families up that way. In the winters, when he wasn't gardening, my father carried coal and sawdust for white families, washed the floors, that kind of work. By the time they had been married twelve years, my mother had had eleven babies. And about 1923 he decided to take us all back to China—we were so poor, there was no food, and no work.

SHIRLEY CHAN: The Chinese Benevolent Association was giving out rice gruel to needy families in those days.

MARY CHAN: So we went back to my father's village. There my grandfather was a rich man. He had lots of fields and houses. But nobody liked going back to China. There was no electricity and no proper heating and the girls weren't allowed to go to school because it wasn't the custom for daughters to be educated. But everybody wanted to go to school, so the people who came back from America and the people from Canada got together, raised the money, and built a co-ed school. That's where I went. I learned to be a teacher and I worked as a teacher for a while in a government school. I got married and then in 1947, after the war, I came back to Canada. My sister sent me money to come over. Two of my sisters, and my brothers, came back before the war, and one of them actually came back on the last boat from Shanghai.

When I came back, there were big changes in Chinatown. The streets were paved, and they had sidewalks. There were lots of jobs, and restaurants and coffee shops. My brother took me out to coffee and everybody was looking funny at me. When I walked down the street, everybody stared at me. So I didn't walk down in Chinatown again. See, there were waitresses but not

Mary and Shirley Chan in the living room of the Chan home, 1978. TOD GREENAWAY PHOTO

many other women in Chinatown. The only women they let in then were the wives of war veterans and native-born Canadians. I lived up on Cambie Street and 26th with my sister, and I worked as a Chinese teacher in New Westminster, and in the family store.

SHIRLEY CHAN: That's the Trans-Nation Emporium that my grandfather and my uncle had started way back in the twenties. It used to be known as the Kuo Seun Company.

NOBUE (MARGARET) SHIGA MINATO

Nobue (Margaret) Shiga Minato was born in Vancouver in 1911 of Japanese parents. Her father arrived in Canada via Manchuria, Korea, Taiwan, Hawaii, and San Francisco. Her mother came to Canada in 1910.

First, when my parents came to Vancouver, it was right down on Powell Street, and I think my father bought a boarding house or something, and my mother was running the boarding house. All the Japanese singles would go fishing or logging, and then in the winter I guess there was no work and so they would board. She said they brought you the money and then you paid for the board and you kept them going like that for years. She would buy meat at the cheapest place and then cut the good part to make sukiyaki, and then the other part for stew. I guess it was an all-day work for her. And then she thought maybe this wasn't for her, and we moved to 920 Cordova Street, when I was about six or seven. Dad was working at the Morrison Wire mill and mother went washing, to the homes. It was a big house and we weren't alone; there were always some new people coming with a new wife from Japan, and they weren't boarding but they would have one room and cook in there. So there was somebody looking after my two sisters, because I was going to school then.

When I was six, I think I went to *just* the Japanese School, and there was an English teacher taught us to read and spell, but the Japanese curriculum was number one. And then about that time, they decided that that was wrong. "These are Canadians, and they should go to the ordinary public school *first*, and then the extra reading and writing in Japanese." And so I was going to Seymour School, and walking to the Japanese Language School on Alexander Street. It was a wooden building and we had the assembly in front of it, and we all lined up and went in to our classes.[46] Then they built the Japanese Community Hall in 1928, next door to it. Where the building stands now—right to the corner was our grounds. On the first of July, we would have sports, and all the parents came to see it and it was quite a big "do" for the Japanese community. There was Mr. Tashiro and then Mr. Sato became principal.[47] The English teacher would come in for a part of the day at Japanese school and she gave us an English name because our names were so complicated. So she said, "May," or "Alice," or whatever, so that everybody had an English name.

Mother had been to Taiwan, and so I'm sure she adjusted right away. And Dad had been all over, so he thought it was a very nice place to settle down. The only thing was the discrimination, but he had a good job in that wire

Parade float on Powell Street, c. 1925. JAPANESE CANADIAN CENTENNIAL PROJECT, COURTESY TAMIO WAKAYAMA

mill, and he spoke, not fluent English, but he understood and he could get along with his broken English, and I think they did well. They instilled in us about education—we sure had to do well at school.

Mother learned to bake bread from our neighbour, Mrs. Monroe. We'd go home and smell this fresh bread and we'd cut it thick and put butter and jam on, and that was our in-between snack, and then we'd walk to Japanese School eating that. After Monroe's house, there was a long tenement house with rooms for single men and then there was nothing but bush and water, not a lake or anything, just little puddles here and there, with skunk cabbage. And in the winter, if it was cold, it would freeze up and then we'd just slide on the ice, and in the bushes we would play "Run, Sheep, Run" and all those old games.

My father started a bathhouse in 1925 at 318 Powell Street. On the corner was Mrs. Hamanaka's confectionery-grocery store, and then next to it, was Nakamura's Florist Shop, and then next to it was a shoeshine. And so the florist and the shoeshine people just had not a very big store, maybe, say, twenty-five feet, and the rest of the back was vacant, and my dad rented it for putting all the wood there, the four-foot-length wood, cords and cords of it for the hot water boiler. We moved to 222 Gore Avenue, and our back door came into this lot where my dad would be chopping the wood. There were two houses facing Gore Avenue, the other house was Mr. Miyasaki's and he was selling bean curds and chicken meat, and so their backyard was facing our dad's wood lot. Now the Sunrise Market takes the whole thing right to the alley. But there were two small houses and then the store, before. And upstairs was our bathhouse—it was the Lion Hotel. It was ten or fifteen cents at the most for a bath, and they were supplied with soap, and two towels, and there was a couple of straight razors there. So even if people just came in from any-where, before they went to even a restaurant or a Chinese chop suey house, they could have a bath first. It opened at three in the afternoon and it stayed open till eleven. And then my mom and dad would clean up, wash everything up, and go to bed, and then Dad would get up in the morning and start the boiler again. Any extra time he had, it was chopping the cordwood. He had some help too, to chop the cordwood for him. It certainly was a lot of wood. It was right against the whole building, all piled up, six foot high—it must have been cords and cords. They would wash the towels every day, maybe twice a day, and then we would help hang them up on this dryer on top of the boiler, there was maybe twenty-five lines there, and then we would just hang them up so that they would dry, and then we'd fold them.

The bathhouse was all tile, beautiful, from floor to ceiling where they bathed. And it had a kind of a corrugated ceiling with skylights. I don't know what it was, but it had designs on it—it wasn't just a flat wall when you looked up. And the other side, where people put their clothes on the knob, had those tatami mattings. In the bath itself, everything was tile. And then you stepped out onto the tatami floor. And they had a kind of a mat, a thick mat, where you would wipe your feet when you come out of the wet onto the tatami floor. The main bathtub where you went in, after you had a wash, was six foot by about ten. But before you go in there, there was a round tub about four feet in diameter, and there's hot and cold water running in it all the time, and you go in there and you wash first, really clean yourself first, and *then* you soak in the big tub. And then you come out and you wash thoroughly, this time—even your ears, and then, you go in and then you come out, and you're finished. So it's quite a ritual.

I never went into the men's tub, but the men's tub was bigger, because there were more single men, and so I think the whole thing was bigger than the ladies' part. On one side the hot water would come in, and so people who liked it real hot would converge around there, and on one side they'd have the cold water tap, so people who didn't like it so hot would turn the cold water on. It was big enough that people could swim a few strokes back and forth, when there's not many people in there. It was called "Matsu-no-yu." "Matsu" means "pine."

My father was an old-age pensioner when we were evacuated from the coast, so it was hard and he had arthritis. Usually, the oldest son takes the parents, but I said, "No, Dad will come with us." My husband was taken to a road camp—one of the first, because we had a store on Hornby and Nelson. We only had half a day's notice. So he gave me power-of-attorney right away, so that I could get rid of the store, and then we went to the Hudson's Bay—it was Wednesday, so it was a half day, and we heard that Alberta was very cold, so we got him leather coats and leather jackets and warm underwear to get him ready. When my husband was leaving, it was March the third, and it was

Girl's Festival day, so my mother said, "Well, he's going, but anyway, we'll celebrate," so we had fish with the head on—that's good luck, and the red rice with the red beans in for good luck, and it wouldn't go down.

We put name tags on all the children, in case we got separated, on cloth we wrote it down, and we put a little sum of money on the bigger ones, and the baby I knew I would carry wherever I went. And we *all* had name tags, in case we got separated, you know, died, or something, well then, they'd know who we were. My youngest boy was two and a half years old and the girl was eleven and the boy was ten. It was quite a shock. Every day there were rumours and there was this curfew where you can't go out after certain hours and everything had to be covered up for the blackouts—we bought yards and yards of black cloth to cover the store windows and we never went outside after sunset. It was really the most traumatic time of our life.

Anyway, I had power-of-attorney, so we sold the store—just for the stock—they wouldn't give us anything for the refrigerator, the counter, or anything, because they knew we *had* to go. We sold it to Chinese people. He was from Canton, and he was so good, he said he'd never had any experience in business—he'd worked in the bank—so he said, "Would you help us?" I said, "Sure." So he came to the store, and we stayed in the back of the store just as we were, in our living quarters. My husband was already gone and there was no way we could call him back. So we said, "Well, we'll go to Lillooet as a self-supporting family so that we can go with my mother, father, and our family." That way my husband could come back to Lillooet and build a shack.

I went to the place where you register for the evacuation, and I was watching, you know, and the man said, "What have you got?" And they'd say, "Table." Well, he would just write "table" and he wouldn't write the amount, or if it was a homemade table or a table that was antique. So when my turn came, he said, "Have you got anything?" and I said, "No, I have nothing to declare." So I went back home and then I packed everything I could, and I asked this Chinese gentleman that bought the store—there was a little shack-like shed—so I said, "Could I put everything there and if we settle somewhere, would you send it?" and he said, "Sure!" So we were *very* lucky.

That way we went to Lillooet for ten months. We weren't in Lillooet proper, we were in east Lillooet, on the east side of the Fraser River. My husband went first, and then there were already people that had started building, so then each guy would help build the next guy's house. Our place was a twelve- by twenty-eight-foot shack—that was one of the biggest ones, because there were seven of us. We had to pay, you see, so what size you wanted to build, okay, you paid. And we didn't ask the government for a *cent* to move from Vancouver to Lillooet, that's one thing I'm very proud of. I thought, well, we won't be a burden on Canada, even if they were kicking us out. It was so hot and you built your house, and we had to dig into the dirt in the summer to make a place where you stayed in the daytime away from the heat,

Japanese Canadian men saying goodbye to their families during their evacuation to camps in the Interior, 1942. JAPANESE CANADIAN CENTENNIAL PROJECT, COURTESY TAMIO WAKAYAMA

underground, and we put rocks in, so that the earth wouldn't fall in on you. It wasn't a cellar, it was to get away from the heat. And then in the winter, it went down so cold, even a rabbit would freeze. We had to buy water; it was fifteen cents a barrel. When they put the water into the buckets, well, it would almost stick to you in the winter, because it was that cold. It was not water, it was going to ice. When it was cold, my husband or I would take turns to be up all night so we'd have the stove going. Even vinegar froze. The house was just a one light plank, you see, and it was wet wood when we built, so it dried up and we had to chink every crack, and there was icicles. There was heat going but, you see, it was so cold that when you were asleep, well there would be ice right by the sheet where your breath was.

I was so worried about the children's education. They didn't start any school in September, and we'd arrived there about May, and they played all through summer and September. So I wrote to the head of the correspondence department at Victoria, and I said, "I have a son who's in Grade 7 and a daughter who's in Grade 8, and they had good grades in Vancouver, and I don't want them to miss a whole year. So is it possible that I could teach them by correspondence?" and she said, "Certainly." So, I got all the things for Grade 7 and 8, and then I started teaching our two. My son was eleven and he said, "Everybody's out in the Fraser River swimming, and I have to go to school!" So I went around to the neighbours and said, "Are there any Grade 7 boys?" and there was, luckily, two, and they were willing to have them educated too. So then I got another little girl to come, the same age as my oldest daughter. So I baked bread, I read at nights to study for tomorrow, and I had this two-and-a-half-year-old, and seven of us, you know. So then, when I started that, it dawned on them that September, October, November, well it was no use letting these kids—these were all *Canadians*, you know—do nothing, eh? So the Japanese community built a school. And there were a lot of people that were university and high school graduates and so that's how they got on there. So we didn't have to worry. The children took their exams in Lillooet proper, at the school there, and they all passed.

My husband went apple picking that fall because there was no labour in the Okanagan. Mr. Howe, his boss, came to Lillooet, and hired maybe sixty young men to pick apples. And there were fishermen and people that never had done labour like that, but anyway they went. And when he came back he said, "There's a high school there and the people aren't friendly yet, but it's good for the children to get to school." And then we wrote back and forth and then Mr. Howe said we could come. So we were the first ones to get out of Lillooet, and they didn't like it because they thought if everybody went out the whole community would fold. In Vernon there was maybe 150 Japanese hired, there were teachers and there were fishermen and dressmakers and professional people. We all worked, we *really* worked. It was wartime and they were growing seeds too, not just apples. Seeds for England, Europe—onion seeds, carrot seeds, beet seeds. At first we didn't know a pigweed from a beet. It was twenty-five cents an hour for the ladies, and thirty-five cents for the men at the start, and then it went up a little. Where we went first in Vernon, it was a bull barn where we lived. They kind of cleaned it up a little bit, put partitions in, and there was two families. We had bunks for the children, and there was one bed and a kitchen—everything in the one room. Every time you washed the wall, it would smell of manure. But it *was* a place to stay, and then they moved us into a real home later, and I lived with Caucasian people, half of the house, and that wasn't bad.

We lost our son in Vernon, he was sick. And we had moved to Vernon because we knew we were near a hospital and near good medical care because there wasn't any in Lillooet. You see, when we were in Lillooet, my son was helping a neighbour chop kindling, and he broke his nose, and so we had to get a permit from the Mounties to go across the river to the doctor. So I said, "Well, we'd better get out to somewhere there's medical attention," especially when you have children. And then my father died at Lillooet that spring, while we were in Vernon, and we got him buried there. We still go to Lillooet once in a while.

STRATHCONA SCHOOL TEACHERS [48]

GERTRUDE DOYLE: My first impressions of Strathcona School? I hated it! As a matter of fact, when I went there as a substitute and it came to the end of the year, I thought, "I hope to goodness I don't get appointed to Strathcona." And I did! What I didn't like was the teachers. They were the

The teachers and the years they taught at Strathcona School:

Miss Gertrude Doyle (1923–58)
Miss E.G. Farrington (1926–69)
Miss E.M. (King) Morris (1930–39)
Miss J.G. Schooley (1928–59)
Mr. V.A. Wiedrick (1928–39)

most unfriendly bunch of people I ever saw. But we got together afterwards, and everything was fine. I stayed on because of the number of nationalities, the kinds of people, and the teachers—afterwards. And I had chances to go to Europe or to transfer to any place around the city, but I wouldn't go.

EILEEN FARRINGTON: It was the same for me. I wouldn't have left Strathcona on a bet. They couldn't have *paid* me to leave it, after I got to know the children and became involved with them. I really loved them all.

ELVA MORRIS: Isn't that funny? I *wanted* to go to Strathcona. I was hoping that was where I *could* go, because I thought the teachers were all so friendly. Now, it just depended who you met, didn't it? And I never changed my mind, they were a great bunch.

JENNIE SCHOOLEY: They were. They were a swell bunch there. Well, I substituted first, and when the word came that I was to go there—I'd substituted in Grade 8, and the boys were all bigger than I was, and I was frightened when I thought of going there, but after I got there, I loved it. Some of the boys were over-age for one thing. They had come from a foreign country and were late in starting to school, but *all* the time we were there, many of the Grade 8 boys were bigger than we were. You know, many of the European boys were full grown. And as teachers, we were all in our twenties, when we started there.

GERTRUDE DOYLE: When I had to go and look up a kid, I had to go to Hogan's Alley and of course, I went at noontime. I went down there in Hogan's Alley, and it was only about eight feet wide, I guess, and every window as I went along had an eye peering out—it was the spookiest feeling I ever had. We got down to the house, and I found the little boy, and there was nothing in the home at all, just the four walls. Another time I had to go up to a Chinese place. There were about three floors, and I had to go to the top floor. Nobody understood English and we went into the office and went up there, and as we went by, every door opened a little bit, and a head appeared out that door. But I found the kid.

JENNIE SCHOOLEY: But we were safe at any time of the day or night. Everybody knew us—"Teacher, teacher." And yet, that was the centre of the "square mile of crime," that's what they called it, that was general talk in town. But we could walk down any street, and we walked down that Hastings Street from Main westward, it was always, as long as I can remember, very tough, and we could walk down there. We were never molested in any way, and never a word was said out of place, to any of us.

GERTRUDE DOYLE: I thought it was my schoolteacher look that saved me.

ELVA MORRIS: There were policemen on the beat in the neighbourhood, because I can remember once I said, "You have to do right," and this boy said, "No, you don't if you give the policeman—whatever his name was—a chicken, it's okay to open your store on Sunday."

GERTRUDE DOYLE: There was no stage in the school of any kind but we had all this talent, and we needed money, so they put all the tables together, right in the end of the hall, and their dressing room was the staff room. The performance was put on on top of these tables, swaying as they were. There were Ukrainian dances with costumes, Japanese costumes, all sorts of little plays and skits and things like that, and it was a howling success. It must have been 1928 to 1930, right in there somewhere. And then every Friday, we'd have a half an hour in the auditorium, and sometimes it would be a Japanese program, sometimes a Chinese program, sometimes Jewish, sometimes Blacks. They took their turns, and it used to run overtime.

JENNIE SCHOOLEY: One of these concerts that we had was "International Day." Miss Roberts put it on and she taught all the children the chorus of all the national anthems. She had all the Italians in one section, all the Ukrainians in another, all the Chinese in another, the Japanese in another, and all the various nationalities in groups. And then, the people of that nationality would sing the first verse of their national anthem in their own language and the whole senior building would sing the chorus, and then they'd go on to the next national group. That was just thrilling. I can never remember when I was there in the thirties and forties any discrimination of any kind. We never thought, this one's Chinese, this is Japanese, this is something else. We just thought they were all children, and they too, they all mixed together.

Strathcona School as it looked in 1907; the building on the right still stands. PHILIP TIMMS PHOTO, VANCOUVER PUBLIC LIBRARY, VPL 5000

EILEEN FARRINGTON: It was the school of many nationalities and only one flag. That was our motto.

ELVA MORRIS: Actually, I always had a feeling none of them were Canadians, that I was the only Canadian in my room. I thought they all felt allegiance to where they came from, and their parents did, too. Yes. You didn't meet many grown-ups when we were young who said they were Canadian, even if they came from England, Ireland, or Scotland, or any place.

EILEEN FARRINGTON: There was a great pupil/teacher relationship. Oftentimes, I would ask their opinions about something. They knew I had respect for them, and they had for me. I remember once I said, "Where would you like this picture put? Would it be better here or there?" and they said, "Now you know very well that you're going to put it where you want to anyway."

JENNIE SCHOOLEY: Only one bad incident I can remember in my thirty years there was the Gypsies. They all ganged up against the Gypsies. I remember going home from school one day, and down on Jackson Avenue there was a fight going on, and I walked right in and here were all the Gypsies and the others, and I just walked in, took them by the scruff of their neck—they both towered above me—and said, "You go that way. You go that way." And they did, they never thought to dispute you. Any of them.

ELVA MORRIS: Once there was the big trouble with Mr. Brown, the principal, because the Gypsies said no music should be going on in the school because they'd had a funeral, and when there was a death, you didn't have music for—was it a year, or so many months? And each of their children would have to go out in the hall, and I can remember the principal saying, "Well, isn't that silly? In a school like this, there's music going all day." So the Gypsy went stamping down the hall. He said, "Stupid school, all they do is sing."

GERTRUDE DOYLE: Their way of life was entirely different. They were out to make a disturbance, wherever they were. And they made it in our school a little bit, too. As far as they dared.

VERNON WIEDRICK: I remember when I was teaching at Strathcona School and the longshoremen were on strike [1935]. There were so-called scabs and the strikers would chase these people all over the East End. One day there was a horde of these scabs running through the school, actually right through the halls, with these fellows with bats and other things, chasing them. This only happened once or twice, but it was a period of strikes and a lot of labour unrest and demonstrations in Oppenheimer Park. People didn't have too much money.

GERTRUDE DOYLE: It was during the 1930s that the Japanese navy was in our harbour. The first thing we knew, the whole navy was up at our school, throwing open the doors, talking with the pupils. We didn't know what to do about it—they just walked in. They came in to see the pupils, you see, they had friends here, and they just came in to see what was going on. Of course, they were feeling their power in those days, too. And feeling around in Canada, I think, and they were letting us know about it.

Elva Morris: Some Japanese students went back and did military service in Japan. Quite a number went back to Japan when they were in high school or through high school, because I remember different ones telling me their brothers had gone back. That was the first I'd ever heard of it.

Gertrude Doyle: Miss McLellan was the only school nurse in Vancouver for many many years,[49] she and Miss Breeze. And later on, when she went in any of the stores around town, she'd meet the head of the store and she'd say to him, "Well, I remember the days when I used to look down *your* throat." All the businessmen of Vancouver went through her hands, one way or another.

Jennie Schooley: If a child was away from school, she'd go down Hogan's Alley, anyplace in town, the toughest parts of town. And everyone knew her—"Nurse, Nurse, Nurse." She was safe anyplace, and she'd go anyplace.

Gertrude Doyle: And those dark, dark nights after school—her hours were till five o'clock, which was pitch-black, and one time she was down just outside Woodward's, and she felt somebody feeling around to the belt of her coat. So she looked around and here was a poor drunk, and he said, "Don't worry, Nurse, I'm just straightening up your belt a little bit." She loved the neighbourhood. She could go down into their homes, you see. We didn't have truant officers or anything, the nurse and the teachers looked after things like that. She'd go into their homes, and they always offered in the Italian homes a drink of something, and she wasn't having any. But that didn't matter to them. She never insulted them about it, she just didn't take it, that's all.

Jennie Schooley: And another thing about her, she knew all the children's problems. If we had a child in our class who had a problem, she'd come to us quietly and tell us. After she left the district, there was one little guy I had, and that poor little guy never once brought his pen, pencil, ruler, and eraser—those four things, and I'd bawl him out. In Grade 8, he ended up in my badminton club, and he couldn't buy a racquet. Another boy, was a pain in the neck but a likeable kid, bought him a racquet and I said, "Oh, that was good of you to buy him that racquet." And he said, "Oh, Miss Schooley, his mother's no good. She's the very worst of those on Cordova Street." Now if Miss McLellan had been there, I would have been told about him. She had a monetary fund that the teachers contributed to—we just gave her this money. And children who needed something that she didn't have in stock, well she'd buy it and give it to them. We also took clothing, and other things. And Miss McLellan would give them these, and the children never knew it came from the teachers.

Jennie Schooley: They had a bathtub down in the Senior Building, and children who were really unclean, were sent down there to wash. But what could you expect—many of the kiddies lived in these apartment buildings in just a cold-water flat. Some of them didn't even have cold water, they had a sink and a toilet down at the end of the hall on each floor.

GERTRUDE DOYLE: That's all they had, and when you went into their buildings and saw how they were living, you *couldn't* make a fuss about them coming to school dirty.

JENNIE SCHOOLEY: But others were absolutely immaculate, clean as could be. Their things might be well-worn, but they were absolutely immaculate.

GERTRUDE DOYLE: Yeah, we had problems, and one time it got too bad with one boy, and Mr. Brown was our principal then, and he took that boy, after lots of warning, and said, "Now, if you come again in this mess, I'm going to take you down to the basement, and I'm going to bath you." So he thought that would be enough, but the boy came dirty again, and he took him down and he turned the hose on him, with cold water, and everybody in the building could hear this kid screeching at the top of his voice, "You're killing me, you're *killing* me." And he never came back dirty.

ELVA MORRIS: They boarded up the house of one boy—a very nice boy. His father was bootlegging and he would keep opening his house again and finally they locked it. I used to be very careful what I wrote on his report, because one of the other kids told me if his report wasn't good, his father just took his belt off and beat the dickens out of him. He was such a nice boy and he wasn't that bright, but I was very cautious what I put on his report. There were all sorts of things like that going on then.

I think I grew up a bit, I don't think I really realized things until I taught at Strathcona School. I was working, and all my family were working and here were all these kids. I remember this little girl, and she would come late and we did watch the girls coming late. So finally, I didn't want to send her to the office and I said, "Why *can't* you come on time?" and she started to cry, and she said, "Because the wood is wet." At their home, this poor little kid had to get up in the morning and try and get the fire started and feed her five-year-old brother *before* she came to school. Well, that finished me right there, because I used to get up and my breakfast would be ready for me. And I think I really started looking at people differently when that poor little kid told me that. None of our friends felt the Depression because we all had enough, but we knew about it from the school. I got a note from a boy one day and they didn't know the teacher's name, but would I pass it on, and it was from his mother, thanking this teacher for seeing that they were always supplied with coal. He had kept them for two years. And I can remember taking it over to him. And it was supposed to be kept quiet, but I can remember looking at him a little differently.

JENNIE SCHOOLEY: I was in charge of the money that was raised for the war effort, and we raised a lot of money. We had these concerts, we had drives, and bazaars. We raised $6,000 one night at a bazaar. It didn't start till four o'clock. Mr. Woodward of Woodward Stores had gone to Strathcona School at one time, and the principal, Mr. Patterson, had a speech all prepared for approaching Mr. Woodward. Mr. Patterson got halfway through it and Mr. Woodward said, "Well"—I've forgotten how many hundred dollars—"would that do? And would so many hundred dollars' worth of goods from the store, would that be suitable?" "Fine." So from all the material, different groups sewed and knitted and made different things for the bazaar, and we got wool, and we got materials and anything we needed, free down at Woodward's.

GERTRUDE DOYLE: Every merchant in the district contributed, *every* store, in one way or another.

JENNIE SCHOOLEY: During the war, the Negro children first went to Miss Hardwick who was in charge of any musical concerts and then they came around to all the classrooms, and they said, "We all coloured folk, we're going to put on a concert, 'Jitterbug Wedding' for the Red Cross. Five cents. Wednesday at quarter after twelve." And the auditorium was filled, and it was this Jitterbug Wedding which they had put on at a nightclub down near Main Street. It *really* was a professional concert. Several of the teachers were a bit shocked by part of it although it had been censored. Three or four of those children are now professional entertainers, well known in Vancouver.

As for the Japanese, we wept with the children, when they left, but we saw where it was necessary, because the day after Pearl Harbor, on that Sunday and the following week, there were some who were glorying in the Japanese victories at Pearl Harbor and Singapore. And so we were sorry to see them leave, but what could they do?

GERTRUDE DOYLE: The parents took it very well. Two or three came to me and they said, "We don't want to go and we feel it's unjust." But what could the Canadian government do? There were a few spies among them[50]— they *knew* there were, and you can't pick a few spies out of 2,500.[51] So they put them all out.

JENNIE SCHOOLEY: That day when they were going, the children came to say goodbye, and they were crying and we were crying—we just hated to see them go. But, as Miss Doyle said, their parents felt what else was there to do? What else?

EILEEN FARRINGTON: But actually, the children did improve their academic careers by moving out.

JENNIE SCHOOLEY: They did, they had a better chance. They might have stayed in that area forever. They were moved out and the ones who went to Ontario did well, they did very well, and also the ones who went to Alberta, many of them did very well.

GERTRUDE DOYLE: It broke up a ghetto, I believe.

ELVA MORRIS: You wonder if this would have happened after the war anyway, or would it have at all, because this is what made them Canadians. I mean, Canadians never accepted them before, really. I don't know if it would have happened anyway or if this speeded things up a bit.

VERNON WIEDRICK: With the children of *all* origins, a thing that has been common, regardless of race or anything else, is that those people came here as immigrants and they aspired to do things. For example, there were a number of Jewish children in this area who were really hard up. And their parents worked hard, they'd go to other parts of the city collecting what we call junk—they began to save money and they gradually came ahead. They were the ones that really climbed out all on their own by hard work, and you'd see them move gradually on along. The Chinese, too, did the same thing. They were law-abiding, they worked hard, and they gradually climbed out.

JENNIE SCHOOLEY: Yes, we learned about life [at that school]. We had a sheltered life. We did, you know. Our parents were comfortable—not wealthy but comfortable, and we took things for granted. We really did. Until we were there. And we all loved it, we loved those kids—they meant a lot to us.

TADAO WAKABAYASHI

Tadao (Tad) Wakabayashi was born in Vancouver in 1916. His father came to Canada in 1892 and worked as a fisherman, sawmill worker, boarding-house owner, and finally as a tofu (bean cake) maker. His mother came to Canada sometime before 1910 as a picture bride.

My religion was Buddhist but the funny part is I went to the kindergarten under the auspices of the United Church [now Buddhist Church, corner of Powell and Jackson]. As I grew older, I was still a Buddhist, and the Buddhist Church used to be on Franklin Street, just off Clark Drive.[52] Then they built a new one on the corner of Princess and Cordova. It's still being used as a church, you can see the neon light, "Christ Died for Our Sins."

In those days, there was nothing for us to work towards, because of discrimination. Quite a few went to university, but they came out and—no future. So a number of them went back to Japan and they have been doing very well. Our parents' main objective was for us to get the education because, and this is my personal opinion—if we can beat them, we'll beat them by education. There was no maybe about it. If we sluffed on our schoolwork, look out! After we finished the regular school at Strathcona, we went down to the Japanese school and took in a lesson for about an hour and a half. Really, we had no time to play, because my dad was in business and any spare moments we had to work. And after we finished work, then we sat down and tried to do our homework, two homeworks, the Japanese and the English.

My first teacher at Japanese school was Mrs. Sato. During the time the Satos were teaching, they graduated about 1,200 students from that school. We were taught the grammar, the history of Japan, and to read and write calligraphy. At Strathcona School they had their discipline, but it was more strict in Japanese school, we had to look up to the teacher. In that way, I think, the Japanese respect authority more than anything else—police department, city officials, schoolteachers, they were the people in authority and we had to behave. You got the strap for talking too much or just making too much noise, not paying attention. At the Japanese school, we were put outside the classroom if we didn't behave. But one teacher knew judo and oh, we were afraid of him. He took one schoolmate outside and the next moment we heard a *bang* and this chum of ours came back and his face was white, and we knew what happened—he was thrown.

About 50 percent of the students at Strathcona School were Japanese.

The Japanese Methodist Mission in 1907, later the Japanese United Church, at the corner of Powell Street and Jackson Avenue. This building became the Japanese Buddhist Church in 1956 and was demolished in the late 1970s to be replaced with a new structure. PHILIP TIMMS PHOTO, VANCOUVER PUBLIC LIBRARY, VPL 6840

And then next came the Chinese. Then the Italians and the rest of them. Personally, I got along very fine with Italian boys. But there was a little bit of animosity between the Chinese and the Japanese even then. I never had any occasion of fighting them, but my brother used to come back and say, "Gee whiz, we got ganged up on, and oh, we had a fight."

Our association with the Occidental group wasn't much. Because we felt as though we were sort of left out. At school, mind you, they were nice to talk to and we'd play sports together but outside of that there was no socializing. But we had our fun. The main sport was baseball, and the Asahi Baseball Club was well known and well liked by the Caucasians and everybody, and they began playing on Powell Street.

We had a judo club, behind the Hotel Marr, right behind there, and we used part of the beer parlour as a judo gymnasium then. So after coming back from Japanese school, we'd have our supper and then we'd go to the judo club and maybe practise for two, three hours. Actually our sport was nice, clean, and there was no rough stuff, and even to this day, I hardly get into an argument because, well, you know the background of judo and your reactions might be slow right now and your reflexes are slow because you're out of practice, but once you get into an argument or fight, you know you can look after yourself.

The Hastings Sawmill was our swimming ground. Every weekend, you'd find a number of boys and girls down there, and some of us used to swim across the inlet to North Vancouver and swim back. We had to be careful because the tides run, so we'd take a certain time to swim. The water was clean, not like now. Because, weekends we used to go fishing for shiners down on Gore Avenue dock or anyplace—the favourite place was the Gore Avenue dock—and we used to pull out fish until we'd get a pail full, then we'd go down to Powell Street to the fish market and sell that fish and we'd go to the movies.

My dad's friend started a fruit and vegetable wholesale, and he needed a helper, so I was it. The work itself was much more than I could handle, going out to the country at night time, picking up fruits and vegetables from the farmers in the Fraser Valley district. You work from six to twelve in town, and then from twelve o'clock, you head out towards Surrey and from Surrey, you go out to Aldergrove and Abbotsford and then cross the old Mission bridge, and then you went down the north side and came home, so it usually takes you over twelve hours and you're not stopping. You go from farmer to farmer, picking up twenty crates of strawberry or fifteen crates of asparagus or lettuce or something. So when I ended up coming home it would be about two o'clock in the morning, and I'd go down to Powell Street to the Chinese chop suey house and sit down and have bowls of noodle or something and then come home, go to sleep and it was usually about three, three thirty. Then get up, be at work at six o'clock. I did that for three weeks and I got sick. So then after that, they made it a little easier for me.

In the thirties the Chinese still had horse and wagon peddlers, but the Japanese peddlers were more mechanized, they had their own trucks. Usually my dad's customers were from the valleys, and they would come in and buy, not too much vegetable, but fish, rice, and bean curd, which my dad was making. He shipped those bean curds out to Woodfibre, Ocean Falls, Powell River, where the Japanese were. There were about three in Vancouver that were in that business, but my dad was the biggest, Wakabayashi Tofu.

Behind American Can Company used to be flats [of Burrard Inlet] and between the American Can Company and the Hastings Sawmill would be what we used to call "jungle." That's where all the unemployed men congregated and built the shacks, and, oh, we were afraid to go there. They built the shacks from *anything*, you know, from tin to cardboard. And during those days, if they were hungry, they went down and broke a window in Woodward's or Hudson's Bay or any place like that and just waited for the police to come and pick them up. That's why Woodward's storefront was all covered up with lumber. That jungle, I was speaking of, you know, when you see that, you'd wonder how people ever lived. And every freight train that came in, men were coming in, and then they're going out. Must have been thousands in there: It went from the Campbell Avenue west. And not just one man in one shack, there's two, three, in one shack. And there's always fighting. Can't help it, because the men are hungry, and they were only getting, what, twenty cents a day to go to the road camp.

There was pride in the Japanese people that they wouldn't go on welfare, so they really helped each other then. Not organized help, it was neighbour to neighbour. It's because, in a way, the Japanese were thrifty. Because our mother and dad's motive, you see, coming to Canada was make enough money, then go home. So they did save money, even if it's a few hundred dollars— that's a lot more than a lot of people had then. My dad went back to Japan a few times. The last time he went back, he built a house, hoping to go home and retire. But he couldn't do that because the war started. So I was the last one to go back and see the house. That was in 1936 and my personal feeling is, I never want to live in Japan. No. The lifestyle is altogether different. In those days the people in Japan knew there *would* be a war between America and Japan, they were already talking about it. And when I mentioned about the government, "Ssh! Not too loud. Somebody might listen."

It's my personal feeling that the evacuation was the best thing that ever happened to Japanese people. If they had left us alone on Powell Street, where would we be today? Still down there? It opened up the field for us. Now you can go across Canada and find successful people, millionaires and so forth. We have our architects, lawyers, doctors. Before the war, we couldn't join the union, now anybody can join the union. And you go to any business establishment, you find Orientals working in there, and quite a number of them have key positions which we couldn't have before the war. The only thing I regret is people my age, when we were just about ready to blossom, so to speak, we were sent to the road camp and the Interior. And people did lose their assets. Take my dad for an example, he was in business and they told us, the BC Security Commission told us, "Write down all the money that people owe you, and send it in and we'll collect it for you." So I was doing the books for my dad so I jotted down a, b, c, d, and it came to over $20,000 because of the Depression. And to this day, I remember one cheque coming.

In 1940 my dad bought a house on McGill Street for $3,000. Two payments and the house belonged to us, you know. My dad put that house in my name and when they wanted to take the cases to court regarding Japanese property, they wanted a Japanese Canadian, a naturalized Canadian, and a Japanese national. That's why our house was put through the court. And we lost the case.

My parents continued with the business as long as possible on Powell Street because people wanted to buy groceries, so it was all right that way. But *every day* people were being shipped out. We had to go to the RCMP and ask for a permit to stay in Vancouver, and they might give you a permit for one month, so we kept that permit and you had to carry it with you all the time. Curfew was on, so we had to be home before sundown. The feeling of the

A 1910 classroom in the Japanese Language School on Alexander Street. VANCOUVER PUBLIC LIBRARY, SPECIAL COLLECTIONS, VPL 86019A

Japanese—the majority was very hostile. Even myself, I felt I was cheated out of being a Canadian. Because we were called for military duty before everything happened. One group was called, and my brother, he went and took a medical, and he came home you know, so happy, said, "I'm Class A." And his friends were all classified physically fit, so he was so happy that he's going to join the Army. Then by the time my turn came along, the atmosphere had changed and they said, "No, we don't want you." You know, we were a "bloody Jap," that's all. When I was courting my wife we came out of a movie, Orpheum Theatre, one night and an Army chap walking in front of us looked at me and said, "If it wasn't for you guys, we wouldn't *have to* join the army." And it's not right, you know. Here I am, I'm *proud* as a Canadian. I'm more Canadian than a lot of these people. And at the last minute they say, "You're not a Canadian citizen. You're just an enemy alien." That's not right.

After Pearl Harbor happened, we didn't feel unsafe on the streets. Not a bit. Only thing we were afraid of was being picked up by police and shipped out to the road camp. The most comical part was that the Caucasians couldn't tell the difference between the Chinese and Japanese. So the Chinese had a button made, "I am Chinese," and somehow or other we'd get hold of it.

So we had our fun, but finally my excuses ran out to stay in Vancouver,

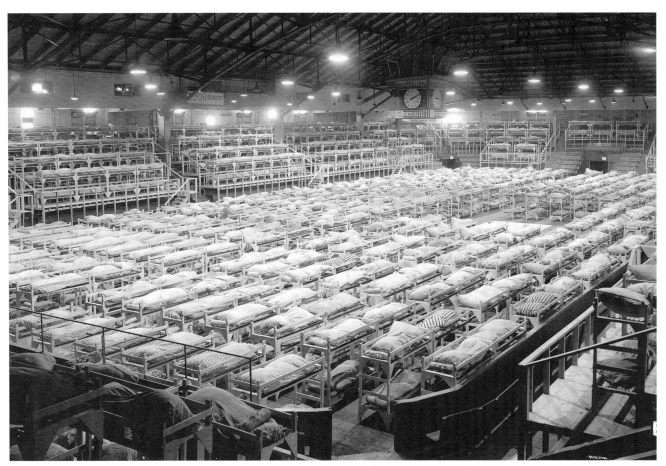

PNE building at Hastings Park used as a dormitory during the Japanese evacuation, 1942. LEONARD FRANK PHOTO, VANCOUVER PUBLIC LIBRARY, VPL 14918

so I thought to myself, "I'll go to Hastings Park and stay and work there," because if you were working in Hastings Park they couldn't say too much.[53] So I worked there putting straws in the mattress. Have you ever slept on that? The men's dormitory was the Forum, and that place was just crammed with double-decker beds. You try to sleep in there and they're playing card games all night. Many fortunes were won and lost in that building. But the most sorry part that I can't erase from my head was when I went down to the Agricultural Building where the animals were kept—each had a stall, and the families were living in there, mother and children. And the only privacy they had was to pull the curtain in front, and that's all. So I ask you, would you live in a place like that? We were forced to.

The people who went to the Slocan Valley—oh, I felt sorry for them because the year of '42 was the *coldest* winter we ever had. Even our place [near Sorrento] we didn't get any windows in our shack. Two-by-four and slap a board across it, put the tarpaper over it, then put the one-by-four to hold the tarpaper in place, and that was all. No insulation. And no windows. The temperature went down to thirty-two below, Fahrenheit. I remember that— because in the morning, you woke up and where your breath was hitting the blanket was all white, coated with frost. We didn't have any winter clothes. You know. We'd just come from the coast, we never expected to find thirty below. When I went to visit my folks in Lemon Creek, that was near Slocan, and I *saw* the house they were living in—they had to move the furniture at least a foot away from the wall because from the floor to about four feet high, frost, right around the house.

Oh, we went through a lot of hardship but now we are able to smile instead of holding our animosity. We realize there's no sense in holding it, because of the event that led everything up to that point, and because it was these rabble-rousers in Vancouver, especially the politicians, who wanted to make hay.

Alec Lucas

I was born on a blanket in the front room of 522 Cordova Street. A midwife brought me into the world. My parents came from Portland, Oregon, and originally they were from Yugoslavia. My father worked in the steel mills in Pennsylvania and when he came to Canada he worked at Britannia Mines. He worked there for a considerable number of years until he had to retire with silicosis.

Logs used to come in on Burrard Inlet, and in those Depression days we would go down and cut the logs up for firewood and wheel the wood home in a wheelbarrow and stack it in our backyard for the winter. An awful lot of people did this because there wasn't enough money around to buy coal. It would take nine or ten cords to get us through a winter because it was a big house in which we lived, ten bedrooms. My mother

Alec Lucas was born in Vancouver in 1916. His parents had emigrated from Yugoslavia to the United States and then moved to Vancouver. He was principal of Alpha Secondary School in Burnaby.

kept a boarding house there for some time when my father was ill. People that came from the old country would stay there and she would help them out. And then once they got working in the mines or in the woods, they would repay her for helping them. Our house was sort of a centre for many Yugoslavians that came out here. In those days most of the Yugoslavian people lived on Cordova Street.

Peanuts were imported in big sacks then and some would fall overboard when they were unloading them. So they'd float in and my brother and I would take the sacks home and dry them out and put them in our kitchen oven. Then we'd buy little paper sacks and we'd weigh out so many ounces in each paper sack and sell them at the Powell Street Grounds where there were baseball games going practically every night. They used to have a large audience because the games were very popular and most of the teams were commercial teams. The Japanese always had a very good baseball team. One fellow I remember, his name was Tanaka, and he was a one-armed pitcher and he was one of the best.

On Main Street there was a farmer's market and it extended right through to Pender. You could go there and you could buy—oh, you could buy meat, you could buy rabbits, you could buy vegetables. There was a big Greek store on the corner of Hastings and Main, and it was the open-style fruit store where you could pick up your fruit outside on the stand and take it in and purchase it. But the stands along Main Street at the farmer's market were almost tents, you know, open in the front with a canvas top. People used to bring all their wares in and set them up early in the morning and they'd stay there and sell them all day long.

At that time [1935], Andrew Roddan was the minister of First United Church, and he used to help people out. Of course, the various churches would have breadlines, including the Salvation Army. And then there was welfare, because there weren't the jobs for them, there wasn't the money. So they had welfare slips and people would go and pick up their welfare on Cambie Street off of Hastings. There were quite a few families in the neighbourhood on welfare, but there were a lot of people who were too proud to go on welfare, so they made do without. The breadlines were mostly for men that were on the move and hungry.

My mother converted the downstairs part of the house to a store so she had an ice-cream parlour and a store, and this is how she earned our keep. The famous fighter, Jimmy McLarnin, lived a few blocks away from us and he used to come to our home in the morning and have breakfast with us because everyone helped each other out in those days, and he knew my brothers very well, and my mother. Most of our friends were Italian. We didn't seem to mix with the other Yugoslavian children as much. The majority of people in our neighbourhood were of non-Anglo-Saxon backgrounds, and we felt there *was* a difference with the west side of the city. Maybe we felt inferior—we *shouldn't* have, but we did in some respects. Mind you, there were Anglo-Saxons in the area, but there was a good mixture of all nationalities, which was a good education because we all learned to get along together.

Most people in the East End are very interested in athletics and sports—it was an outlet for them. We played basketball together, soccer together, and we even went out to Brockton Point to train there two or three nights a week. Andrew Turner had this boys' club, and for many years he cared for these boys and trained them, not only in soccer and basketball, but especially in track.

There were quite a number of churches in the area. In those days, all the Sunday schools competed with each other, they all had their boys' clubs and girls' clubs, and we had soccer leagues that played on Saturdays, and we had the annual Sunday school track meet, and then we had other dual meets during the year with the other Sunday schools. The Sunday schools then also had the gymnasiums, so these were centres to keep boys and girls off the streets at night and give them something worthwhile.

When I was growing up there was a curfew at nine o'clock at night, so if you were under fifteen years of age I think it was, you had to be indoors, before that. The policemen of course walked the beat in those days. The other way you knew it was nine o'clock at night on Cordova Street, the water wagon used to come along and wash the street off. There were drugs in those days too, but it was minor compared to now. The drug addicts were always getting into trouble and the police were always chasing them. We knew them. And there were an awful lot of holdups. It was the East End. But still at night you felt safe walking around. You never felt that anyone was going to slug *you* or hold *you* up or anything. If there were holdups, then they held up people who had money, or who they figured had money. It was just the way of life.

KIYOKO TANAKA-GOTO

I was born in 1896 in Tokyo, somewhere in the Shinbashi [high-class geisha district], but my mother came from Kyushu so that's where I grew up. It was a terrible childhood. From the age of seven I was helping my mother farm. Father was in San Francisco, he had left us when I was four years old. He sent her a letter and asked her to come over to San Francisco, but she didn't want to leave Japan, she didn't want to live with "strangers." So he got quite upset and wouldn't send any money to us. We farmed and we sold bean curd, gathered firewood in the mountains, sold flour in town, which was four or five miles away—we had to walk to get there we were so poor. Then when I was nineteen [1916], I came to Canada as a picture bride. My husband was also from Kyushu, although I didn't know him. It was arranged by our neighbours who knew how hard I'd been working since I was a little girl, and they figured that a woman who was getting married in North America had to be very healthy and a good worker. I could have married a doctor in Japan but I decided to get married in North America because I wanted to find Father and send him back to Japan. My plan was to stay in North America about five

Kiyoko Tanaka-Goto was born in Tokyo in 1896. The following is compiled from earlier interviews in Japanese by Maya Koizumi and translated by Taki Bluesinger, and from a recent additional interview by Taki Bluesinger.

years, find Father, save some money, and then go back myself. I never did go back although I did send Father back.

My husband and I milked cows at a farm on Vancouver Island for a year and then we went to Saltspring Island where my husband worked for another farmer and I cleaned out chicken coops three or four hours a day. On my way back from cleaning coops I'd pick up laundry at the hotel and do it at home. I slept about four or five hours a day, the rest of the time I was working. After four years of that I came to Vancouver [1920] with $2,000 I had saved and I bought a whorehouse at the corner of Powell and Gore with three other women. We turned it into a restaurant, the kind of restaurant where people came mainly to drink. Of course we didn't have a liquor licence, and there was singing and dancing and a lot of noise all the time so we got hustled by the police fairly often. The first year business was so good I couldn't believe it. There weren't many women around then, you know, and a lot of our customers were fishermen and loggers. They worked out of town and whenever they came back to town they spent their money fast. So I made a lot of money, but I spent it fast too. There were twenty-four restaurants here then but none of them had a licence, so the police were constantly coming around.

There weren't any real geishas on Powell Street. The people who came to Canada before the war weren't that kind of fancy people—they were all fishermen and farmers. But many waitresses pretended to be geisha girls. They played the shamisen and sang songs, not nearly as well as real geishas in Japan, although some of the older women weren't bad. But it was good enough for most of the fishermen who hadn't seen real geishas and believed there were lots of them on Powell Street.

There were lots of grocery stores here then. The largest one was Maikawa Shoten at 365 [Powell Street]. Next door to it was a fish store owned by Maikawa's son—that's where we bought our fish for the restaurant. And next door to it [349] was a Japanese bathhouse. I took a bath there every day for more than ten years. Sometimes the place was really crowded and then we went to the 200 block, where there were two more bathhouses. Upstairs at 358 and 354 were gambling clubs. The one at 354 was run by a sort of Japanese gangster. They hardly ever paid their bill at our place, and it was the same at other restaurants too.

The Japanese bank, Tamura Shoken, was on the corner of Powell and Dunlevy. But right in front of us was a sort of financier's, Sanban it was called. We kept all our restaurant money there and I had my own savings there as well. About four people were working there but they were drinking all the time and I didn't think it was very safe so I took all my money out, but the restaurant stayed on with them and none of that company money ever came back to us. They drank up all their clients' money and then they ran off. Lots of fishermen kept their savings there too, and nobody got it back. It was a sad story.

This happened about two years after we opened the restaurant and at almost the same time I got rid of my share in it because I was sick and needed medical treatment. One of my boyfriends had given me a nasty disease.

I had to get penicillin shots, twelve of them, and they cost twenty-five dollars each. A man I knew who was boss on a CPR construction crew suggested I go out to Kamloops with him and he paid for my medical treatment and took very good care of me. So I worked for him and his crew for five years, washing their clothes, cooking for them—oh, their clothes got dirty fast!

I came back to Vancouver when I was thirty-two [1927] and bought a lease on the upstairs of a hotel at 35 West Hastings. Now it's the Palace Hotel but then the main floor was a medical clinic, and I turned the upstairs into a whorehouse. You see, buying the lease was very expensive, so was the rent, and there were only thirty-five rooms. You couldn't make a profit on it if you ran it just as a hotel. So I hired twelve prostitutes and took commissions. Usually the owner would take 50 percent, but I just took 30 percent, so I got on well with the girls, they liked me. Those days you could get a white woman for two dollars and a Japanese woman for anywhere from three dollars to five dollars. The Japanese women cost more because they were more in demand. At first I hired someone to look after the business because I didn't know anything about it, but after a year I knew how to run it myself. My job was mainly being friendly with customers and with the police. If a policeman wanted a woman I arranged it for him. And of course they didn't pay, I paid the girls, but it's cheaper than getting arrested. And then I had to check our customers to make sure they didn't have a disease the women could get. Very often I asked them to take their pants off and I learned how to check them quickly and efficiently. They were all kinds of people—Japanese, Chinese, white people.

Business was tough the first year. Then, luckily, a new chief of police came in from Kamloops. I'd known him when I was there, so that made things easier. Other people got arrested, but not me, and when they were arrested they often went to jail for quite a long time so my business really picked up. So I ran this place from 1927 to 1941, and then World War II came along and I lost everything.

I didn't want to go to war camp, I wanted to stay in Vancouver, so I went into hiding in my hotel. But three Mounties came and arrested me. They sent me to Oakalla instead of Greenwood, and I was the only Japanese there. The radio newscasts in jail were talking about the war all the time and I got so itchy. Everybody called me "Jap." I hated it, and I'd yell back, "Shut up, keto" ("barbarian," only used for foreigners). They kept me there two and a half months and then they sent me to Greenwood where I had to stay for four years. I was the first Japanese to come back to Vancouver from Greenwood. You see, in Greenwood the Mounties told us that we all had to go back to Japan. They offered us $210 to go back and some poor Japanese took it. But

Mrs. Kiyoko Tanaka-Goto, 1978. TAKI BLUESINGER PHOTO, COURTESY OF ROYAL BC MUSEUM, BC ARCHIVES

I had a Chinese friend who came out from Vancouver and acted as guarantor for me. He brought me back.

The first year I got back I worked in a Chinese restaurant on Keefer Street. It was really busy but I didn't feel too uncomfortable because I'd known so many Chinese people when I was running the whorehouse. My Chinese is almost as bad as my English, but I got along. Then I opened a gambling club on Powell Street with my Chinese partner. It was on the main floor of the Lion Hotel [316 Powell] which is where I was living then too. The business went really well. I made about $30,000 in three years. So then I opened another on Pender Street with the same partner and a few other new Chinese partners. That went really well too.

You don't often find business relationships between Japanese and Chinese people, but my boyfriend is Chinese and I've found them so reliable they won't cheat you out of a penny. In a way it's much easier than with the Japanese. Here's a good example: three years after I quit my partnership in those two gambling clubs, I opened a new one at 358 Powell. It went quite well too, but after a few years my Japanese partner ran off to Japan with all our business funds. That made me so angry I haven't gone into the gambling business since. Well, I did start betting on horses, but I lost a lot of money. So then I opened a restaurant on Powell Street, but I didn't do a very good business at all. Everything's changed since the war and the police are much tougher. I couldn't get a licence, and although I still served sake in a teapot, I lost a lot of money, so about ten years ago I sold it to Aki. Since then, I've more or less retired. There's nothing more I want to do, except visit Japan before I die. I want to see the graves of my ancestors, and I want to ask Honganji [the main Buddhist temple in Kyoto] if they'll take care of me after my death.

ELISA MARTINI NEGRIN

Elisa Martini Negrin was born in Vancouver in 1917. Her parents emigrated from northern Italy in 1913.

There were six daughters born and I can remember back to 1925 when we moved to Atlantic Street and my dad couldn't stand to see empty lots and he said, "My goodness! We could do something about helping ourselves. We can plant a garden and we can…" We had chickens 'cause I can remember chickens all my life and with chickens he expanded to goats so that we could have milk. That wasn't enough so he said, "We'd better get cows." That was quite a battle with City Hall but he knew about sewerage and cement work and he told them just what could be done. He said, "You support my kids or I get a cow and support my own." He got his permit—even in those days you had to get a permit and, of course, city inspectors came to see that it was built properly. The barn was all from old ties off the Great Northern Railway and planks that were brought up from Stanley Park. We were very independent and made ourselves useful. Anyway, he got his barn built and he had four cows at that time—one, then two, and then two were fresh and two were expecting and then it always kept going like that. We had a few customers for milk and Mother made cheese and butter, and we had all the cream we wanted. We didn't have money but we had plenty of food.

When we came into our teens, I was a herdswoman because there was no boys in the family. To herd the cows, we went down on what we called the Great Northern Flats which was really mucky clay. Boots and all or feet and all, we were in it as knee-deep as the cows were. Yes, and they used to come all the way up to the Grandview district and the roundhouse there, in fact, all the way up to Nanaimo Street. And that took a lot of running, I'm telling you! Sometimes there would be thirty or forty cows—there was my family's, the Piccolos', the Zanatas', and "Big John's." There was only about half a dozen families in town that had cows and there wasn't any English families that had them. In fact there was a battle there too, thinking there was going to be odour and this and that. Let's face it, the poor cows couldn't have a chance to have a job and the people were ready to pick it up for the gardens. Nothing was ever wasted! No way. We had the cleanest streets in town. And never mind, people used manure for medicinal purposes, we had people with eczema coming—they believed the old housewives' tales that the morning dew that settled on it was to nurse wounds and they believed it was a cure. Oh yes, they came from all over—these were the British people, the Russians and the Ukrainians who were great on that, but we didn't know the potions. They even picked these mushrooms, puffballs, and picking up this liquid, the dew, they made a potion or something to use for sores.

We kept all the boulevards nice and neat, cutting the grass for hay. Our truck drivers were the young fellows, our own friends, and they thought it was just great to be able to sit down and picnic with us and that's the way it was done—a lot of singing, a lot of fun, a lot of teasing, a lot of fooling around. It was summertime, that was a holiday for then. And maybe you'd hear Dad say a few cuss words at them—horsing around at night and the haystack would go over and he'd want to know who the son-of-a-gun was, eh? We'd start at six o'clock in the morning and we'd go on until eight or nine at night, until it got dark. You had to cut it and then it was just left there and then we'd go back and forth two and three times a day. Where Nanaimo Street is and where Raymur is and Atlantic Street, now that was all done by foot, all on foot.

The city pound would be picking the cows up, always on the alert, but when they found out it was our livelihood, they knew there was no point, and they knew the girls were trying to get them because my other sisters were out with me too. Once the cows went astray, the first thing *before* you went after the *cow*, you had to go home and get somebody to come and help you, eh? Especially when you were up in the Nanaimo Street area, it was almost bush area and a lot of grazing land, and if kids saw a cow, "My goodness, a cow!" you know, and instead of staying clear of it, they wanted to go close and scare the cow and away it would run in different directions again.

I think it was after 1936 when everyone thought they'd had enough of it

Elisa Negrin, c. 1927, in the backyard of the Martini home on Atlantic Street. ELISA NEGRIN COLLECTION, COURTESY OF ROYAL BC MUSEUM, BC ARCHIVES

The Piccolo family haying on False Creek Flats in the 1920s. COURTESY OF AMERICA BIANCO

and then the restrictions from City Hall came in. After all, it *wasn't* farming country—we were in the city, let's face it!

The Barnum and Bailey circus, now that was in '26 or '27, with the big top. That was the boom, that's when the Italians made themselves rich. Dad recruited different Italians and they had to lay out all the sawdust, and on the flats it was all water, eh? They worked hard and that was good money then. Plus, Americans, they're used to liquor for their crews, so they said, "Well, where do we go?" The Italians all had their beer, they had their wine. It was moonshine too, because it was open house to everybody and there were no restrictions 'cause it was primitive, those early years. This was when—I don't know if they call it bootlegging or what—but it was manufactured all over the place. And that kept the circus men happy, and that set a lot of families on their feet. It was maddening to all the British subjects to see all these "immigrant children" as they called us, going in free. We *worked* for them. We figured we did our part to make them happy, so we all saw the big top.

We didn't speak Italian on the street. No, no. Oh, we would be called— you know what they would call Italians. They didn't call me that too often, because I had a good swing! But you just couldn't [speak Italian on the street]. And my dad, he wouldn't permit it anyway because he said, "This is your country and you learn English." But Mother always spoke Italian and we understood it but we would always answer in English. The younger sister didn't even know a word and wondered what the heck our parents were talking sometimes. You more or less had to speak English, because in our [neighbourhood] you had your coloured, you had your Japanese, you had your Chinese, you had your Russians—you *had* to speak English to understand each other.

I just went to Grade 7 and we had a lovely school nurse, that was Miss McLellan. I got training from her, I just loved to help people and I thought I'd go into nursing but I had to get out of school at age twelve to help the finances in the family. Mom and Dad lost two teenage girls inside of six months [from tuberculosis] and that drained their funds. I was a burden to them and I was only twelve, so I thought, enough of just babysitting, I better get out and see if I can get a fifty-cent piece somewhere. So I was fortunate enough to have Mr. and Mrs. Giuriati take me under their wing and they put me into their grocery store. I did that for about two and a half years. That wasn't enough because Mr. Giuriati was helping everybody—he was a good Samaritan, helping all the underprivileged. And then, Dad became ill and he couldn't get to work although he did work for the City of Vancouver and he just hated the fact that he'd have to go for social assistance.

By the time I was sixteen, things became kind of rough and I was strong and healthy and should get out to work. Also, the welfare authorities said I wasn't to live with my family and Father said, "No way! I'll break her legs so she can stay home with me!" He said, "You're going to put my daughter out to work for someone else for nothing? I can keep her. I've got enough to eat—I can't dress the girls very well but they're covered. I'm not going to have her scrubbing and wearing herself out for some rich fool. They can put their own kids to work!" There was quite a hassle there. I almost felt like a convict because I had to always be running away and back to some other place so I

Looking north over False Creek Flats in the mid-1930s. LEONARD FRANK PHOTO, VANCOUVER PUBLIC LIBRARY, VPL 7917

wasn't found at home with my parents. Then Dr. Fox was a lifesaver there and he said no, I was needed at home with Mother because Father was ill.[54] And finally, I went to see Miss Williams and Miss McLellan, the school nurse. They were a great help too, it was rough going but they could see it and the authorities let me stay home.

ROSA PRYOR

Rosa Pryor was born in 1887 in the United States. She came to Vancouver in 1917 from Iowa via Seattle and established the city's first southern fried chicken house.

That winter I saw the people just dropping on the street. I never seen nothing like that flu. And I never caught it at all. The man that ran the undertaking business, Mr. Edward, down in the half block where I lived, why, he had bodies just dead laying out in the alleyway, and he couldn't take them in to get them ready to bury. He'd put a canvas over them till he could work on them. And I used to have to go down that alley at night. I'd see people, and they'd say, "Well, I'll see you," and then I'd wake up the next morning and it was the same Mr. so-and-so who died last night. They just died so fast they'd be just standing talking to you and just drop dead. Oh, it was awful![55]

About that time I opened up the Chicken Inn, and I was there for forty-two years. I thought, well I'll get those live squabs in the Chinatown, make little squabs and maybe people around there, close to the Stratford Hotel...

Well, when I first opened up the Chicken Inn, I didn't have a nickel. Didn't have a quarter. I got everything ready to open and I looked around and I didn't have any licence money. And I had to have twenty dollars for a licence. I didn't know what I was going to do. I looked at my husband and you know, I'd just as well been looking outdoors. He sat right there and looked at me. I said, "Well, why don't you get out and maybe you'll find some money on the street, 'stead of looking at me, 'cause I don't have nothing." "All I can do is to write to my mother and get the money." Well, I knew that my mother didn't have any money, but my mother lived in the country where she was acquainted with the rich white people around there, because she worked for them. So I had to write to her, because the man was waiting for my twenty dollars. Well, my mother wrote me that she didn't have the money at first and she was around trying to borrow it from different places. There ain't nothing on earth that a mother won't do, you know. So she borrowed the money and she wrote me in a hurry on a paper sugar sack, some kind of sack which she split open. And it said, "Rose, I'm sending you some money. I have had a hard time getting it. I didn't have any money in the house and I went from place to place and it's hard times here."

But by then I had *borrowed* the money. I'd found a woman running the racetrack and she took me to the races every day with her. That woman said, "You want to buy? Here, you take two dollars." I didn't want to put it on a horse, I wanted it myself! But I'd put it on my horse, you know, and I'd lose every time I'd bet. She was paying away and she just had a pocketful of money. She came from down in California, but she said she just liked me—she liked to talk and she didn't know anybody, and I'd do the talking, but I wanted some of that money. I wanted twenty dollars! My God, that woman had so much money and was just buying stuff for me. She was drinking, and buying. I couldn't drink. I couldn't do nothing. I wanted that twenty dollars. Well, I couldn't get no money from her, she was a *stranger* to me. But she said she liked me, so I just asked anyhow. I said, "I'm going to open up a Chicken Inn..." She just looked at me, said, "Well, you don't know me. I don't know you. I'm just spending my money. My husband came up here to bring this money and just have a good time. But I don't know anything about you." Well, she *didn't* know anything about me. She said, "If I give you the money, when are you going to pay it back? How are you going to pay it back if you don't have a nickel?" I said, "If you give me the money, lend me the money, I'll pay it back in two weeks." Oh, she bawled me out like a dog. She talked bad, too. She said, "Well, if I loan you this money, then don't you frig off with my money." So by God, she lent me the money. Oh, she had a great big thing of money.

Rosa Pryor of the Chicken Inn in 1952. COURTESY OF ROSA PRYOR

On the first day, I asked the different people to come and I didn't really expect they all were coming. A man came in and said, "Ain't you got them chickens ready?" I said, "Yes, I've got them and I'm *just* ready to open up. Come back in half hour—you'll get your chicken. I couldn't afford to buy but two chickens at a time—I'd run my husband over there to buy the chicken and he'd just cut them up right quick and I'd wash them and I'd get them on frying. Oh, he liked the chicken. I gave him a good dinner. I kept saying to my husband, "Now you stay right here in the hall so you can run quick over to the Chinaman's and buy another chicken." And then I'd commence talking, "Oh, yes, yes, so and so and so," and I'd talk to take up some time until I'd see him come in, then I'd say, "Well, I must get those chickens on." Then I'd get him to pay and I'd say to my husband "Now, you get two more." So, I got by that way. And that night, the woman who lent me the money came there and was fooling around, watching me. But she was alright, that woman. On the next day, I just paid her the money. "That's alright," she said, "I knew you'd pay me or I wouldn't let you have it." I thought to myself, "No, well, I had to *beg* for it."

And about two weeks later, the money came [from my mother]. The doorbell rang, said, "Registered letter here for you." It said, "Rosa, I had a hard time getting this money. I had to send all over everywhere to get it." And shoot, I had about a hundred dollars then all saved up and plenty of chickens and everything. I was a big person. I just took the money and got it together and put it right in the envelope and sent it right back to her. And I've never had to borrow a nickel from anybody since that day.

I was the first person who ever owned a "Chicken Inn." First person who ever fried any chicken. They didn't know much about fried chicken here in this country like they did in the States.

I remember lots of funny things happened. I've done lots of fighting in there, I know that, with every damn fool coming in there and one thing and another. There was lots of people who were going to fight me but I'd fight them back. I never went for no police the whole time I was there. Oh, and fight! But I had a husband that weighed 200 and some odd pounds and I wasn't bad myself, and so if they'd start the fight, well, we'd always win. I had a stick. Always. Right here under my apron. By God, I'd draw that out—they'd leave. I never lost a fight. Had some bad ones, too.

It was awful bad in the thirties, but I just kept one girl and then me and my husband done the work, and so we got along pretty good that way. Didn't have to have no outside help. But it was a long time. But I know we didn't take in nothing—we sat up there and played whist all night. You weren't getting any money then, but you weren't spending anything. Oh Lord, it was hard. When you get a dollar, you better hold on to it. 'Cause they all make out like they are going to give you this and do you that, and one thing and another, but oh, God, when you ain't got it! And then you are looking at a bare floor or looking at a man and he's doing nothing. Oh, I haven't ever been broke since, no.

FRED SOON

Fred Soon was born in Canton, China, in 1908. He immigrated to Canada with his uncle and cousins in 1921.

When we landed in Vancouver, we were put in the Immigration Building—you might call it like a jailhouse—and we were there for three weeks. My father had to go through a lot of red tape and that was done with paying a head tax of $500 and then I was able to stay in Canada. In the Immigration Building, we each had a bed. No furniture, naturally, not even a night table. There were probably a dozen people in a big open room. No privacy, everything was public, you couldn't even write a letter. Those are the days we don't like to remember. The past is the past and I really don't want to dwell on it.

When I first arrived in Vancouver, I regarded it as a hostile land. I mean, I had to tread very carefully—that was my impression when I landed. But my elders always taught me not to make trouble when you don't have to.

In those days, you were called a "landed immigrant," but there was no such thing as a full citizen, because you were not allowed to vote. You didn't have the franchise and you were not naturalized. We weren't naturalized until 1947, after the Second World War.[56] Before then, you were treated just like a political football, like an object and it didn't matter how badly you were treated. There was no way to vent your sorrow and be able to do anything about it, because what the political parties were doing was for the privilege of their own citizens.

The CCF was one of the groups that protested, but not just one group or one party, a lot of people protested—conscientious people protested. There was discrimination against the Oriental in general. And jobs were very limited. The Chinese mostly confined themselves to lumbering, restaurants, farming, sawmills, and logging camps. In other words, they did manual or menial labour work.

The Chinese children who were born here had no trouble integrating with the white children. It was the immigrant children like myself [who had trouble]. Naturally you come up with a lot of discrimination amongst children because some of them don't want to play with you, and you can't blame them because it's just like a chicken and a duck, they don't talk the same language.

We lived in community houses along Keefer and Pender. There was about ten or twelve people there, all single. They all came from China, and they left their wives in China. There was a public kitchen and everybody had their own room and the house was rented. Very seldom people bought a house.

I didn't have the opportunity of higher education. My father was a worker, he didn't have too much money. I wanted to finish high school and he said, "Forget it, you won't get very much ahead." Then I wanted to go to a technical school, I wanted to be a mechanic or an engineer and start out in the technological field. I tried to do that, and before the season was half over my father took me out of that school. "Are you crazy? You'll never get a job, you'll never get anything like that. Even in a garage they won't hire you." I took a commercial course, because he said when you take a commercial course, you don't have to rely on people to hire you, you can own a business, you can hold on to your job.

During the war years, I started work in a shipyard. It was probably the

Detention shed where Oriental immigrants were held for processing, c. 1910. CITY OF VANCOUVER ARCHIVES, CVA 153-2

only steady job I ever had. Before then, just touch and go, you know. But in the shipyard, we worked four years, from the beginning to the end, until V-J day. All the fellow workers were pretty friendly and the management gave us promotions. I started out as a bolter upper, bolting steel together at seventy-nine cents an hour and I was promoted to a sheet-metal mechanic and I finished off with a dollar and a quarter an hour as a mechanic. And that was marvellous wages.

I operated a grocery store after the war. And after the grocery store, I went to the shingle mill. I worked there for two or three years and then I was drafted to work for the union. The International Woodworkers of America was looking for somebody to be their agent, to be an organizer. I was on the international staff for a while and then they put me back to the Canadian staff. I worked there for five and a half years.

When I first started mill work, the Chinese workers had a camp of their own. Maybe it was not of their own choosing, but for expediency. In the logging camps, they paid the Chinese crew less for the same job that the white worker held. And they sent the Chinese in to do the tough jobs, mostly doing the track work, all back-breaking jobs. Anyway, as soon as the union got organized, more and more we got the operators to toe the line, and openly they didn't dare say, "We pay the Chinese that much less."

ABE GUREVICH &
RITA GUREVICH GOLDBERG

Abe Gurevich was born in Russia in 1901. A skilled locksmith and gunsmith, he was unable to find that sort of work in Canada. His daughter, Rita Gurevich Goldberg, was born in Vancouver in 1931.

ABE GUREVICH: I used to rent a horse and wagon and peddle junk house to house. I tell you the truth, I used to go around and I didn't know where I was. I couldn't talk English then, only a few words. One place I came in and she had a lot of stuff and I didn't know what it was, I didn't know what it's worth, I didn't know what the name was, and I didn't know how to even approach her to buy it. So I said, "How much?" That's all I knew. But then *she* said, "How much?" So you see, there was no end to it. So I went to my pocket and grabbed a handful of money and I said, "How much?" So she took that and I don't know how much she took. So I put it on the wagon and went back and I sold it and I made seventeen dollars that day. Well, that was a lot of money! I said, "My, that's a good game!" So the next day I went again, and it's not so bad, you see.

Then I made money a little bit so I said this is not so good, too slow. So I went and bought a Model T Ford truck, first. And then I had nothing to do—with the horse and wagon you can go and peddle, and with a truck you can't do that. So a fellow came in and said, "Come on with me," you see, "I'm in the food business." So I went with him and bought a carload of apples, borrowed some money that way and came back, bought two carloads of potatoes. We used to get up every morning, early in the morning, I used to go at break of day, and buy forty boxes of apples, and by two o'clock we used to sell everything.

Rita Goldberg: Once he acquired his truck my father put benches alongside the back and all the neighbours would come in with their picnic baskets and we'd take off to Stanley Park on Sundays for our weekly outing. About three families with all their children and everyone would all crowd in the back and we'd all take off, normally to around Lumberman's Arch, so that there's the swimming. And the main thing was that there were big stoves, so they would bring their food, you see, and warm it up for dinner. The men would sit around the table and sing and play cards, and the women would gossip.

Abe Gurevich: The first times we went, I didn't yet have the truck so the kids were small and I had two kids by that time. So I used to put up one kid on this shoulder and the other on the other shoulder and take two suitcases and walk with them from the streetcar stop. Oh the streetcar, the shaking and so on! It used to fall over almost in the park.

Rita Goldberg: It was very, very rattly.

Abe Gurevich: Then you see, my late brother was in cattle business and his partner left him so he said, "Now is the chance you should come with me." So I went with him and we did pretty good. Until we lost everything in the Depression. I used to go out around Fraser Valley to buy some cattle to sell to the slaughterhouses. I made pretty good. But in 1930 I used to take away cattle for nothing and I couldn't even pay for my gas expenses. I had to give the truck back to the company. Depression times—it touched everybody. The first thing, we couldn't get any jobs. The second thing, if you do get a job you have to work almost for nothing. Well, we weren't lazy, we tackled *everything*: a dollar was good to us, fifty cents was good to us. One time in 1936, it was so slack I couldn't get a job, and it kept raining, so I went out looking for something to do. I saw a load of wood laying by a house and I asked the lady, "Can I throw in this wood? You know, work?" So she said, "All right." And I threw in that load of wood, got soaking wet, piled it up, and in the end she gave me twenty-five cents. And I was married by that time. I went out and I bought a loaf of bread and a dozen eggs for twelve cents, and ten cents for a half pound of butter, and we lived for three days on that.

Rita Goldberg: The Sabbath occurs at sundown and my mother would always prepare the chicken soup and the chicken, and we knew that this was the Sabbath and everything would be—the tablecloth and the candles, she always would light the candles for the Sabbath, and there would be wine. My father made his own wine and we made a lot of sauerkraut and fruits and pickles in big earthenware crocks.

Abe Gurevich: And then we had some little wooden barrels that we did sauerkraut in.

Rita Goldberg: On top of how hard he worked, my father carried on the tradition that his father had: this is the Burial Society of the Jewish faith

[Chevra Kaddisha]. A body is not left alone until it is buried, and it has to be prepared by this society. He is still one of the members of the Burial Society after all these years.

ABE GUREVICH: Already forty-two years. We go and sit with the body and we wash it and we put on a garment of linen to cover it with, and a casket, a simple wood casket. Lately we've started to line them, we didn't line them in those times, just very plain wood.

RITA GOLDBERG: People eventually moved out. We were one of the last Jewish families to move out of that area, in 1944. I guess after the war had started there were more opportunities for work so there wasn't that poverty that I remember—people waiting in line for sandwiches next door at the church there on the corner of Princess and Georgia.

TOM WYLIE

Tom Wylie was born in Calgary in 1909 of English parents. He came to Vancouver that same year. He later lived in Richmond and Sidney before returning to Vancouver in 1926.

In the course of my seeking work in 1926 I was successful in getting a job with the Linde Canadian Refrigeration Company situated on Campbell Avenue, near Georgia Street. Not having any particular permanent residence, I immediately proceeded to seek out a room near Campbell, so I wouldn't have too far to go to work, and I was successful in obtaining quarters in the 500-block East Georgia. I had a room with nothing in it but a bed and a dresser, and my room rent was $2.50 a week. The rooms were above, on the second floor, below which were two shops—the western shop was occupied by Abraham Kolberg, kosher butcher, and the eastern shop was a Mr. Costanzo, Italian grocer.

I got acquainted with some of the younger people around the district, and became active in MacLean Playground, as a volunteer. I had already had some experience in gymnastics in the YMCA in Victoria. So I furthered my own abilities on the rings and the high bar at MacLean Park working completely over asphalt, and with no mats or grass or anything else, and we learned to have a lot of courage. MacLean Park had been scooped out on the Georgia Street side and built up on the Union Street side. The bank around the Georgia Street side managed to nurture a modicum of grass coverage; however, the playground itself was entirely covered with tarmac—it was a hard-surface playground. There was a running track around the edge of it, and a sort of a rail fence, one rail on the top of posts. There was a wading pool in the southeast corner, and the apparatus was generally toward the northwest corner of the playground.

I ultimately was employed by the city in the capacity of city fireman because I was interested in sports and perhaps because my father knew the deputy chief. It helped. At the age of eighteen I became a city fireman with the understanding that if anyone complained about me being underage, I would have to be let go without notice. I mainly worked in Number Two Fire Hall, which was actually the headquarters in the 700 block on Seymour. We had lots of chimney fires, and sometimes these were quite dangerous in that you had to scramble up on these old-fashioned houses, three or four floors high, with steep, sloping roofs on the top.

I had gone to bed one night, about ten or eleven o'clock, and I was just going to sleep when I heard shouts, screams, and glass breaking, and that was not a terrifically unusual occurrence in that part of the town. However, I got up and looked out of the window to find that the house directly across from me was in flames. Immediately I turned in the alarm by telephone, dressed and rushed across the street. There was one poor gentleman who had got out of a top-floor window, slid off the verandah roof and, on the way down, clutched the guttering with his fingers. The guttering was still strong enough to hold him. And there he was dangling, being slowly toasted. My one rescue that I made in my three years as a fireman consisted in braving the heat, grasping him firmly by the ankles and yanking him off the guttering, where he fell only about five feet to the ground.

I was ultimately forced to leave the rooming house on Georgia Street due to (a) bedbugs; (b) rats. My treatment on the rats was merely to buy a trap and, being statistically minded, I tallied them on the wall, and some nights I would get two, but every night one, for sure. I would tally one, two, three, four, and then the cross line for five, and when the line got right across the wall, I decided I should move somewhere else. I think you can stretch loyalty too far. I seemed to have an unending supply, as far as my own place was concerned, and all I had to—it wasn't a question of leaving things out for them to eat, except what was on the trap, and I couldn't find out where they were getting in. The building must have swarmed with them and I would assume then that the district did as well.

At that time this neighbourhood was the hub of the Jewish community of Vancouver. There was no kosher cafe in Vancouver at that time, and visitors who wanted kosher food came to the Bobroff family who catered to outside people. I was good friends with the younger members of the Bobroff family, and there was a verandah and we used to sit on the verandah, and sometimes if I were sitting alone on the verandah with Bertha, the eldest daughter, the old ladies who walked by would shake their heads sadly and say, "Bertha's sitting with a shegitz," and Bertha and I would say to each other, "Those old yachnas!"

Sadie Mandleman was one of my favourite kids on the playground. She broke the main rule that we all adhered to, that girls shouldn't run more than a hundred yards. I did a lot of running at that time, I used to run every night, sometimes for an hour. And she was the only girl who would run with me for more than half a mile. Sadie was a very, very good runner in that respect—she would have been a good middle-distance runner, but *then* there was no such thing as middle-distance running for girls.

There were at least four little boxing clubs around the Lower Mainland at that time, and we used to hammer hell out of each other for five bucks.

Tom Wylie in his African imports store, 1977. TOD GREENAWAY PHOTO

It was the beginning of the Depression and if you could get three fights in one week, you were doing as well as anybody who had a job, and during one winter I had perhaps over forty bouts, and then I started getting a little better and started going to Seattle and Spokane and Bellingham, and I reached the point where I had to sign a contract and I had to get into the racket as a piece of property, if you like. The man who wanted to "manage me" had a stable of horses and prostitutes and I didn't feel like identifying my noble art of self-abuse—it is a form of self-abuse, boxing—with a string of prostitutes, and I thought he could get his own string of boxers if he liked, but I refused a contract with him, and shortly after that, got a job and got out of boxing.

Chinatown at that time was the same size as it is now. There probably weren't so many Chinese people living outside of Strathcona at that time. I would say that most Chinese people probably lived within a mile or so of actual Chinatown, which was mainly Pender Street between Gore and Carrall. In the 200-block East Pender, there was a downstairs poolroom, an underground poolroom, where I occasionally visited. In this poolroom were hanging on the wall a fairly full set of Chinese musical instruments, and they seemed pleased by the fact that I was interested in their musical instruments and it was there that I started playing Chinese flutes, something which I've kept up ever since.

In July, 1926, I remember going to the Pantages Theatre and there experiencing my first encounter with electronic sound equipment. They were displaying in the lobby upstairs an Egyptian mummy that would answer questions, and you could ask it questions and then you could put a stethoscope on its chest and put the stethoscope in your ears and you would hear a voice answering questions on the stethoscope. This was probably an early use of radio technology and speaker technology. I, and everybody else at the time, was considerably impressed by this performance—this mysterious voice that came out of the chest of this fake Egyptian mummy.

IVY KAJI MCADAMS

Ivy Kaji McAdams, daughter of an English nurse and a Japanese Canadian medical student serving overseas in World War I, was born in Edmonton in 1920. She arrived in Vancouver in 1921.

My mother and father married in England. He was a Japanese soldier overseas there for Canada. She was an English nurse. He had been sent out to Canada by his family to attend McGill University as a medical student. And then, when the war broke out, he volunteered and went overseas. He brought her back in 1917. He went into the sanatorium when I was three with very advanced tuberculosis, which he had contracted in the trenches in France. He was in there for five years, he died when I was eight, and I think I only saw him twice.

I remember my mother had a rooming house when she was on a soldier's pension, and then shortly after he died she went on a widow's pension. We moved several times and all the time I was going to school my mother was quite ill. She was always in bed, and trying desperately to keep a house and keep the two of us, and I'm sure a lot of times she was hungry but she'd say, "You kids go ahead and eat, I've already eaten." When the ambulance finally did come to get her, I remember the doctor telling this friend of my father's that she was suffering from advanced tuberculosis and bronchial asthma, *and* malnutrition. So they put her in the sanatorium, and intermittently she'd come home for a month or so, and then she couldn't cope because she'd be up and trying to look after us, you see, then they'd send her back to the sanatorium again.

Ivy Kaji McAdams in her home, 1978. TOD GREENAWAY PHOTO

I went to Chinese school, because all the kids in my tenement [Second and Main] were going to Chinese school after public school and I had no one to play with. It was Christ Church of China [340 Keefer, from 1923]. There was a missionary there and he taught Chinese—speaking, reading, and writing—and he was very English. I couldn't imagine how a white man could be speaking Chinese, and they told me he was brought up in China with a missionary family. It was mandatory, as far as the Chinese families were concerned, that all their children learn their language. Later, when I worked in restaurants, the fellows, the cooks, used to say to me, "You look like Chinese girl, you learn to speak Chinese, so you don't talk in English anymore. You come in the kitchen, you speak Chinese, or you don't get any order." "But they're not talking in Chinese out there. We've got white customers." "I don't care. You talk Chinese all the time when you talk to me. I don't want to hear you speak English." So, for a while there, that's all I did. I spoke Chinese, and talked to the kids, and they always talked to me in Chinese and they thought it was funny, because naturally I spoke pidgin Chinese as much as they spoke pidgin English.

I can remember many people talking about being afraid to walk in Chinatown. You know, ridiculous things like, "You mustn't walk down in Chinatown because my mother told me that they've got manholes where they pull the girls down into those opium cellars." Well, I was just a little shaver and I'd run up and down those alleys because I knew that where the gambling joints were on Pender Street, the back doors were always the restaurants. They would set up a little kitchen, you see, to keep the gamblers in there, because it would be rainy and where else were they going to go anyway? So they'd set up a cooking effort, with a counter, and the food was so much better in those gambling places, because they had to keep their patrons there. So I used to run up and down those alleys, and, "Oh, there's the green door and the red door, and the orange door"—we knew which ones to go to, because those cooks were very good to all children. You just had to knock on the door and look at them, and they'd say, "You want something to eat?" and then right away we'd be sitting in at the counter. We were little moochers, but we knew, we were the good-hearted ones.

I spent most of my time around Chinatown because this old Chinese friend of my family was working around Chinatown—as a matter of fact, he put in a lot of the wiring there. I'm extremely fond of him because I know,

Interior of the Chinese Theatre, 1923, with cast and audience. W.J. MOORE PHOTO, CITY OF VANCOUVER ARCHIVES,
PORT N479

without him, we would have starved to death. He more or less adopted us as
his family, because he knew we had no father and he was going to look after
us, so he just went all over Chinatown, all the chop suey places, and he told
them, "You see those two kids? If they ever come down here and want to eat,
you give them anything they want, and their friends, and give me the bill next
time you see me. Just charge it." He was a marvellous old man.

There were two theatres in Chinatown as I remember. One was in the alley going south from the Mandarin Gardens, which is now the Marco Polo. It
was an old red brick building, just on the alley, and you walked in past a little
box office and then through two great, huge doors, ornately decorated with
Chinese dragons and things. It was a big theatre. It was all stage performance,
with a type of orchestra pit where all the Chinese orchestra was sitting, mostly
brass, you know, a lot of clanging and banging of these great, huge, brass
cymbals, bang, bang, bang, and then all the high-pitched voices of the real
Chinese singing, and many gestures with the long kimono sleeves. Each actor
would come out in different colours—beautiful satins and the embroidery
and the sequins and beads.

They'd bring in these acts from China, and they'd be advertised for many
weeks in advance that this great actress was coming from China, and this
traditional play, which was very well known in China. And of course all the
nationals probably knew it, you see, because they had gone to them when
they were in China and of course they'd flock to these theatres and they'd

be full. They started fairly early in the morning, say, about ten thirty, eleven o'clock, and they went on steadily. This Chinese friend of my family, he used to always give me some money to spend and my great treat was to go to the Chinese grocery store and buy a nickel's worth of dried shrimps, and a nickel's worth of dried beetles. I'd be cracking them like peanuts, just crack open the beetle shell and then pop the body in your mouth, you know, and they were treated and dried with some kind of flavour on them and to me they were really delicious.

This very close friend of our family lived in the Sam Kee Building at the corner of Carrall and Pender. The room was six feet wide and they had little narrow cots all along—it was just one long hallway. That was their living quarters, you see. And they used to carry coal up there and they had it stacked in a big box on one side, and their bed would be on the other side, and then they'd have a little black cast-iron stove and they'd cook their meals up there.

I remember we had lots of East Indian friends who lived in the area around Second and Main. They had little houses around there where several men lived in the same house, bachelors, you know, and they had different turns at cooking. I remember my brother used to go out with them at four or five o'clock in the morning or two, three o'clock in the morning, whatever time their appointment was in the mill to go pick up their load of wood. You see, they'd have to make appointments so all the trucks wouldn't be there at the same time. They'd line up and make their appointment at the mill, then go down and get the slabs of wood—half cord or full cord, whatever size the truck would be, and then solicit from door to door to sell these loads of wood.

My brother was very good at sports all the time. I can remember when we were going to public school when the sports meet day came and all the schools were competing down at Crystal Pool. That was something that was unforgivable. My brother was the only Oriental in the class and he was competing and he *was* a good swimmer. He came back from the swim meet and my mother asked him how the class made out and he said, "We didn't swim." She said, "Why not?" He said, "Because in Crystal Pool they've got a rule, 'No Orientals allowed in here.'" They had singled out my brother and said, "He can't swim because we don't have Orientals in here." So the rest of the boys said, "Well, if he's not swimming, neither are we," and the class all stepped back.

We were the only Eurasians in school, the only ones. There wasn't really any slot you belonged. You were either accepted or you weren't, and you sort of stayed back until you realized whether you *were* going to be accepted or not. Sometimes you were accepted on the ball team and sometimes you weren't, you know. They'd say, "Well, we don't want *her* there," or "She's not getting in *our* picture." There was always these slurs and reflections.

Powell Street had so many great smells down there—all the restaurants, you know, and there was something like an ice-cream parlour. I remember every time we got a nickel, we used to walk from Second and Main down to Powell Street to get a little dish of chopped ice with a syrup on it. I don't remember what we called it, but boy, we all used to scramble down if we ever got a nickel.

I remember the first Japanese bath I ever went to. That would be somewhere about where the World Hotel is at Dunlevy and Powell, a building or two over. We went into a long hallway on the south side of the street, and I could hear a lot of voices. I had never been to a public bath before and you know how modest you are at fourteen, fifteen. This woman who took me there said, "You take all your clothes off now," and I walked into this room, you see, and all these women were sitting around, all ages and sizes and shapes, you know, and I was just standing there and I thought, "Oh, I've never stood naked in front of anybody in my life before, except my mother." And I was looking and she said, "That's okay, that's okay. Now you come and you soap up." They used a bar of white soap, I think actually it was Castille soap, and she told me to soap myself all over everywhere until the soap dried on me and it was all white. Of course we all looked so grotesque. You've seen the Japanese stage makeup? It's almost like a medicine man's mask. You leave little bits of your eyes, you see, and your mouth is showing, your nostrils are showing, and all the rest of you is just caked white, you know, and your dark hair. I was astonished to see that women were in there nursing their babies, they were sitting there naked, with all this soap on except around their nipples. And I thought, strange way to live. She said, "Every night they come down to the public baths." You see, there wasn't too much in the way of plumbing in those older buildings.

So first you soaped yourself down very well until the soap dried and then you went around and visited. I could hear all the men on the other side, they were all laughing and talking, men and boys on the other side of the bath, just a very small partition. I was hoping it would be about ten feet high, you know, because I was expecting to look up and see two eyes looking at me. I don't know how I thought I looked like anything better or worse, or funnier than anybody else, but I was *so* embarrassed, and so self-conscious, and finally she said, "Okay, it's time now—you go and wash yourself." You had to soap and wash yourself before you climbed down into this lowered hot steaming bath, and there were little seats inside where you sat down, you see. But you had to be clean before you went in there for the rinse off. So she said, "You like that, eh?" "It's, uh, nice." I said to my mother, "Don't ever let her take me down there again." She said, "I thought you'd find it interesting." And it *was* fascinating, you know.

Her husband was a friend of my father and he had a tempura-sukiyaki house. All the fishermen would come to his place to drink sake, it was sort of a social gathering place. And he'd serve food, he and his wife, and his wife was a geisha girl. She was very nice to us and she said, "Well, if you want a job," she said, "I'll train you how to be a geisha girl." She was a very gracious and lovely-looking woman, you know, beautiful skin, and I was fascinated by her and her hands. And I said to my mother, "Gee, she's sure pretty, isn't she?" and she said, "Yes, she's lovely." She said, "He brought her over from Japan and she was one of the head geisha girls in Japan. She wants to teach you all the Japanese customs." And I said, "Well, I don't really think I liked the Japanese baths, so," I said, "I don't think I'm going to like the customs very much."

I remember, when the evacuation started [1942], walking down Powell Street looking at all the people's faces, and they were gathered in groups talking and so depressed and everyone looking so unhappy. It was really a sad street. Any merchant up in any other end of town knew he was going to get a bargain, so he'd be down there. It was like a big flea market. They had to leave in "x" number of days, and they had to try and salvage *something* out of their belongings or their businesses. It was a great exodus of a lifetime of savings and business and effort, and their families being uprooted and wrenched out of their environment, and children out of their schools and wondering where everyone's going to go, just a total collapse of their world.

I woke up one morning to pounding at the door. It was about seven o'clock, the usual time for the iceman to come, so I just opened the door and walked away and told him to put the ice in the icebox. He said, "You're under arrest," and I said, "What for?" He said, "This is the RCMP, and you've failed to register as an enemy alien." And I said, "Because I don't think I am one." And he said, "Well, we think you are, and we have orders to pick you up." "You're not coming in," I said. "You don't have a warrant to search the premises, and you don't have a warrant for my arrest. I don't see how you can take me." He said, "You're classified as an enemy alien because your father was a Japanese." "He was Japanese," I said, "but he was also a naturalized Canadian, and he fought with the Canadian army overseas for Canada." "That doesn't matter," he said. "You'll have to come up to the RCMP headquarters, so don't try to get out, because you're surrounded. Don't jump out the bedroom window." I said, "Well, I think you're treating me like a murderer or a bank robber, and I don't think they have this many people to arrest *them*."

So he took me up [to RCMP headquarters] and asked me to speak to this Japanese girl at a typewriter in the office. She started asking me for my height and weight, and she put down my complexion and all my description, and she says, "Now, you must carry this card and be fingerprinted and photographed, and you must give me your National Registration Card." I said, "You can give me all the cards you want, but I'm not giving you *any*. And you'd better find out what you're going to charge me with, because you're holding me in custody and you haven't charged me with anything yet." So she said, "I don't know what you're charged with. I just have orders to put your description down and issue this card to you. You'll have to show this card whenever you're stopped." So I said, "Who is going to stop me?" She said, "Well anybody might stop you." So I said, "Well, I'll take the card if you're giving it to me, but I'm not giving up my National Registration Card. I haven't got it here, I've hidden it. I want my rations," I said, "and if I don't have that card, I can't get any rations." She said, "Well, if you'll just sit in that room there, we'll talk to someone else." So I said, "I demand an audience with Austin Taylor. I hear he's the head man down here, so I want to go and see him." She said, "Oh, he's in the Marine Building."

So they took me down there and I went and I talked to Austin Taylor. "Well, young lady," he said, "I hear you're raising quite a fuss." "I certainly am," I said. "I've been classified as an enemy alien, and I don't think I am. My father was the first volunteer in the Japanese Canadian contingent to go to France and to England," I said, "and he came back as a returned soldier and he got a pension as he fought for Canada." I said, "I was born in Canada, and my mother's a British subject. Did *your* father fight for Canada?" He said, "No." I said, "Were you born in Canada?" He said, "No." I said, "Well then which one of us is really the alien? You classify me as an enemy," I said, "and yet I have more to do with Canada than you have." He said, "Well, this is a unique case. Normally you take your ethnic origin from your father." "But I didn't even know my father, or my father's relatives; I have no communication with them whatsoever," I said, "I don't speak, write, or read the language, so how could I be a threat? You treat me as if

Notification of Japanese Canadians that they are "enemy aliens," shortly after Pearl Harbor, December 1941. PHILIP TIMMS PHOTO, VANCOUVER PUBLIC LIBRARY, VPL 1343

I'm on an espionage ring or something, and I've got to be dragged in here, and arrested. For what reason? You haven't given me a reason yet." So he said, "Well, I think we should make an exception in your case. We'll have to write to Ottawa." "Well, *somebody* write to Ottawa," I said, "because if you won't, I will." I said, "I'll get to the *Vancouver Sun* and they'll write this up." So he said, "Well, I don't think there's any need to be hostile about it." And I said, "Maybe not where you're concerned. But where I'm concerned there is, because I want to be where I can see my mother. She's very ill and she's in Victoria. Now you ship me out to Tashme or Greenwood, then I can't get into the protected area again and I can't go to visit her." "Well," he said, "we'll see what we can do."

Then a few days afterwards, I got this permit to stay in the protected area, providing I complied with all their wishes, rules and regulations, and my curfew of nine o'clock. And, he said, "It's against the law for any Japanese people to take pictures, or to have any shortwave radios in their homes." I said, "Yes, I understand that you've seized all their radios and their cars and their fish boats and their homes, and they've lost their jobs," and I said, "I don't know what you're doing to them, but I think it's criminal. And what you're doing to me, too," I said. "I can't speak for all of them. I just feel very sorry for them."

I know what it did to my mother. I'm sure it's what really gave her the relapse, you know, where she became so despondent that within about three or four months of the evacuation, she died. When I talked to her night nurse, she told me how she spent many hours with my mother when my mother couldn't sleep and she'd say, "I can't understand why they're treating my children like that, because my husband fought for Canada." She was worried about what was going to happen to us, because she knew we weren't really brought up in the Japanese culture.

Some of the tragedies that come out of that time were just incredible. I was friendly with the boy who was shot, Yosh Uno [January 16, 1942]. The family had this little grocery store on the corner of Fourth and Alberta and just eked out a living with it. His mother was in the store one day, they lived in the back, and four young [white] kids came in with a gun and they held her up. Yosh ran out from the back to protect his mother and they shot him dead. So then these kids were charged with murder. Then the headlines, "Four whites for one Jap—is it fair?" And oh, there was this commotion started. It was enough to lose the boy but to suffer all the slurs and everything, like, "Japs are killing Americans, so what difference does it make if four Canadian boys shoot one Jap? Why should these boys be tried for murder?"[57] Well, they were afraid to even open up their store, you know, because the police had laid the charge, naturally, but the public went up in arms about it. The feeling was very, very strong at that time.

SHINICHI HARA

Shinichi Hara was born in Wakayama, Japan, in 1900. At the age of ten he went to work in an Osaka shipyard. He worked at a series of jobs in Japan until December 1924, when he came to Canada.

When I was twenty-four my uncle said I was ready to work in his saltery on Galiano Island, so I came here. I landed in Victoria on December 21, 1924. Next day I came to Vancouver and stayed in a rooming house on Powell Street.

Powell Street was much cleaner [at] that time. The stores were all clean. I still remember the Japanese people, when they got up, first thing in the morning they cleaned the front of the store. They used brooms on the sidewalk, same as the Italian people. Everyone was washing windows, cleaning the sidewalk, cleaning up. No Indians then, and no drunks. Soon as any Indians came into town, police caught them and took them back—it was bad for Indians, [at] that time. Nobody had extra money to spend on themself, everybody had to work, no fooling around. Lots of people worked at Hastings Sawmill, I think about a couple of hundred. Because all the work was by hand, you know. And cheap labour.

My uncle took me up to North Galiano at Christmas time but I didn't know Christmas. I worked Christmas Day, New Year's Day, worked them just the same, no holiday. My uncle had fishing boats and we'd catch the herring, bring them in to camp, put them in a ten-ton tank, all by hand. Soon as we finished in camp then we'd go out fishing again. Lots of herring then, and I worked for two years at it.

Then I started selling groceries by truck. From Vancouver to Port Moody one day a week—lots of Japanese were there, and the sawmill, so I went camp to camp, made a few dollars. And next day New Westminster, next day Port Coquitlam, next day Haney. I was fish and tofu [bean curd] and kamaboku [fish cake]. [At] that time I asked white people round that way, you want to buy fish? But nobody ate fresh salmon. A big salmon: ten cents! In 1926, yeah, I *gave* it away. Then I worked for Mr. Millerd [Francis Millerd of the Millerd Packing Company], but he went broke, so the company stopped. It was a hard time for everybody. And I was broke too myself. My friend said, "You want to work, come to Port Alice, BC Pulp Company—forty cents an hour." Pretty good money. So I worked fourteen months, never stopping, worked every day, and I saved a little bit. I went to Japan in 1929, and in 1930 I married there. *Then* start the hard times, yeah, the hard times.

I came back in March 1930 by myself. If you could see what I saw! People hungry and dying down on the beach. Three stakes and a sack, that was home for them. You just went down to the foot of Dunlevy Avenue where Hastings Mill used to be, and there were lots of them, both ways. Hungry people. And then the trouble in the city started. People had iron bars, they broke windows at Woodward's and everyone went in and helped themself. You see, they had no jobs and no food, and the police couldn't do anything with so many—a whole city! And the garbage cans: on Hastings Street, Granville Street, people ate from them. I saw a mother with a baby pull out some chicken bones, set them on the garbage lid and right away three, four kids were standing around eating chicken bones. I left Vancouver that spring.

I jumped on a train in the shipyard with half a dozen young fellows. We'd gone to a butcher shop because we were hungry, "Have you got any leftovers you can give us?" They gave us old bread and meat we put in a sack. Any butcher shop you asked would give you liver free. There were more than half a dozen of us, about twenty-five, twenty-six years old, on that freight train. We hid under the lumber and we wanted to go to the other end of Canada. But when we got to Vernon, it started to rain and we were all soaked, so we had to get out. Two of us went down the Okanagan and we had nothing to eat for two or three days—pretty hungry. We ate anything, we ate grass. We got a job with a fruit company picking apples, but we only picked sixty acres. Three hundred acres we didn't touch, they were lying on the ground. There was no market for them. In Vancouver apples were three dollars a box, three dollars! and here they were lying on the ground and people were hungry.

I came back to Vancouver in 1933 and I worked for Mr. Nelson [of Nelson Brothers Fisheries Ltd.]. My wife came over that year. I said to Mr. Nelson, "I got no money and my wife is coming." He lent me $300, and I bought a house. I was working for him, very good money that time, pretty near five, six hundred a month—buying fish. But that big money lasted only the season, and then hard times start again. That's the story of my life.

We used to live on Cordova Street before the war. Cordova Street was mostly poor people—most Japanese were fishermen or common labourers, sawmill workers, poor people. From St. James Church on Gore Avenue to the end of Cordova, it was all Japanese both sides of the street.

By 1941 I had a few thousand dollars I borrowed from friends here and there and I leased a coffee shop at Hastings and Carrall for eighteen years. I started my own seafood place, called White Cap Seafood. I spent $11,000 on that place—big money, but I owned another seafood store, a high-class place, I made good money and I thought this time I'd make a million dollars. Then the war came.

I had a friend working in the Japanese community, and he said, "If you stay here, they'll catch you and put you in a camp—you and your children and your wife in separate camps." And the next day two RCMP came to my house. A friend of my wife telephoned, "If you go back home, they'll send you to a camp in Ontario." Because, you see, ordinary working people they didn't bother about very much, but me, I had quite a few employees and two stores. This was a dirty war, you know, governments make this war. So I left and went to New Westminster and I didn't come back. That was the last time I saw my coffee shop.

On March 6 [1942], my friend said, "Hara, you've got to go. They're going to close the bridge at twelve o'clock and they'll seize your truck and everything after that." So I left, I crossed the bridge one hour ahead of time.

Jungle shelters of the unemployed men at the old Hastings mill site in 1931. COL. R.D. WILLIAMS, CITY OF VANCOUVER ARCHIVES, RE N10.09

I was by myself. I planned to get to Kamloops, where I'd been once a long time ago, try to find a place, then try to get my family. It was a bad road then, slide time, March and April, it took me four days. And then when I got to Kamloops, there was all this newspaper propaganda and everybody was scared—"Lots of Japanese spies coming to Kamloops." Even the Indians were scared. So I thought I'd better go and see the head of police. He said, "Very bad news for the Japanese. I don't know *who* wrote this propaganda, but you fellows all come from Vancouver to Kamloops and they call it a 'Japanese army.' So you're not going to stay here because somebody will kill you." I went to Pritchard.

[After the war] I sold my farm and came back here. And with that money I bought the fish store on Main Street. I worked and my children got university educations.

HARRY HALPERN

Harry Halpern was born in Poland in 1902.

I came to Vancouver in 1930. I came to Keefer Street, to my sister's house. I was going around trying to work, to make a dollar, to look for a job. A friend of my sister's offered me a job. He offered me a job, shall I work for him? I started, he told me he was going to give me two dollars a day. I started Monday, I came Saturday to Vancouver, on Monday I started to work. I saw people, old people, using a sledgehammer and breaking engines from cars. That was in 1930.

After ten o'clock, I heard a whistle. I didn't know what a whistle meant. I saw one throw the hammer. I threw the hammer too, and he ran to his box lunch. He was drinking coffee. I had no box lunch, I had no coffee, I stayed and watched him. I saw he finished the coffee and he took the hammer, and he started breaking the engines again. I took the hammer too, and I broke and I broke. Twelve o'clock I heard another whistle. I didn't know what he was going to do. What did I know? The same man, I just watched, you see. And he went to the box lunch, started to eat the lunch. Twelve thirty, a whistle, he finished, he ran and he took the hammer and started to work. There was three people working, and I was the fourth. I was a young boy, I was twenty-eight years old—those people that were working, maybe sixty, fifty-five. Three o'clock, another whistle. And I got nothing to take—no coffee, no sandwich, nothing. I didn't know about restaurants. Four thirty, another whistle. Finished. He left the hammer and he got changed, and I did the same thing.

I went outside to Main Street. I waited for a streetcar. I said to myself, I don't know which way I go. Is it this way or this way? I think I paid the conductor seven cents and I said to him, "Stop—Keefer Street! Keefer Street!" So he stopped and he said, "That's Keefer. Where do you want to go?" I said, "I want to go to the 900-block Keefer." He said, "Go straight, straight, straight, straight." My sister said, "How did you like it?" I said, "If I knew when I came to Vancouver, I'll have a job like this, I'd never left. I'd stayed in Poland." "Well," she said, "what did you think? Were you figuring the money grows on the trees? You've got to work." Well, I never said nothing. She gave me supper. I wanted to go to sleep—it was seven o'clock. I was tired, you know, I'd never done that in my life. Before I came to Vancouver, I did nothing like that in any country, I was a butcher. I went to lie down but my brother-in-law lay down and he took a rest, and when he got up at twelve o'clock, he went to his bed. And I was waiting for him to go from the couch to his bed! At seven o'clock in the morning, my sister said, "Hey, get up, get up. You've got to go to work." I looked, my hands were all blisters, big pieces like dimes, quarters. I said to myself, Oi, I've got to go to work.

And then I got dressed and I went from Keefer Street to Main Street. I saw an old man driving a horse and a wagon. And I said to him, "What are you doing for a living?" He said, "I buy *shmatas*." That means rags in Jewish, old clothes. He knew I noticed he was Jewish, and I was Jewish. I said, "Listen, can you take me in your wagon, and show me the town?" He said, "Oh, I don't want partners." I said, "I don't want to be a partner, just show me the town. I'll sit with you in the wagon and you go around." He said, "Okay. But I promise you I'm not going to give you nothing." I went with him to Twelfth Avenue, to the lane. And you know what he did? The first thing he said was, "Junk! Rags! Bottles!" I said, "You've got to do that?" He said, "Well, if I'm not going to do that, nobody will know I'm a junkman." Mein Gott, I said to myself, I've come to Vancouver to do things like that! Where I came from in Poland, there was a fellow doing this business. Now, he was rich, he was so rich, and he had daughters. He would never let anyone take out his daughters. And everybody would say, "He's no good, you know, he's a cheap man. Anybody that wanted to buy junk, a junkman—cheap." That's how it was in our country.

Anyway, I went around with him and he talked to me and he asked me about our country things. Then he said to me, "Well. It's twelve o'clock. I'm going to sit down and eat dinner." He had dinner, he gave the horse a little bit of oats. One o'clock, by the children going from home to school. He said, "Okay we'll go peddling now." Three thirty, he said, "See, the children are going from school already. I never spent nothing. That happens some days, you don't spend nothing." He said, "Let's go home." He never went home on Main Street, he never went home on a street, he went in the lanes. Back and forth. Tenth Avenue in a lane, Eleventh Avenue in a lane, Thirteenth Avenue in a lane. He was not hauling junk anymore, he was going home. Closer, closer to town. One lady said, "Hoo-hoo!" He stopped, and he said to me, "Stay. Wait here. I'm going to see what she wants." Well, I stayed and I waited—half an hour. I saw him going down in the basement, and he never came out. I said to myself, well, I'm not afraid. I'd better go take a look what he's doing down there. I went to the basement door. I was not a baby, you know, I was twenty-eight years old. When I came to the door, I never rapped on the door, I just opened the door. Well, the lady saw me. She jumped to the ceiling, she got scared, she was scared, boy, she was scared. She said I'm supposed to knock on the door, and I never did that. Ahh, you know what he was doing? She had lots of rags, and he was filling up sacks, sacks of rags.

It took a long time—he filled up one sack, he left it, he filled up another one, he filled up the sacks, you know, and when I came he was talking to her, you know, he talked to her. After he said to me, "Okay, give me some help." I didn't take two sacks, I took four. He took two, I took four, and I never carried them, I pulled them. He said to her, "How much do I owe you, lady?" The lady said to him, "Oh, mister, nothing. Thank you very much for taking it away." She was happy that he cleaned up the basement. He said to me, "Well, we'll go to the junk place now." He was going to sell them. Before he went to sell, he came to another lane and he saw a section from an old furnace. He saw one section laying in the yard by the garbage can. And he stopped and he said, "Wait a minute. I'd better go ask the lady what she's going to do with it. Maybe she doesn't want it. Maybe she is giving it to the garbage men." He went to the door and he said to the lady, "Lady, I see you've got a piece of iron by the garbage can. What do you want to do with it?" She said, "If it is any good to you, take it. If you want some more, I've got the rest in the basement. I just took out one piece for the garbage man. If I give him a little piece every week, he'll take it." He said, "Okay, lady, I'll take everything."

He went in the basement and I went in too. I helped him and we put

Harry Halpern in his daughter's home, 1978.
TOD GREENAWAY PHOTO

everything in the wagon. For nothing, too—he never paid a penny. And he took it to the junk place. He weighed the rags, two cents a pound and then the iron. He took in $9.78 for the rags and the iron. I said to myself, He never spent a penny, and he got nearly ten dollars, that's good money. I said, "Are you going to take me tomorrow, too?" He said, "Where shall I pick you up?" "You pick me up at the same place, Keefer and Main, that's the place I know." He came in the morning, eight o'clock, and he picked me up and I went with him.

He bought bottles, you know, beer bottles, the price was twenty cents a dozen. If you called him in for five dozen bottles, he'd give you forty cents. Or, if you want to give him a dozen for nothing, that's nobody's business. When he went over to the junk place at five thirty, he took the bottles and he counted them, there was over fifty dozen. Do you know how much he made on a dozen? Seven cents. I figured, fifty dozen, even if he paid twenty cents a dozen and maybe he's got a dozen for nothing—still, fifty times seven, he made $3.50. Still better than if you take a sledgehammer and break engines!

After that, I said to myself, I'm going to be in this business. Junking. I met a fellow and I said to him, "Oh, you're peddling, you make money." "Huh!" he said. "Money! Huh! You want to buy my horse?" "Sure, I'll buy your horse and buggy," I said, "what do you want for it?" He said, "Forty-two dollars." "I haven't got forty-two dollars," I said. "Can I meet you tomorrow?" I wanted to see how the horse goes, if he's a healthy horse. Okay, he took me around in the morning. A dollar, he paid a lady for a buggy, a baby buggy. I said to him, "You still can sell the buggy?" He said, "I don't care if I throw it away. I just bought the buggy and I put it in the back of the wagon because I want the people to see that I'm a junkman. I don't like hollering, 'Junk, Rags, Bottles.' If a lady sees the buggy in the wagon, she will say, 'Come on, I've got something for sale,'" she'll call *him*. Next day, I said to him, "You don't want to take forty dollars for the horse?" He said, "No, forty-two dollars." I went to my sister and I told her I wanted to buy a horse and buggy. "Horse and buggy? You want to be a peddler?" I said, "Why is it not nice? It's better than going with the sledgehammer and breaking iron." Well, I was a couple of times in this junk place where they buy junk. There was an old lady, the wife, and she had a daughter and she asked me if I was married. I said, "No." Oh, she was happy, she was thinking I'll get married to her daughter. Anyway, she said, "What's your trouble, Mr. Halpern?" I said I needed forty-two dollars. I wanted to buy a horse and buggy. She said, forty-two dollars is not much. You've got to have a few dollars spending money, you know, to buy something. I'm going to lend you fifty dollars." I said, "Oh, thank you very much, lady." Then she said, "Now, anything you buy, you shall bring it to here." I said, "Lady, if you're good to me when you're buying the things, why shall I sell it to somebody else?" "Okay," she said, "you look to me honest." She gave me fifty dollars and I bought the horse for forty-two dollars and I had eight dollars in my pocket.

Once when I was peddling, I came with the horse and buggy to a fellow one block from Nanaimo Street. I stopped the horse, and I saw he was taking water from the ground. I asked this fellow for a pail. He was a farmer, an old man and when he came here, he bought the place. I looked at his calves and I said, "Mein Gott, how many! What are you going to do with that calf?" He said, "She's only three weeks old." But for Jewish people, after one week you can kill it. When the calf is five days, six days old, it's against the Jewish religion. I said, "I like the calf. What do you want for the calf?" "Oh," he said to me, "eight dollars." I just thought, Mein Gott, eight dollars for a calf, and my wife, when she buys a piece of meat, she pays over a dollar. Anyway, I bought it, the calf. I took the calf to the wagon and brought it home, and I showed it to my wife. We were living then on Jackson, in an apartment. And she said to me, "Ah, you're looking for trouble. Who's going to clean it?" I know she knows I can clean it, see. Anyway, I went to the rabbi. But he won't kill it, he can't do that—a chicken, yeah. And I'm not going to take it back. I went to the Jewish butcher, and I said to him—my wife reminded me all the time—I said to him, "Listen, I bought a calf, and the rabbi said he can't kill a calf. He can kill a chicken, a goose, a duck. No calf." I said, "Come and take a look." And he came upstairs and he took a look, and he said to me, "I've got no money. I like the calf, but I've got no money." But my wife said to me, "Okay, if he's got no money, trust him." My wife is that kind of woman. I said, "Okay, you'll pay me when you have it. But you know, a calf doesn't eat, you've got to give her milk." He never paid me back—you know what he gave me? From this calf, when he killed the calf, he gave me the leather. Jewish people like the leather, you know, calf leather is good. It's not pork leather. He gave me the leather. The leather, I'll never forget, cost me eight dollars. Nice man. See, he was a butcher and he couldn't afford it. I said to myself, "It's too bad he's not a junkman!"

GLORIA STEINBERG HARRIS

Gloria Steinberg Harris was born in Vancouver in 1924 of Jewish parents. Her father had emigrated from Russia via Germany, and her mother came from Romania in 1911.

Whether you were Italian or Yugoslavian or Chinese or Jewish, your parents were all immigrants together and there was such a *warmth* in this neighbourhood, I can't begin to tell you. In 1944, my mother became very ill and she was in the hospital a number of weeks. When she first came home, we'd never know what we'd find on the back porch: it could be eggs, it could be vegetables, or else somebody would bring over a hot dish of something. And then there was the respect for each other's religion. Every Sunday morning we would sit in the living room and watch the exodus to Sacred Heart Church—the *whole* Italian neighbourhood. And this was just part of our life. Sundays, in the warm weather, were a beautiful time. Kids would be on the street playing catch. Three doors up the street were the Santagas. On Sunday afternoons they'd be sitting on the front porch, and he'd be playing the accordion, and she'd be singing. It was beautiful. Even with all the hardships, it was still beautiful.

Living in that neighbourhood was such a melting pot. Mrs. Cibular was from Scotland and she had the Scottish and Jewish accent combined, which was really something to hear. She was the neighbourhood "yenta." She would come and give everybody the news, and if it was bad news, so much the better.

And then Mr. Marino lived kitty-corner from the Barro house at the end of the block. He was a fruit peddler, and when he came by our place he was probably on his way home after a day's work. He'd be selling watermelon, only it wasn't watermelon, it was "wa-ter-mel-OWN!" this beautiful musical thing.

Gloria Steinberg Harris in her home, 1978.
TOD GREENAWAY PHOTO

None of the teachers lived in the neighbourhood. You must realize that the teachers that came to us came from a better financial class of home—I don't say better class of home, but a better financial class. As a matter of fact, we found that if you were bright, or if you tried, the teachers were understanding. They saw how we came from backgrounds where education was uppermost, and we all tried, it didn't matter what we were. For anybody of any ethnic background, education was your only weapon—as far as you could afford it, which wasn't too far for most of us. If we got through high school, we sent up flares.

The one time I had any trouble at Strathcona School was with an Italian boy. I had a little suitcase to hold my books. I was a fair student, and studious, and I was a year ahead of myself, unfortunately, so I took a lot of abuse because I was the youngest in the class. Well, he called me a "bloody Jew," and he took my suitcase and threw it down the aisle so the whole bottom just scraped right off. I was a milquetoast kind of little girl, I didn't assert myself too much at that time, so I came home crying, and my mother says, "Well, I can't go and fight your battles for you, but," she says, "the next time he talks to you, you just call him a 'bloody dago.'" And I'll be damned, I did that and this boy fell apart, he just couldn't take it. On the whole, our close relationships were strictly with Caucasians. We did have friends among the Japanese—mind you, they left in '42—and friends among the Chinese, but all my fondness and closeness is with the Italian people.

My father and mother would speak Yiddish at home and I would speak English. But they spoke English too, and they could both read the newspaper, self-taught. You must realize that being foreign was a very delicate problem then. We were never, ever allowed to forget that we were foreign. I was born in this country, but I was "foreign." So we were very touchy about being Jewish, or being Italian, or being Yugoslavian. If we got on a streetcar and my mother spoke Yiddish I'd pretend I didn't know her. It was *sad*.

My connection with the Jewish religion was deepest at home. My mother and father had a traditional home and Friday was the big deal. My poor mother would be exhausted. We had a wood and coal stove, of course, and

Mrs. Cibular, neighbourhood 'yenta,' selling plums at the corner of Hastings and Carrall in the 1930s. GLORIA HARRIS COLLECTION, COURTESY OF ROYAL BC MUSEUM, BC ARCHIVES

every Friday the kitchen floor was washed, with newspapers laid over the floor for Friday anyway, so it would be clean for one night, and a fresh white tablecloth. After my mother did the dirty work, I remember she'd put on a clean housedress and a clean apron to do the baking, because you shouldn't have a dirty apron when you're handling food. So Friday night, no matter how hard up we were, was a beautiful time. And then the holidays: after the synagogue on the high holidays, the family got together and we had a big lunch. On the high holidays my father didn't light the stove—on Yom Kippur morning particularly. On Rosh Hashanah, my mother had to heat up the lunch, so she lit it, or else my father banked the fire in the stove so it would not go out completely. But Yom Kippur, my father never made the fire because you didn't eat anyway, you were supposed to fast. The kids were never forced to fast, and I remember my Yom Kippur morning fare was a piece of honey cake and a glass of milk. And that morning would be pretty chilly, you know.

My dad was the politician in our family, an armchair general, you know, afraid to vote his way because of impracticability. Basically, he was a socialist, a very religious socialist, but voted according to what would avail him of a job. Where your bread and butter was concerned, that came first in those days. And I don't think this was peculiar to my dad.

I remember boys coming to the house, because we weren't far from the CN railway station and they came across Canada, these boys coming to the house—nice, clean-cut boys, looking for food. People were a little nervous about the young lads coming in because there had been some violence, but my mother never was. We always had bread and butter in the house, and tomatoes. I remember this one case—I couldn't have been more than ten years old—this young lad came to the door and he was begging for food but he wouldn't come in. So my mother put newspapers on the front porch and she spread a napkin out, one of the napkins with my grandmother's monogram, because in those days that was part of your trousseau. She gave him milk or tea and a bunch of tomato and bread-and-butter sandwiches, and he was so grateful. We were all poor together, but these boys were absolutely *starved*. I think, when you're poor, if you go to somebody poor, you'll get a better response. Let's face it, you have a rapport, an understanding. That's why, no matter how poor we were, we always managed to give the boys something.

As a youngster, I remember my father peddling, you know, looking for scrap and so on. And then there wasn't anything in that so he gave that up, and I remember he and my brother buying fruit from the wholesale, and vegetables, and going from door to door selling it. As soon as my dad started working full-time, and this was in '42, the first time I remember my dad working full-time, he immediately went and paid the baker, the butcher, every penny he owed them.

In 1939 I remember getting ready for bed in September—it must have been September the third—and a newsboy running along the street yelling, "Extra! War has been declared on Germany!" I can feel the goosebumps today, the frightening feeling. We relied on the newspapers for everything and the newspapers were *so* sensational. I'll never forget that night, trucks, running, driving down, and boys running from one house to the other, selling papers about the war. Our whole life was emotional, rent with emotion, really, when you think about it.

I remember the fear associated with the evacuation of the Japanese. I remember the soldiers that were ready to march down to Japanese town, and they stopped them. People were really all fired up. They *said* that some of the Steveston fleet were wired with radios. I don't know how true it is, but the kids that I knew were just ordinary kids. A lot of people say, "Well, at least they came out of it with their lives." But that's not right. These people were born here and brought up here. And yet there *were* a lot of young men in the thirties that went back to Japan for military training.[58] I never understood that.

Even in '41, when I was just out of high school, anti-Semitism was rampant still. I remember some food place where I went in and applied, and the form asked for nationality, so I put down "Canadian." He says, "That isn't enough." I says, "Well, I'm born here." And I knew what he was getting at, he could see I was Jewish, I had a Jewish name. But I thought, well I'm going to push this as far as I can. I knew I wasn't going to get the job anyway, so it didn't matter. "Well," he says, "we have to know, because we're not going to hire Japanese or anything like that." I says, "My name is Steinberg, and I certainly don't look Oriental. Why don't you just admit that you don't want anybody other than someone English? Why don't you just say so?"

All the people, when I was growing up, were working people, and their whole life was just to keep working to provide for the children, get their children educated. Every other block, I think, had a bootlegger. A lot of them, by the time their kids were grown up and getting their education, probably quit. Because we did end up with a few educated people in the neighbourhood, good chartered accountants, and so on. And where would they get the money to send their kids to university if they didn't do this? So what was *really wrong* with it? And it was the wives who ran a lot of these bootlegging places, because the kids needed things. What easier way to make a dollar? A hundred percent profit. No taxes.

In those days, people of ethnic backgrounds had jobs according to their nationality. I mean, the Swedish people were usually loggers, and so were the Ukrainians and Russians. The Yugoslavians were also loggers but became fishermen. The Jewish people were peddlers, and eventually went into the second-hand business. The Italian people—a lot of them were labourers and bootleggers, and then when education reared its head, finally and fortunately, they became highly educated and among our best legal minds in the city. The Chinese had the little stores. A lot of the Japanese women were seamstresses, and of course the men were fishermen. Everyone seemed to have their own vocation according to their nationality almost. Because, I guess, they were

The Morris Steinberg family in the backyard of their Union Street home, c. 1916. GLORIA HARRIS COLLECTION, COURTESY OF ROYAL BC MUSEUM, BC ARCHIVES

forced into it. It's just like earlier, the Chinese working on the railroad. That's an ugly thing. I've seen people, particularly Anglo-Saxons, walk down Pender Street and stare at these old men walking around, not knowing the history of why they looked the way they did and how their wives were back in China.

But during the forties, people became a little more prosperous and men had steady jobs, there was a little more work—things improved during the war. The older men who finally got steady jobs saved their money and were able perhaps to buy a little house up in the Nanaimo Street area, the Italian people particularly. So the Italians left. The Jewish families had already left, except for one or two. All the Yugoslavian families left, because the fishing, you must realize, was taken over a great deal by the Yugoslavian families after the Japanese had gone. Anyone who made a little bit of money during the war invested their money in property elsewhere.

ROSE BEZUBIAK, LORNE BEZUBIAK, HANNAH BEZUBIAK POLOWY & ED POLOWY

Rose Bezubiak was born in 1905 in Mundare, Alberta, of Ukrainian parents. Here she is in conversation with her son Lorne Bezubiak (born in Vancouver in 1933), her daughter Hannah Bezubiak Polowy (born in Mundare, Alberta, in 1927), and her son-in-law Ed Polowy (born in Wayne, Alberta, in 1923).

ROSE BEZUBIAK: In 1929 my husband lost his farm in Alberta so he thought we would come to Vancouver. He went to Vancouver himself, he didn't pay for the train, he rode the freight train. Hannah was sixteen months old, so I came on the train one month later with her. I was working housework in Shaughnessy and Dunbar and all over the place. We were living in a two-room apartment on Georgia and Clark Drive, the building is demolished now. They'd have maybe one baby, a nurse and a cook, and even chauffeurs. When I was coming home, it took me an hour, I'd have a snooze on the streetcar, I'd come home and start to do the housework in my two rooms. And my husband went logging for a little bit, not too long—the jobs were scarce. One crew would do a little bit, and then the other crew, and so on. But the people had to work and they were glad to get the jobs. We had five kids in seven years. Well, my husband went on help—we had "relief" at that time. And he worked for it, two days a week, cleaned the parks.

We moved eighteen times, *eighteen times*. I'd always have two kids in a crib, so we'd bring those cribs into the middle of the house because the walls were with holes and very dirty. And we'd have to paper right away and patch the holes and everything. And the cribs in the middle and the kid crying and we papering the house. So we painted and cleaned up a house and it was sold in four months and we'd have to move again. It was lots of times like that.

HANNAH BEZUBIAK POLOWY: My mother brought this kimono home once, beautiful silk kimono with flowers all over it and she said, "You can have it." Someone had discarded it and given it to her, but she said I was not to wear it now because we had one of those pot-bellied stoves in our living room and it was too cold. She said, "One day we shall have steam heat and I'm going to have floors that look like polished glass and you will put that kimono on and you will stand by the steam heat." My mom and dad always had hope.

Ed Polowy: Mom and Dad and the three of us children came in 1930, from Edmonton. In 1931 he started up the first delicatessen east of Main Street, at 740 East Hastings. It was an ethnic type of delicatessen—Ukrainian-style sausages and salamis, and head cheeses, herring, kielbasa, a Ukrainian garlic sausage. My mother was the driving force behind the business, she had the physical strength and my dad was the brains behind it. This was in the deep part of the Depression, and I just say that we, as kids, didn't suffer 'cause there was always stock in the store. Many people sort of resented the fact that Mom and Dad had a store, but little did they realize the hours they put in, that they took bum accounts and had to carry them and lost most of them. Taking somebody's word that they're going to come in with a relief cheque, and it's not there. It wasn't till the war that the business really got onto its feet; it was just an existence, that's all it was. We lived in the back, five of us in two rooms.

My father was the first Ukrainian sausage maker in the city. We made the sausages right on the premises. It was up to my brother and I to help out as much as we could, after school and such. There was wood to pile for the smokehouse and wood to pile for the house itself. Our smokehouse was located near the back of the alley, so that meant walking up dozens of stairs, up and down with sticks of sausages in the raw form to hang in the smokehouse, and then carry them back after they were smoked and cooked. Many times on our return trips, we'd find a stick or two missing. Somebody would be watching and help themselves to it and it would represent twenty-four rings or your profit for the whole works. So we had to do it in shifts then, always somebody watching. Dad was up early in the mornings, down at the fish docks picking up salt herring. And down to the food stands early in the morning, to pick up food for the shop. As a matter of fact, we stocked our shelves, many times, on Woodward's specials. It was cheaper buying it from Woodward's than from the wholesaler. But there was always a limit—two per person, or whatever it was, so the whole family took their turn, maybe twice, to get enough for the stock.

There was always lots to do. The Ukrainian Hall was right in the centre. They had dancing, choir, Ukrainian school—language school, music, drama, social affairs, the whole bit—concerts every Sunday, sometimes matinees.

Lorne Bezubiak: We were always busy. We did pick music up from other sources later, but basically it was down there because it was the Ukrainian Community Centre and it was free. My father was a fiddler, he could read music but he could pick it up quicker by ear. And he played a violin very unorthodox—just the way he held it, his own style, the way he held the bow, the way some of the noises or sounds that came out of the violin, well, you couldn't duplicate them. It didn't come from a regular piece of music because a lot of that wasn't written. An awful lot of the things that he played were

The Polowy delicatessen on Hastings Street in the 1930s. Ed Polowy's father was the first Ukrainian sausage maker in the city. ED POLOWY COLLECTION, COURTESY OF ROYAL BC MUSEUM, BC ARCHIVES

songs that were handed down and the rhythms, unfortunately, we haven't got them.

ED POLOWY: The Ukrainian Hall had an active role in the Post Office sit-in by the unemployed in 1938.[59] It acted as a hospital, a field hospital—the grounds were littered with the wounded, and those who were badly, really badly hurt were inside and overflowing. There was a soup kitchen and everything else.

HANNAH BEZUBIAK POLOWY: Off we went with our mandolins to the Ukrainian Hall that day and I remember walking into that hall and it was just full of men lying on the floor. There were a few doctors there. Dr. Lyle Telford was there and he was bandaging people's arms and heads and legs. There was a soup kitchen downstairs and there were a lot of people cooking and getting food ready. I could remember standing there and looking all around and feeling—this is the Ukrainian Hall, I know this hall, but what's happening here?

LORNE BEZUBIAK: In 1944, they turned around and took our halls.[60] Right across the country, the government seized them all, and we were all out. And they turned them over to very right-wing groups that favoured the government. And this way, we had no place to meet, we had no place to sit and criticize, as a group. And our schools continued, our dancing school, our language schools, under different conditions, different halls, but we were still active.

ED POLOWY: And raised thousands upon thousands of dollars for war effort, sending over bundles to the Red Cross.

LORNE BEZUBIAK: They had them for about four years. And finally we had to petition the federal government to give us back our halls.

ED POLOWY: We were a Ukrainian group with our halls and they took them away from us and gave them to the other element of the Ukrainians, which were the element that were crying for the Ukraine, who said that the Ukraine hasn't died yet and so forth, and they wanted to get the Ukraine back. The Soviet Union, at that time, was an ally of Canada. These people, by their very nature, were opposed to the Soviet Union, but they got our halls.

LORNE BEZUBIAK: They were really a fascist element. They were more supporters of Hitler than they were of Canada. And then the move right across the country was, "We're going home." I can remember those marches. We all got organized and big banners, and we marched back to the Ukrainian Hall at 805 East Pender and officially opened the door and we went in.

ED POLOWY: There'd be a yearly affair, the May Day parade, made of trade unions, labour groups, women's organization—thousands upon thousands of people.

LORNE BEZUBIAK: Blocks and blocks and blocks and blocks, and everyone was carrying banners.

ED POLOWY: They'd march from the Cambie Street Grounds. That whole area was a big football field and that's where they set up, and then they marched all down Georgia to Stanley Park. There were labour floats, so to speak, and unemployment groups, all types of groups. And then when they stopped them going to Stanley Park, they went to Oppenheimer, which is Powell Street Grounds, and had them there as well. 'Cause then there was a period they were stopping them from parading completely.

LORNE BEZUBIAK: And in the latter years, it went up Powell Street to the entrance to Hastings Park and it was the Exhibition Grounds. And then that was cut off. There was Tim Buck from the Canadian Communist Party speaking the odd time because, of course, he was national leader. He always made sure that there was always some speaker from our organization, because we were part of that movement, we were part of that feeling, and we were part of the sympathetic group of people that were unemployed. I'm talking about the later fifties. We marched in one of the last May Day parades they had.

ED POLOWY: Many of the organizations that marched in the early thirties were religious groups and such. They had something in common, they were unemployed. Discriminated against, in many cases. All of us saw the Winches at Powell Grounds.[61]

LORNE BEZUBIAK: We knew exactly what he was talking about. You know, even kids knew what he was talking about: the suppression and the exploitation of our fathers. We knew what he was talking about. You know, someone from the outside would laugh, but we knew, 'cause we had experienced it. We saw it every day. We lived with it.

HANNAH BEZUBIAK POLOWY: In the Depression, I can remember walking down the street and there would just be a clump of furniture sitting out on the street and people around it, and then the neighbours would come and maybe try and take that furniture into their own homes and offered people food or some shelter until they could find another place.

LORNE BEZUBIAK: The sheriff's office would come and just take it out. It was put into a great big pile and then you were given so much time to get it off there, a couple of hours to get it off the street or they'd just come and take it away. Some people would come with carts and wheelbarrows and help them.

HANNAH BEZUBIAK POLOWY: Across from us on Princess Avenue we never did know those neighbours, because that was a very famous bootlegging joint. They had no children, and they had drawn curtains all the time, and these great big cars would pull up. They never bothered anyone and you'd just see these people get out of these great big cars and go into the house and then later on they'd come out.

LORNE BEZUBIAK: But you know, I always worked for bootleggers squeezing grapes in the wine season. Prominent families used to come into the neighbourhood or they were on delivery routes. We had the odd mock police raid, and when you're twelve years old you're scared. But they would just say, "Don't worry about it, just stand still," and the police would come through, and they'd leave after they were given whatever they wanted.

HANNAH BEZUBIAK POLOWY: My sisters and I washed floors for some of the bootleggers, and they were also running other kinds of facilities but that didn't bother us. I can remember going into Smith's place and washing his floor and having to change the bed, and there was a big wad of money under the pillow. He'd just done a couple of abortions, I guess, and there was all this money. Well I never thought of taking it. "Mr. Smith, here's all this money that was under your pillow," gave it to him and changed the beds and did the floors.

But that was a safe neighbourhood, very, very safe. I guess one of my first jobs was at the Westcoast Woollen Mills, and I had a job there from four thirty to twelve thirty a.m. Well, I was really afraid walking up Hastings Street where there were lights even, more lights than down Princess, but once I hit Princess I felt safe. There was a cafe on the corner there, Home Apple Pie, and that's where all the gang used to hang out, that Zoot-Suit gang, Home Apple Gang.

LORNE BEZUBIAK: We used to hang around the street lights, and you'd be playing kick the can at eight o'clock, and usually around nine o'clock the police would come and say, "Okay, stop kicking the can and go in," or you'd hear someone calling you anyways. The mothers would be out on the front porch, and they'd just call. You know, not like it is today, you'd *hear* them calling. And you'd go, you'd go home—the tough gang suddenly had to fold up for the night. In many ways our mothers were very militant in those days. It's not like today where a lot of parents just don't know where their kids are. You know, even when you belonged to these gangs, your

Group of marchers in one of the May Day parades of the 1930s. VANCOUVER PUBLIC LIBRARY, SPECIAL COLLECTIONS, VPL 8790

mother knew where you were—you were on the street, but you could hear her. And if you were there, it was like a telegraph system, you could hear them in the distance—it was like the jungle—you'd carry on the message, and everyone always got home.

The Bull Gang I was in, was made of just very young kids and we never did anything maliciously, you know, there was never any property damage, we didn't do anything like that. But if there was a way of, oh—I don't know, just somehow, articles would suddenly come to the forefront, where they came from no one seemed to know, and we didn't do any stealing or breaking-in or this type of thing. There was some of that in the later forties, when I really didn't associate with them too much. But we sort of roamed the streets—more for the idea of looking for outsiders that were coming into the neighbourhood. We were sort of a protective force walking around.

Hannah Bezubiak Polowy: The Zoot-Suiters were older, they should have been in the army and somehow weren't. And they wore the zoot-suits, the big hats, and the very tight pants, the chains.

Lorne Bezubiak: You know, it was a big-enough deal to go behind the garage and smoke. We would never accept anything like drugs. There was a very high code of ethics. You did certain things, and you didn't do certain things. It was nothing to get somebody that came to the neighbourhood and beat the pulp out of him. That would bother you sometime, depending on how bad you beat him, but no, there was a limit. And there was no drinking.

And with all the wine available to us, there was no such thing as taking a bottle, and we could have taken bottles.

We'd have situations where the Bull Gang and the Zoot-Suits joined forces and we all had jobs to do. For instance, when the Marines came, the U.S. Marines, our job was to get clubs and baseball bats. The story was circulated that the Marines were going to come down and clean out the neighbourhood, they didn't realize what a tightly knit neighbourhood they were coming into. So they came down with a little bit of a band and they were marching down Hastings Street, coming east on Hastings. We first picked up the signal when they were past the Patricia Hotel and we were all more or less stationed along the road. Of course, the neighbourhood heard about it so they were all out there and the Zoot-Suits were all intermingled with the neighbourhood and everybody was cheering the band as they were coming down. The Marines were all slicked up and coming down the street and they had little billy clubs that they were going to clean the neighbourhood with. All of a sudden, everyone attacked and I think it was all over in about fifteen minutes because the Marines were lying all over the sidewalk and all over the road and their instruments were smashed. There was just nothing left of them. There was the situation where a Marine or two pulled a knife and they had to break their arms to get it off them, but you know, you can do it very easily with a club. Of course, the whole neighbourhood was just cheering one way and the good guys won.

Hannah Bezubiak Polowy: We didn't like it when people came in from Kitsilano or from Kerrisdale. They'd come in to—I guess they would call it "slumming" or whatever—but we didn't like it.

Lorne Bezubiak: Then when Wallace Transfer opened up, in the early forties, it was great, because suddenly we had vehicles in the neighbourhood, such as six-ton flat-deck trucks, and when it snowed you could stock your snowballs with stones and ice and we used to visit the Kerrisdale area on flat-decks and just really give it to 'em. And we'd go out there very, very carefully, and it was all covered up with tarp, and then all of a sudden open up and smash their windows—we'd do everything. And then, come back to our neighbourhood and of course wait for them to come, and we'd be waiting for them because we were going to protect it. And they never did come too much after that, because they were afraid.

Hannah Bezubiak Polowy: But there was that real sense of community, and when you think that we get so uptight about language being a barrier—it wasn't a barrier. People couldn't speak English too well, and they tried and they spoke whatever language was their first language, and people just accepted it. It was a European background neighbourhood where there was a strong work ethic, there were morals—it didn't matter what you did for a living but they had high morals and they had high expectations of their kids.

Lorne Bezubiak: Sam Barrett with his fruit, he was a character and the kids loved him because he went down the street selling and he used to holler out "watermelon" and "bananas." We would follow him but we had no money and we wouldn't follow him because we were going to steal something, we just knew that eventually he would break down and he would give us some. The gang of kids would become too massive and he had to sort of thin it out, so he would thin it out by giving us a part of a banana or some watermelon—it was great.

HANNAH BEZUBIAK POLOWY: "Crazy Mary" she was a pathetic person, but she was accepted. Nobody ever saw her sober, and you never expected to see her sober.

LORNE BEZUBIAK: She'd stand there on the sidewalk and watch us and we'd keep on playing cricket and then she'd walk away and go home. We never bothered her and no one ever called her names or taunted her or anything. It was just "Crazy Mary" and there she was.

When I first experienced discrimination was when I went to Britannia [High School] because we were getting people from what we call the "upper part of the east" and the Grandview area who were using the terminology "bohunk" and "chinaman" or "chink." And they were Anglo-Saxon, so as we shifted from Strathcona School to Britannia High School we went as a group. It was fine and dandy, let them try and use a word like that and they had ten of us—we'd put them in lockers, lock them up, turn the combination on them! If they tangled with us once they never tangled with us again because we were just too organized, we were a very, very tight group. I think this was the experience of all groups that came out of that neighbourhood. See, suddenly you're exposed to discrimination that you know is there but you don't think people would actually throw it at you. And suddenly, it was.

LEONA RISBY

My parents moved from Texas to Oklahoma, and from Oklahoma to Alberta in 1911. They brought most of their materials and all their furniture and their horses, and they even brought a dog. They chartered a wagon train, I remember my dad saying, him and four other men. They chartered this car and they brought all their belongings in it, and the menfolks slept in this car, but the women and their children they stayed on the train. They came to Edmonton and I was born in a tent there. Then they took us all to Athabasca and most of my childhood was spent in Athabasca, one hundred miles north of Edmonton. My mother's Indian, a southern tribe, Cherokee. My father's Black. Oh, there must have been tons of coloured people that came up from Texas. I don't like to go into that because it hurts and I won't talk about it, but I heard my father tell these stories of why he came to Canada. It makes you feel hurt inside, it makes you feel bitter, and you don't know who to feel bitter to, so it's best not to talk about it.

I was frightened when I first arrived [here] because Vancouver was rough—when I came to the coast here it was *rugged*, really rugged. It was a

Leona Risby was born in Edmonton, Alberta, in 1911 and came to Vancouver with her husband and children in 1933.

sort of a red-light district in there on Main and Hastings. All around Hastings and Main and Alexander, but it wasn't down in Japtown. I was scared to death. I used to take the streetcar up as far as Woodward's and then I'd get home as fast as I could because it was *really* rough. I think it deserved to be cleaned up. They were not giving the young girls any protection, and there was so many young girls in that type of a mess, just to get a dollar. Kids, young kids. I knew girls that were fourteen and fifteen years old that was in such stuff as that. Some of 'em got there for the money, some of 'em got there to help support their family, sometimes their parents put 'em there, and sometimes the men put them there. The girls in that type of work wore these clinging satin pyjamas, they had these big wide legs to them, these pyjamas did, and they'd have on these beautiful pyjamas and all made up. Then you'd just pass a little house, there'd be a man across the street, and you're walking across the street, and there'd be "ping, ping, ping"—they're knocking at the man to come in. That's an awful thing. Now I think the town has cleaned up from that. Whatever they do now, you don't see it. Mama Pryor said when she came here [1917],[62] you didn't go in that part of town that was a red-light district, but the red-light was all over Vancouver when I came out here—those bugs were lighting up everywhere! Well, the law got in there and they closed up *all* of those places. It was Mayor Telford that got in, and it was cleared up good in 1939. You didn't see no "pinging" on the window and I'm sure it was Telford because all of the people were fussing at Telford. They didn't like Telford, but he is the mayor that cleaned up the city.

Most of the Black families lived out [of Strathcona] and not too many that lived downtown. Maybe the old pensioners that couldn't get around much, and didn't have much money for carfare, so they'd get a little room and crawl in it or something. Our people never lived close together, only with the people that lived down where we say the slums are, across from the church [Fountain Chapel]. They lived in those little places because they couldn't afford to get any other. But the Black people did pretty good for themselves here. They used their money well, most of our people used their money well. I won't say all of 'em 'cause some of them wouldn't have a job if you put it in bed with them. When they could buy something, they got it, 'cause they hadn't been used to getting money—just like myself. I've never had too much in life, but everything that I got, I earned and I earned it the hard way, and I pinched pennies.

When we lived around there, there was a lot of people living there, the odd drunk, and a few winos, but it wasn't rough. Nobody got robbed. And you could go to work safer—walk to work and back. I lived on Prior Street, in the 300-block Prior, used to walk back and forth to work in the early parts of the morning and nobody bothered me. Most of Mrs. Pryor's business came from the Stratford. A lot of the loggers used to stay there and they were all clean-cut working men. You'd see the odd old wino laying around sleeping someplace, but actually they don't bother, too weak to bother and they just want a little wine and they go out on a sleep and their face is all red and they look pitiful.

Then there was Hogan's Alley where they danced and they sang. Maybe one person was pretty high that would want one song sung all night and the same song, because it reminded him of something, and they'd be putting money in the kitty, and then when they get "Will you sing that song?" "Yeah," they'd say, and they loved that old song, and they would be wanting that played, just some song or 'nother.[63] And it was a small place, there would be a few around dancing, and a few sitting around at the table drinking until they fall on the floor, and pick 'em up and drag 'em and lay 'em out in Hogan's Alley.

Later [mid-1950s] I owned a place on Powell Street that was a Japanese fish market Mother Alexander bought, and I bought it from her son after she died—old, old place and it was between two big stores and it was kind of falling under. Well, my husband and my daughter, they didn't want it. "Oh, this old place will fall down. You don't want it. You're just wasting your money." So I said, "I'll call the city building inspector and ask his opinion." Well he came and he looked and he said, "Well, one thing I can tell you—that it will never fall down, because there's a building to hold it up on one side, and one to hold it up on the other." So I took the place, and honest to goodness, I never knew what I was going to do with that place. I sat downstairs and hour after hour I shut my eyes and visualized how to fix it. So I called the inspector and I told him what I wanted to do, and he looked at me and he said, "Well, I'll tell you what I'll do, Mrs. Risby, if you'll fix it, I'll pass, it." It was the worst-looking building inside that you ever saw in your life. So I just sat down and I drew some plans, and it took me about three days to visualize how it would look, with my eyes shut. So I just got me a bunch of gyproc, and I just—*schzoop*—right over one side of the building just closed up all those windows, windows up and windows down, you never saw such a place. And the other side, I did the same. Then I painted it, put the rough ceiling on, and we built a nice little log cabin front. When I called the inspector, he came and he shook his head again, "Well, I don't know how you did it, but," he said, "if you think you would be able to open up on New Year's night, you go ahead and open up—I'll pass it."

We landed a nice business there. Had a lot of nice customers, and we had all sorts of banquets. We had banquets for A. Phillip Randolph,[64] we had banquets for the baseball teams, we had band banquets, and we did a real good business. My husband was a good cook and so was I and we worked together. Sometime I'd have as many as six people—I'd have to employ that many. We usually opened about five in the evening, and we closed around seven in the morning, and sometimes we'd have a house full of guests at three o'clock in the morning. When the other nightclubs would close up, they'd come over to our place. And then we used to sing gospel songs. We got a write-up in the paper, you know, the only nightclub in town that when they're not doing any work, they sing spirituals! We would all sing together and it was like a real big family—everybody knew everybody. We had most all the taxi drivers, people from the sugar refinery, the longshoremen by the carloads.

You've got to *earn* what you get in this world and I feel that our people, some of my people, not all, some of my people are very good at going ahead and doing and helping and getting places—but there's a number of my people that just sit back for Providence to send them a flag. And if they don't get the flag, then they don't like it and it's "because we are coloured." If you get out and *do*, then there's no person born with nothing, like myself, no education, that can't go ahead and do—like Mrs. Pryor and so many other people. You've got to have a *will* to want to do a thing and if you make one step forward, the other nationalities will help you.

This play *Roots* crucifies me! They speak of religion, our people are supposed to be the most religious people in the world. Yet they don't forgive nobody. Now the people that *caused* slavery—all those people are dead. There's not one person living that was in slavery. Now why should you go around and be mad at their offspring because of this slavery? I think the quicker we get all this out of our minds, forget it and live in the future and not in the past, the better. I say I'm not worried about where I come from—I'm worried about where I'm going!

AUSTIN PHILLIPS

Austin Phillips came to Vancouver from Athabasca Landing, Alberta, in 1935.

Corner of Main and Union was the Bingarra Hotel which has been torn down since the new viaduct opened. Then you went down the alley, down Park Lane, to this place called Scat Inn which was, oh I'd say they cooked a few chickens and steaks and played a lot of music and people danced. They cut a few walls out of an old house, sold drinks, a regular bootlegger at that time. Whisky was twenty-five cents a drink, beer was twenty-five cents a drink—that's bootlegging prices. Then the real part of Hogan's Alley started right at Park Lane and it ran right straight up between Prior and Union, ended around Jackson Avenue—that's when you were out of Hogan's Alley, the rest was just called an alley.

Oh, the things that used to happen there! I came out here in '35 and that's about the first place I run into. I didn't know anybody in town and I just got off a freight train somewhere out here by the ocean and started to walking. Just walked right down as though I'd been in town before and ended up in Hogan's Alley. Going through the alleyway, you'd see some people laying on wagon wheels—they had a bunch of old broken wagons out on this old-time lot with the grass maybe growing up around it about a foot high, two feet high. And people, some of them bums, would just sleep in the wagons, sleep in the grass.

There was one thing about it, none of them were big boys around there. They'd get all the play mostly from everybody coming in and out getting their drinks, and they'd have a room where you'd have a dancing space. Then there was Buddy's over on Prior. The Chief of Police remembers him from now. He was the only man that was known to take a set of square dice and throw from two to twelve on 'em and never miss. When he died, the Chief of Police made this statement in the paper. He says, "He's the only man I ever saw say dirt to me because I bet him two bucks he couldn't do it." He had an ex-fighter, most everybody knew him, Joe Wilson, and he used to play piano for him.

Another one down there, the big boss of the place, was Lungo. This was the big Italian, he was 310 pounds, six foot four inches. His house was in the middle of the alley and they called him "The King." He made homebrew wine, you know. He'd make this wine and he would sell it for forty cents a quart and the fella across the road from him, this West Indian guy, used to buy from him and sell it for ten cents a glass. So you can imagine the profit he was making.

There was nothing but parties in Hogan's Alley—night time, any time, and Sundays all day. You could go by at six or seven o'clock in the morning, and you could hear jukeboxes going, you hear somebody hammering the piano, playing the guitar, or hear some fighting, or *see* some fighting, screams, and everybody carrying on. Some people singing, like a bunch of coyotes holler—they didn't care what they sounded like just as long as they was singing. Oh, I used to go from one place to the other playing guitar. They never paid you a salary. They had what you call a kitty, a little tin box with a horn like a phonograph on it. People wanted to tip you, they'd want to throw a buck, ten cents, whatever it was—well, they'd throw it in the kitty. That was *your* money, that's what you made. Then if you didn't want to drink whisky, well you'd ring for the houseman, the boss, and he'd bring you Coca Cola for rum and tea for whisky. Then you'd get that two bits for yourself, see.

So I can say, myself, I was making my money going from place to place, you know. There used to be a bunch of chop suey houses on Pender Street—always has been—and I would go from restaurant to restaurant and play from booth to booth. I've seen myself make as high as twenty-five dollars a night in those days. And then go back down and go into the bootlegging places again. I was playing the songs that come out then: "East of the Sun, West of the Moon," and "Don't Get Around Much Anymore," and, oh, just mostly all those songs. "Stardust" was pretty well famous in those days, and "Am I Blue," that was one of the favourites. And "Beale Street Blues," "St. Louis Blues," and "Beautiful Lady in Blue," "Paper Moon." Those songs all got famous around '36, '37, then they died out. There's been thousands of them. I can't remember them now until somebody requests them, and then I try to remember all of 'em. I would take my guitar, throw it across my shoulder and go from one place to the other. I play all string instruments—piano, guitar, banjo, steel guitar, ukulele, mandolin, violin. Somebody want a party played for, I'd go all over town. I'm a pretty good singer in my time, and I

Austin Phillips at home, 1977. TOD GREENAWAY PHOTO

always dressed pretty well, always ready for an occasion, and I've made a lot of parties.

Back in '38, that was after [Mayor Gerry] McGeer was out and Taylor was in, anything went. [Prominent people] would come in a place, and if they didn't want anybody to know, they would buy it out, say $100 or $200 a night—just whoever they wanted to stay there and drink with [them]. And Mayor Taylor used to come down and drink if he went to Buddy's or Dode's, or Mother Alexander's for chicken and steak.

There weren't too many guns around Hogan's Alley, it was more black-jacking and mugging and stuff like that. There was more killings in the West End, even at that time, than there were in the Alley. I can't recall of anybody except this one guy getting killed. Another guy was shot in there, and some of them was stabbed in there, but they all lived. But this guy, this Lungo's son, never knew his name—he's the only one that was really killed. Coloured guy killed him with a wrench over a dogfight. What happened was, this guy they called Ernie, he was setting back near the Scat Inn in the summertime you know, and he was strumming away on my guitar. And the dog starts a fight down the alley right in front of Lungo's place. His son was hitting the other dog that was fighting *his* dog, and he hit him with a stick. All of a sudden, Ernie goes down and he says, "Don't ever hit a dog around me," he says, "dog saved my life overseas," he says, "you hit the dog again, I'll hit *you*." So the guy kicked the dog and, well, he hit him with a wrench—very light tap it looked to me like, but it was enough to kill him.

Well, there was always somebody in fights, or threatening. But then again, you take all the other guys bumming, no matter what nationality they was, they was on the bum for dimes and nickels—and some of those fellas was bumming could stand on a corner and they'd bum more than the average guy working a day. They could eat cheap too, but nobody would refuse. These people that had the money with them, they'd give them ten or fifteen cents, a quarter. Some were generous, some made a winning and they'd hand a guy two bucks, tell him to "Go git your clothes cleaned" or something like that. But they was always good that way. Unless a man was something really out, like he was considered an informer or something, a stool pigeon. Then he wasn't liked, he wasn't welcome around that part. Even the police didn't like him. They'd use him till he was no more value to them, then if the crowds want to get him let them get him, he's served their purpose. But that's the way it run, off and on, like the fish in the sea: the big ones eat the little ones, if they could have them. You never know when that little guy might come into the luck and make something, might be able to get it back.

There was a guy came out of the logging camp—I think he was a don-key puncher, 'cause he was making good money. But he came down in this Hogan's Alley with a girl I knew, a regular clip-artist. She picked him up, or he picked her up, in the beer parlour there, and on a foggy night he comes down with $800 in his pocket. Well, she give him the knockout drops in the drink, and he walked outside and she rolled him, and when he finally did come to, he was on a pile of rubbish out in the alley. He went down and he made a complaint to the police, and they says, "Have you ever heard of Hogan's Alley?" He says, "No, I really haven't." He said, "You've heard of the East End, haven't you?" He says, "Oh yes, I've heard of the East End." He said, "You mean to tell me you didn't have any more sense than to come down here?" He said, "I'm a policeman, I wouldn't pack that kind of money with me in this part of town, and I've got a gun." He said, "If you're stupid enough to go down that end of town with that kind of money on you, I would say you deserved it, and we're not wasting our time looking for nobody we couldn't find anyhow."

There was gambling going on practically every place. Sometimes there'd be guys over from the American side, and I seen as much as two or three thousand dollars on the table. And some of the little places had penny-ante games you could buy into for twenty-five cents, and they'd play as hard for that as they would for the big stakes. Practically every house around there, they'd just start up a game, but there was only a few of the houses that had big games. Old Buddy, he was quite a man on the dice game, and he used to get all the big shots from across town, big-time gamblers, and he gambled them. They were shooting two hundred up to a thousand bucks a shot, rolling dice. But he was one of the rich men there, he was top bootlegger, and that's all he did was bootleg and gamble.

There was junk that passed around there too. But maybe out of a thousand you'd see one dope-fiend in those days, that's how few they were. Not because some of them couldn't afford it. Because it was so cheap in those days they could go down and get a prick of morphine for about a dollar and a half. But very seldom you'd see dope-fiends.

But every place you went to, practically every place in Hogan's Alley bootlegged. If you could afford a high-class place, you went to the Scat Inn, you went to Buddy's Beer Garden. He served beer and he'd serve hard stuff—rum, gin, whisky. Then there was the two Macaroni Joes, one guy was a little one and the other a big one. The little guy, he sold everything from wine to whisky, anything at all, right up until he died he was still a bootlegger. But this other big Macaroni Joe—I'd been buying wine off of him for probably a couple of years, and he had good wine he was making out of apples, it was sweet, and I like sweet wine, and it was a little bubbly, you know. So I was setting in his place one Sunday morning, right on the corner of Prior and Park Lane, and I said to him, "Joe, how do you make this wine?" So he says, "I got some mash on now, I go show you. I making with feet." Well, I seen pictures of girls running around with their feet to make wine over in the old country—that's girls, they wash their feet. But this guy, he pulled off these blue woolly socks and his feet were sweating, and in between his toes you could see this black he called toe-jam. He rolled his britches up, and he's got apples in a tank about four feet high, and it's bubbling up, and he just stepped right in there. He never washed his feet and he weighed about 250 pounds. Oh God.

We used to know a few of the police in town. They used to come down—they liked to get in on that gambling. One night two of them was off the beat and they'd come in and they'd put their money in the bank together, and they were dealing. Blackjack. They had a whole stack of money and everybody was betting the table, as many people could bet. All of a sudden, in comes the Chief of Police. What he was doing there I do not know but he drove up, I guess he must have seen the car parked on Union and wondered where they were at. So when he walked in the door, he said, "What are you guys doing here?" They just *dropped everything* and went out, left their money on the table, they just went away! Well, everybody had a ball with the money, everybody was grabbing away. They used to be pretty good, pretty good. They didn't pay any attention to prostitutes or pimps, they didn't bother them too much. What they were really hot on was dope-fiends, and there wasn't many of them. If they caught them, bingo! And anybody that was selling it, well, that was it, because they're worse against that than they are on murder. They didn't bother about gambling.

This town, it just run itself practically. Some of them were paying off. That's before Gerry McGeer took over [1935]. When he got to be mayor, he closed everything in town up, everything. He tightened on and he chased all the prostitutes out of town, all the bootleggers he was clamping down on them, he just cleaned up the place. The only good thing that he done, that I said to myself, was when he put Joe Celona in jail.[65] That's a guy you couldn't even be decent with—the guys he was paying off to, the cops he was paying off to. And he was just a young man but let go long enough he'd of become another Al Capone. But he ended up with a twenty-year rap on him. He got that time just before I come out here in '35, that's when he first got sentenced. He did half his time and they finally gave him parole and he was out *one week* and the church people, all the people, signed a petition to put him back in. He did his time.

There was quite a few Black people around. That old Mrs. Pryor, that big woman, she used to weigh about 350 pounds, I liked to see *her* come in. She'd come down about once every three months. She used to bring a sack, one of them leather bags, and she'd have it full of silver dollars and fifty-cent pieces. And she would set me on her knee, and say, "Play my song! You come on and you play 'Maggie.'" I didn't know "Maggie," I'd just sing what I knew of it and every time I'd sing "Maggie" for her, she'd give me a silver dollar. And curse me out, curse me out all the time! "Oh, play me that song 'Maggie' again!" Probably have to play it for her about fifteen times a night, but if you got through, you got a dollar for every time you'd sing it.

Most everyone from Hogan's Alley is dead. I'm about the only one that was ever around there that's still living. And that is the lowdown rundown on the way things went at that time.

RAMON BENEDETTI & IRMA BENEDETTI

RAMON BENEDETTI: My dad was born in Abruzzi, in the mountains, a little town called Novelli. And my mother was born in Vancouver, but her family was born in the town of Chieti, which is a part of Abruzzi but another little village. So we're sort of what you'd call *paesani*—the old man was up in the mountains, and my grandmother was down in the foothills. What brought them out here? Misery. There was no work in Italy. The oldest brother, Joe, he came out first. And then my dad came [c. 1902] and then came the younger brother. They came to the States, everybody migrated to the States, nobody came to Canada then. They lived together, pup tents, and it was pretty rough, a lot of snow. They worked in these different camps and there were a lot of gyppo camps that hired these men, put them on room and board, and then when it came time for payday two or three months later, they just disappeared. Nobody got paid. And then just looking for work they migrated across the border.

They came to Vancouver and my dad told me the toughest thing that he found was to have some money in your pocket and not know the language. He said you'd go into a restaurant and they'd hand you a menu and you couldn't read, you couldn't write, you couldn't order, you couldn't do anything. You'd just look around at the plates that the people were eating and you'd see something you might like and you pointed at it and just said, "That's for me."

This was all Italians, this neighbourhood. Basically a lot of boarding houses, a lot of places that would take in single fellows and feed them, give them a room. And I think this is where all the fun came in, really, because there was always something going on. There was card games, and nobody was working that much. I know my dad used to board at Cima's place and she was a fantastic cook, they'd tell me. There was a lot of boarding houses, nobody stayed in hotels then.

IRMA BENEDETTI: What they did for excitement, say, on a Saturday night, someone would get up, a fellow that plays the accordion, and then they would kind of have a little dance at somebody's house. This was their entertainment when they first came. And then they would have a glass of wine. There weren't very many women, very few.

RAMON BENEDETTI: One night my father got lucky—he was always a gambling man—he got lucky playing cards with the boys and he won "x" number of bucks. I don't know what it was. And he thought, "Well, it's time to go into business for myself," so he bought into this store [c. 1912].

He had a partner with him in the store, but it was an ice-cream parlour then—chocolates, ice cream, like the Italian type of shop, you know, cigars, boxed chocolates, banana splits; they didn't have any spumoni and things like that. Anyway, he and his partner had different ideas, so my father told him,

Ramon Benedetti was born in Vancouver in 1928, and Irma Benedetti was born in Vancouver in 1930. Both were from Italian immigrant families. In 1912, Ramon's father, Alphonso Benedetti, established Benny's Market, which became an importer of Italian foods. The business is still in the Benedetti family.

"Well look, okay, fine. You give me so much for my share and you take over." And the partner said, "No, you give *me* that much, and *you* buy the place." So, it was precisely what my father had in mind.

He never went to banks. He went to a friend down the block here and he said, "Guilliermo, I need five or six hundred dollars." "Okay, Alphonso," because this guy had a lot of money. He was one of the guys who used to deliver beer. You had your own jobbers, then—this was before the government had any control. And these guys had the horse and wagon and they'd deliver you a barrel of beer, so this guy was like a beer wholesaler and a whisky wholesaler.

He says, "Alphonso, how much you need?" And he just peeled it off. They shook hands, and that was it. That's the deal. I mean, no papers—like the bank managers, you've got to go through a short-arm inspection and everything else to get a fifty-dollar bill from those guys. It was all done on handshakes, eh, because your honour meant more.

So this is how he got the place. And he stayed there in the store for, oh, years. And he kept telling the Chinese people, "Now, look, I would like to buy this place. Don't sell it out from under me." And two or three of his friends tried to buy from under him, but Woo Shoo came to him and he said, "Look, Alphonso, you've been here 'x' number of years, so I'm ready to sell. There's your first chance."

We had showcases. My mother had to put special locks on them because she used to have bulk chocolates, like snowballs and all that, and I was about six and I used to sneak in there and grab the chocolates. I remember boxes of chocolates with dolls on them, done up beautifully, pen and pencil sets, all this. And then on the other side we had a big showcase just full of cigars and chewing tobacco and pipes. And we had a humidifier—a big jar in there with a big sponge—to keep your cigars moist, and the top opened up. On the showcase was a punchboard, always was a punchboard. Gambling was legal then, punchboards and the whole bit. There was distributors that came along and you bought a board.

IRMA BENEDETTI: My mother-in-law said that when people got married the groom would take the bride to Benny's and sit and have an ice-cream soda on their wedding day. That was sort of the thing to do.

RAMON BENEDETTI: You know, my father used to open that store up at eight o'clock in the morning, and close it at midnight, *seven days a week*. And he could say there was some days he never took in two bucks, three bucks.

We had a pot-bellied stove right in the middle of the store, with a big pipe that went about fifteen feet up. We'd sit around there when we weren't really working—it was like kind of a meeting place. We'd roast chestnuts on the top of that stove, in season, and they'd always peel an orange and they'd put orange peels on the stove, and the orange peels would burn, and it would take away some of the smell of those rotten Italian cigars that would peel the paint off the wall.

They'd play a game like *briscola*; it's something like whist or hearts. And

The Benedetti family outside their grocery and import store on Union Street, 1977. TOD GREENAWAY PHOTO

they had another one, *scopa*, which means "sweep." And they'd be arguing with one another, like: "Stupid, I give you the signal. Why didn't you play *hearts*? Why did you go into *spades*?"

IRMA BENEDETTI: Whoever lost paid the other fellow a drink. Well, the people that owned the boarding houses would have the wine, and then they would get the money. Meanwhile, they're having a little enjoyable game and, at the same time, the people that own the house, they're making a little bit of money to help. Like in those days everybody was on relief; they *had* to have something.

RAMON BENEDETTI: Everybody made wine. In the early days with our family we went dandelion. My old man used to go dandelion. Who had the bread to buy grapes? You went out and you picked dandelions. You made dandelion wine and you made homebrew and a lot of raisin wine.

In later years, when the grapes started coming in and people had a few more bucks, you could afford to buy grapes. There was a lot of headache with them when they'd take a long time to get here. The early importers of those grapes lost a lot of money because sometimes there was no system. The rail car would get up here and oh, the juice would be *running* out of the cars!

And we used to have games—"Union Street Princes" against the "Prior Street Rats"—roller hockey. We'd all buy the Chicago skates because the

Chicago skates were great. Even when you wore the wheels out they still went around. If you had Chicago wheels, now, you were a real dude, because they are like the Cadillac of roller skates. After you wore the wheels off, you still had the rims you could ride on. And our big games were the "Wops" against the "Japs," down at the American Can Company every Sunday. It was a fierce game down at the American Can because they were the only guys that had some nice clean cement down that you could play on. Then we had Vatican Row; it was Atlantic Street—those were all the holy guys that never missed church, every Sunday. A nice bunch of guys, but a little, as far as the Union Street gang was, a little bit too much. Well, they were pretty good athletes— not bad, not bad.

Father Bortignon was quite a character. He's a guy that used to go and play cards with the old man. You know what I mean? He was a funny guy. My mother would say, "Gee, Father, I would ask you to stay for dinner, but we're having roast beef and it is Friday." He'd say, "Well, that's quite all right. That's understandable," and then, crossing himself, he'd say, "Okay, I'll stay, I'll stay."

Do you remember the little guy, used to graze goats, with the little moustache and the boots with the leggings on? He was like in the army and he'd pick up the cows. This lane between Prior and Union was called "Cowshit Alley" all the way up, and he used to drive the cows up Cowshit Alley from where the stables were, this guy with his little white dog and his little switch. This was his job. He'd take 'em down to the dump to graze and at night time he'd take 'em back. And everybody paid him so much a month.

I guess that most of the people lived off the yard, with the vegetables they grew, and with a few chickens and a few rabbits. The Health Department stopped it all. During the war they started a little pressure, and they laid off for a while; then, "No chickens, no rabbits. Rabbits bring rats." And, "No cows; cows are tubercular."

IRMA BENEDETTI: There was this Bollestri down here; he had a little store. Behind, he had chickens galore, and everybody bought chickens from him. But he used to make the salami and sell them in the store. Even families made sausages. My dad and my uncle, they used to make sausages but they would do it in sort of two families because the pig was too big. But you had to have the equipment; not too many people had the equipment. My father always had somebody else, because they had the equipment.

RAMON BENEDETTI: They had a salami bee, just like in the old days they had a building bee. "Okay, now it's my turn, eh? All right, so I buy my pig and you come over and you help me."

Nobody could make sausage like Orazio. His sausage was the best. This Orazio used to live in the 700-, 800-block Hawks Avenue, down there. You'd bring your pig to him and you helped him and he used to make your salami. There was nothing like homemade salami, really. It was coarser grind, but it was pure meat. And he'd make fresh sausage and musetti where you used all the gristle, like, from the head, and you seasoned it and then you boiled it with your beans. The sausage was stored in the wine cellar, always in the wine cellar. You hung them up in the cellar, and there was the long whiskers, the mould on them. Some of the guys kept them, golly, for a year, two years.

IRMA BENEDETTI: And then they used to get together and play bocce.

RAMON BENEDETTI: There were all these boarding houses and all these bocce alleys, and the idea was to make the rounds, and even a lot of times a husband who *had* a bocce alley would leave his wife and go and have a drink with his competitor and they went all around. The wives looked after the home and the man went out. Now the idea was to be able to make the rounds on a Sunday and get home for supper standing up. You know what I mean? You had one here, maybe two there. By the time they got up to the 500-block Union Street they've already had about fourteen drinks. They started down the 200 block, so by the time they'd get up to the store they'd be half smashed, so any of the kids that were around there, they'd buy them ice cream. And remember Nicky? He used to sing all the time: "Rose Marie, I love you..." And all the kids would come in, so: "Hey, come on, come on, I'll buy you ice cream." [He'd] bring them all in the store, buy them ice cream, chocolate bar, throw his money down, threw his money away like crazy.

IRMA BENEDETTI: Almost every block, I think, would have maybe two alleys, or three alleys. They just built them in their backyards, inside the yard, next to their garden.

RAMON BENEDETTI: And school—I can remember my father, going back fifty years ago, with great respect to a teacher—you took your hat off: "Dottore, dottore, si, maestra." A schoolteacher. They could do no wrong: "You're teaching my child; I don't question you. My children are going to school— that's happy." They never *considered* the type of education or anything. They didn't look into it and say, "Well, what are you teaching my child? Let's see. What are you doing?" Because what could they compare it with? They never had any school. My father had one year of school and they took him out *to go to work*. He had to move a wheelbarrow to help his father make a living. My father was self-educated, taught himself to read, write, everything himself.

I would say they were good teachers at Strathcona School. And you know why I would say so? Because I think that those days you had to be dedicated to be a teacher, because the pay was *horrible* and only the rich could afford to be a teacher.

I had a good friend, a fat kid, [a] Japanese guy, and he was a good-natured guy. His name was Akiya Hamigami. I never forgot him. And the war came along, and then the war was over and I was working on the waterfront, part-time—going to school and working on the waterfront. I was working general cargo this time and we were hand-trucking big rolls of kraft paper. And this guy calls me, and I looked. And there was a whole contingent of Japanese people going back to Japan. Akiya Hamigami was one of them, with his family, going back to Japan—this was after the war, after they had been interned—and, you know, I kind of choked up when I saw him. He went back to Japan and he worked for the Americans, the American Army and that.

IRMA BENEDETTI: Before the war the other side of Hastings was all Japanese. They referred to it as "Japtown," and we were referred to as "Woptown."

RAMON BENEDETTI: Cordova, Powell Street, Alexander, were Japanese, with the exception of the odd bawdy house in between. They served the neighbourhood—all these single men that were fishing and working the camps and mines and logging and all that. I think every neighbourhood should have a couple of good whorehouses, don't you?

IRMA BENEDETTI: I remember a woman telling me that they were beautiful. She said they were always better behaved than some of the people that lived in the neighbourhood. You would never hear them use a bad word or being vulgar. They kept to themselves, they didn't even walk around the streets. The only time we'd see them was if we went on Hallowe'en, knocking at the door, because we'd get money from them.

RAMON BENEDETTI: I'll tell you one thing: they were the only ones who would give the kids a treat. The rest of the guys were a bunch of cheaparoni!

Nowadays, more and more Italians that come out here can speak English. You don't have the "stupida booba" like you had fifty, sixty years ago, the poor guy that couldn't go to school, had difficulty learning the language and everything. These people now are *educated*.

Now it's great, I think, to have your ethnic groups, in a sense. I think that in one sense it's good, in another sense it's bad, because I think it's got to stop—this way of thinking "Italian," "French," "Chinese," "German," et cetera—that kind of thinking is sick for the country. You've got to consider yourselves as Canadians.

INES PETRIN LELAND

Ines Petrin Leland was born in Vancouver in 1927 of Italian immigrant parents. She has raised her family and remained an active resident of the neighbourhood, working for local improvement groups such as Strathcona Property Owners and Tenants Association and the Strathcona Community Centre.

Our homes were clean homes, they weren't dirty homes, you know what I mean? They *scrubbed* their floors. Oh, and it was a thing with the Italian women—their curtains were white, that was tradition, white curtains and lace. All the Italians at one time or other sold liquor in the house. And it was a traditional thing, but it was against the law. My mom sold it. And all she was trying to do was make a living because my dad was sick. He got TB when he was a very young man and he couldn't work anymore. She didn't make much money actually, she made a few bucks just to live on. We were all young, we were eleven, twelve, at the time, see, she didn't want any social assistance, she got fed up with it. First she started with rooms and then boarders—it was usually loggers. At that time she had ten boarders, and she would charge them fifteen dollars a month for room and board. So I mean, where was she making money? It was just to live. Some people made a lot of money, but then they were more on the, I would say, "racketeer" side. My mother would give [her boarders] meals, wash their clothes, wash their sheets, all by hand in a tub. I remember her first washing machine was when I was fourteen—an old Beatty she bought.

I think we were all pretty well proud of being Italian. In fact when I went to King Edward High, I was amongst a lot of Jewish girls and a lot of the girls were ashamed because they were born in this area, because we were branded slums by that time. And I was never ashamed. Of course we had what you call a red-light district. Personally, I think it kept a lot of us girls safe on the streets. There was a difference. If the boys came of age and it was run properly—they had their madam, it wasn't done by pimps, it was a house. There were about ten of them, all along Gore there. Oh, we knew the difference.

Our school was noted for its "league of nations." We all got along. It was nothing for me to say, "Hey, you wop," or "Hey, you hunky." And all in fun. There was no snobbery at school. It didn't matter what you wore—I mean, nobody looked at your clothes. And if you did get something new, everybody thought it was great because all our parents sewed at that time, or knit. There were a lot of kids that didn't have anything. We had holes in our shoes. I can still remember putting cardboard in my shoes because there were big holes in them.

There was Miss McKinnon, she was a softie, but she thought all us kids were underprivileged and she used to take us kids to her place where she had a nice home living with her mother. And we weren't underprivileged, I mean, we had everything in our homes, you know, like food and entertainment but she thought we were all very poor. Maybe we were, but we were rich in other ways.

Sure, a lot of families didn't have lots to eat, but the relief—we did get food. We always got a box of apples and raisins in those days, and dates, which we thought was a big treat. And there was a lot of grain in the boxcars. Our mothers would go, just like in the old country, with their aprons, and fill their aprons with grain to feed the chickens. It was actually a little bit of Europe here. Some families had cows, some had goats. Giardins had horses. And there was Mr. Marino, he used to sell vegetables on his carts, just like Sam Barrett sold vegetables with a truck later on. And another fellow might sell fish with his little cart. A lot of them kept their own horses in their own sheds, but the ones that had a team of horses, they had a place down on Main and Prior Streets. It was like a stable under the viaduct. They demolished it. And I remember the horseshoes. They used to go down there for the old horseshoes when they used to play horseshoes.

As we got older, we had little recording sets given to us for Christmas, you know, they were those little crank-up things, and us kids would all get together and dance. The coloured kids were the ones that taught us how to jitterbug. We danced to jive. Strictly Duke Ellington, Stan Kenton, Glenn Miller, Tommy Dorsey. We had Happyland. It used to be the roller-skating rink on Saturday nights, Friday nights we used to dance there. And we were

The Leland family on their back porch, 1977. TOD GREENAWAY PHOTO

the "Zoot-Suiters." We used to wear zoot-suits like today they wear the very popular flares. We got a bad name for wearing those.

When the big bands came into town we were all there for a buck fifty. They used to have it at the Hastings Auditorium mostly. Duke Ellington got sophisticated—we used to go down to Stanley Park, to the Bowl. That was no dancing, that was concert. And then we did a lot of dancing at our MacLean Park, outdoors. The Parks Board used to put the speakers up for us and we used to get a record player. And then we depended a lot on corner restaurants where we used to hang out, like Ernie's Cafe with the Wurlitzer.

I danced every night from the day I was fifteen until the day I got married, twenty-one—just loved to dance. All the kids loved to dance in the neighbourhood, and we were kind of restricted because the church wouldn't let us dance on Sunday so we used to go up to Happyland. There was an old couple running this place and there was hamburgers, hot dogs and milk, and us kids used to hang around there on Sundays. Mind you, some of the kids got in trouble through fighting, because the Grandview-area kids would fight with our Strathcona area, and the West End would fight with the Strathcona area. The Home Apple Gang, that was the toughies of our time. Now if you were to meet those kids today, they're all prominent, they're businessmen, and yet they were toughies in our days. We had a little problem with fights, yes. But it was fist fights, nothing dirty. It was usually after the dance. Mind you, we were forbidden to drink. Now we were all getting to be about eighteen, nineteen, so we used to steal wine from our parents. The kids had their drinks, and this was when the problem started. Our crowd was not drug addicts. If we did do anything, the worst we did was have a few drinks, you know. So I mean, that was our big hullabaloo, a couple of drinks and we thought we owned the world.

But there was a lot of kids that didn't drink, a lot of kids that didn't smoke. We could drink at home but we were not allowed to take that wine out. If I went to visit my godmother, there was "Ines, do you want a little shot of vermouth?" It was traditional. But not to go out, no way, that was *taboo*!

We did have drug users. There were about five from very good families. But most of them were transients that used to come into the neighbourhood. I had a girlfriend that went on drugs. It hurt her family tremendous, but her parents were so strict. They wouldn't let her go dancing with us. If she came to the dances, her older brother would come and drag her home and call her a "prostitute" or a "whore," this sort of thing. And she says, "Well, I've got the name, I might as well do it." So she went all out. First it was hustling, then she got involved in drugs. I remember I used to talk to her. "If you want to be a good prostitute," I says, "*go ahead*, but for goodness' sakes don't get on drugs."

Japanese, Chinese, Jewish, Italian families, our parents protected us too much. The only thing that wised us up was that we had the prostitutes and we had Hogan's Alley where they were all alcoholics, but they were harmless. And the fact that some of our parents bootlegged. We've seen the good side and the bad side, we've never seen just the good side. But you go into a lot of the West End, you know, where you get your rich people—those kids would come down to our area for kicks. You *have* to have a variety of people. I remember there used to be a gal that used to get really drunk and she would strip. Now us kids—the boys would normally you'd think go and peek, eh? No, we would go home and try to get something to cover her up. I mean this was the way we were raised. *But*, there was a certain police officer in this area at the time, he took advantage of this girl. He would take her behind the back lane, and they would shush us kids away. We knew this girl. She is dead today, but she was a harmless drunk and I think they took advantage of her. You see, these are the things we had when we were growing up.

We used to play with the gypsies, but we did not let our parents know. Oh they were beautiful dancers. And their families accepted us kids very much, so they used to tell our fortunes for nothing. They were part of our life when we were sixteen or seventeen, the age of dancing. In fact one of the fathers wanted me to marry one of his sons because he said I looked like a nice little gypsy girl. I couldn't see myself sleeping on the mattresses the way

Prior Street in the wartime years. INES LELAND COLLECTION, COURTESY OF ROYAL BC MUSEUM, BC ARCHIVES

they used to have them all laid down, but they were *good families*, believe it or not, even though they had their ways. During the war years, that's when I first realized there were gypsies, because I was working at this restaurant on Main Street and next door was gypsies and the man was practising welding to work in shipyards. I think that was the first working gypsy I knew. Then, as the years went on, I got to know their moms and dads and they loved music as much as we loved music, you know. If there was Duke Ellington in town, even the fathers came with their children. Mind you, the stories that they used to knock on windows and call the people in and tell fortunes and roll them—yes, that's true, but not to us kids. Always the woman told the fortunes, the women did the work so to speak, and the men lived a life of leisure. They were dressed immaculate, always with the latest clothes from back east. Oh, they were sharp, and handsome too. And they brought the latest dance steps from back east. The women wore their long dresses, peasant dresses, and the ones that had status, oh, they loved their gold. The boys danced with us but their sisters more or less had to stay home. They were very well protected, the daughters. About seven or eight families would come, usually related somehow.

I got a job at Tosi's store. They hired me when I was sixteen—that's when you got your unemployment insurance book. That was the only Italian store in Vancouver then, wholesale and retail, he used to have a big staff. A lot of rich people from Shaughnessy came down and bought cheeses and macaroni, and I can remember this one particular fellow came with a chauffeur. Oh, he was elegant! I couldn't take my eyes off of him and what surprised me was— I'm so used to the Italians buying cases of macaroni, ten pounds of beans and Romano cheese by the pounds because they had big families, and this guy came down—five cents' worth of this, five cents' worth of that. And I turned to Mrs. Tosi and I said, "Who's this cheap son of a bitch?" I can remember saying it, and she says, "Ines, in this store you don't use that language!" She says, "You serve all the customers with a smile." And then she went on, "Just remember, a store is like a home. You keep it clean like a home, and you keep your manners, just like you're raising your children. My customers are like my children," I learned a lot: I learned discipline, and I learned to respect Mr. Tosi.

I remember I even delivered the flyers when the war broke out. My god-mother's son was a newspaper boy at the time—actually it was *his* job but us kids didn't realize really what war was. We thought it was another event! Two or three of us, we all went out and helped deliver all the flyers to the whole neighbourhood. "War breaks out!" But we made a big deal out of it. Being young and stupid, we didn't realize how serious it was, and we were delivering all these papers door to door, "The war! The war!" And all the Italians were, not swearing at us, they were saying in Italian "brutta bestia!" It means "You dirty beast," really that's what it means. But in Italian it's more "Don't you realize what's going on kids? Don't make it sound so happy!"

We were very, very quiet after the war began. I remember the boys joining the service when I was about fifteen and sixteen, that's when I noticed, because I was in high school at about that time. We had training, cadets, and I was so proud with my blue skirt and my white shirt, marching. It wasn't like the Nazi sort of thing, it was fun, you know. It was a lot of exercises, and drilling and "left! right!" I was so short they didn't know where to put me. But it was very quiet around here. I remember all the parents were sitting on the porches in the evening, which was a great thing. My mom would sit with us kids there, Mrs. Stefani with her kids, the Pastros with their kids, the Barichellos, we were all sitting. I remember there was not much conversation because quite a few Italians belonged to the Fascisti, but not the Fascisti that was in Europe, it was just a little club they had in Vancouver.[66] They called themselves the Blackshirts and they had an Italian school. I remember going to that school, it was where we had our catechism. I think they just carried on what they heard from Europe, I mean it was never pushed on us. But we sensed the worry that a lot of them would be sent to the concentration camps. The RCMP did raid different homes in the area where they suspected the Fascists, just like they sent the Japanese out of Vancouver at that time. As a youngster, all I know is that everybody was so sad and quiet.

MAX JAFFE

We came across the country by train to Vancouver. It was all quite exciting, even electric lights were very fascinating, because when we left Lithuania, electricity was only in the odd part of the capital city.

Our first house in the neighbourhood was one we rented at the corner of Princess and Union Streets. You couldn't be more central than that. It was close to the synagogue, and my grandfather was a religious individual, in fact he was a functionary of the synagogue, which was on Heatley and Pender and so within walking distance. This was very important for him, being an older man, because on the Sabbath it was not customary to ride, it was customary to walk.

My father was educated, but not trained in a skill. In Europe, he had worked for a distillery, amongst other things, and his job was to travel to small towns to arrange to buy grain. When he came here, his first job was cracking eggs in a plant, culled eggs that were not suitable for the market. Not exactly what you might call an interesting job for him, but he did it out of necessity. It was very difficult finding work when we arrived. But one of my sisters was a milliner, and within a few months she was able to get work in a ladies' dress shop on Granville Street doing alterations for five bucks a week. My other sister was a Hebrew teacher, and she was hired by the community to give Hebrew lessons to children in the school at the back of the synagogue.

My job was hanging around street corners near fire hydrants, like anybody else. I remember the coal man, with a big felt hat and a black dog and

Max Jaffe was born in Lithuania in 1924. He immigrated with his family to Canada in 1933.

a horse and wagon with loads of coal. He always had one or two dogs following him and he was as black as the coal was. And the Chinese vegetable man used to come to the house 'cause my mother would buy a lot of her fruits and vegetables from him, as most of the people did. He had an old-time hand-scale, and at Christmas he gave all his customers a package of ginger and a package of lychee nuts.

I used to play in the flats, what they called the hobo jungle, near where the trains came in. It was a large fallow area, and a lot of individuals, whether they were unemployed or just people who had no place to go, built little shacks out of discarded tin signs and some old lumber, and insulated them with paper for warmth. We used to play in that area because there was bush and trees and a little bit of a lake, more like a swamp. The people in those shacks were hard up—I mean that was *obvious*—and they came asking for tea and sugar and coffee. We had very little at that time, but my mother always would find something, some sandwiches or some meat or something cooked to give them. You can't send a person away hungry. They spent a lot of time in the shacks amongst themselves, and, well, *I* like to sit and drink coffee or tea, and there is no reason why they didn't. A lot of them were young men, from about eighteen and up. They had come from different parts looking for work, which there wasn't. The jungle ran from where Bemis Bags is [Bonar and Bemis, 900 Parker Street], south of the ball field on Prior Street, almost as far as the train depot. It was one large area, and the swamp was about dead centre.

Max Jaffe in his tools and equipment store, 1978.
TOD GREENAWAY PHOTO

I remember [the Strathcona School teacher] Miss Doyle who is still around these days and she was a holy terror. She wouldn't think twice about grabbing some poor wretched kid and giving him a good slap when he certainly deserved it. But she was a very fine teacher. And there was Miss Williams, a little Welsh lady, couldn't have been five foot. A diminutive little creature, and a sparkly, perky, very peppery little gal. She taught history and geography and she was quite opinionated. She used to throw in little zingers. I remember when we were studying about Ireland—this was in the mid-thirties—and she said, "You know, it's a funny thing about the Irish, they're bloody dirt poor, and when the potato crop fails they're starving. So what do they do? They go to America, and they work hard and do very well, and some of them get very wealthy, and then they stand on the docks in New York, looking over towards Ireland and weeping about good old Ireland. Have you ever heard anything quite so silly as that?" I guess she wasn't in sympathy with pandering to cheap emotionalism, you know.

I hold those teachers in the utmost awe and respect, from the days I went there to this day. Because they did, for children of humble background, more than they were paid to do. They used to check the teeth and check the hands and fingernails. They taught the kids manners, they taught the kids social graces that in 50 percent of the homes were not even known. Many of the children weren't aware that you had to blow your nose instead of wipe it on your sleeve, or that it wasn't proper to sit and pick your ear. They emphasized cleanliness. In fact they used to give out combs to some of the little wretches, 'cause they never owned a comb, because probably their parents never *saw* a comb.

It seemed to be a policy directly of the school, or on the part of the teacher, to de-emphasize the people's origins and backgrounds, and try and concentrate on the now and the present and the Canadian. They made a point of trying to avoid the petty arguments and fears and hatreds people may have brought from their homes. At that time the neighbourhood was predominantly Italian, Chinese, Japanese, Russian, Ukrainian, well, that's of course counting Canadian or English-speaking groups, and a small percentage of Jewish kids, mostly Eastern European. Kids always fight. When they see a different face and a different hair and a different appearance, they always scrap a little bit, but after a short time you would see a group of kids walking along, playing together, friends of every mix. There was no clannishness that I recall, except for a certain amount amongst the Japanese. Of course at that time Japan was going through a militaristic period and there were strong influences. In fact, a lot of the parents used to send their kids back to Japan for summer holidays to go to school there, and those kids would not mix too readily with the others the following year. But the emphasis at school was not on different backgrounds. The emphasis was on getting an education, getting a job later on, and that was the main concern of most people. On certain holidays, one was Dominion Day, and also on November 11, Armistice Day, there was a ceremony in the school where, more than anything else, they stressed the unity and the Canadian aspect of life, of ways of doing things.

Playing together on the streets, we did what kids do. We chased the vegetable trucks and tried to grab the odd vegetable sticking out the back of the truck when the driver wasn't looking. It's a childish delight. *That* was not the making of a criminal. And kids made skateboards, a different type in those days. They got a piece of two-by-four and they got an old roller skate and they mounted one set of wheels in the front and one in the back. I don't know. I spent a lot of time listening to radio and reading in those days, because, when we came here, I did not know one word of English at the age of nine or ten, and I had to learn. So I used to get a lot of *National Geographic* magazines from school or from the library, and I used to bring home bundles of encyclopedias. You know, in an encyclopedia there's pictures and the words underneath, so I used to spend a lot of time looking at them.

The teachers used to stress the use of the library and push the kids to go. That was the old Carnegie Library. It was quite a large library and very good, and it was free, which was very important. Saturday was library day and it was a continual hubbub. Kids were coming and going, lugging bundles of books, and it was a good place to go and meet other kids. Normally, where in the hell would a person get books and things to read? We didn't have the money to buy magazines even. The main floor of the Carnegie was a library, but up above was a museum, which was very interesting. They had everything:

spears, Indian masks, a lot of African masks, the odd little cannon from the old wars, guns, sabres, spears, and shields from Africa. Because some of the early settlers had served in the Boer War, or maybe they had served with the British Territorial Army on various occasions.

Outside the library was a drinking fountain above ground and a public washroom below ground. There was an attendant there, and you could have a bath or a shower for about two bits, with a couple of towels. A lot of people would come off the CN boats or they'd come off the CN or the Great Northern, or people working in the Interior, they'd waltz down there, change their clothes, and have a good hot bath and a shave and walk out another person.

The Exhibition parade was always a great deal, because it passed by on Hastings—it was an exciting moment in a kid's life. And then there were the May Day parades that ran from the Powell Street Grounds to Stanley Park. I heard a lot of the political speeches at Lumberman's Arch, because, being curious, we used to walk along and see what was going on and hear some of

Carnegie Public Library and City Market Hall (which was the site of Vancouver City Hall from 1898 to 1923) on the corner of Main and Hastings streets, 1932. After 1923, the Market Hall building was used as a library annex until it was demolished in 1957–58. PHILIP TIMMS PHOTO, VANCOUVER PUBLIC LIBRARY, VPL 3395

the thunderous demagoguery. I heard Harold Winch and I heard Sam Carr.[67] The CCF [Cooperative Commonwealth Federation] at that time used to muster a considerable group for the parade, and so did the small Communist Party. There was a communist magazine issued then called *The Clarion*. And a friend of mine who was a house painter, an older man, was a communist, and I'd give him a hand distributing this magazine. It sold for a nickel and you would see it on street corners.

Along Union there was quite a few houses with girls where men would go. It wasn't a rowdy situation. In fact, I used to walk by on the way to the streetcar and a lot of times wave to them, you know. But it wasn't a centre of evil. If you walked along the street and you knew house "A" was a bootlegging establishment, and house "B" was a house with girls in it, so what? So people came and went, but it didn't seem to have any influence or direct bearing on your everyday activities or life. It was one of the situations of the times, and that situation was compounded all over the country, wherever the restrictions on liquor were the way they were. It didn't seem to breed any murders, and burglaries were almost unheard of. In fact, the doors in the summertime were open, front and back. Remarkable, you know.

As far as criminals go, the neighbourhood exported a lot of its crime. A lot of drug addicts, oh sure. It raised some bank robbers, thieves, scoundrels. And I'm sure it must have raised some heroes as well—a lot of them went to war and died. It just so happens that Strathcona had a reputation of producing a goodly number of criminals. Whether it was due to the polyglot mixture of people, whether it was due to poverty—I'm no sociologist, and sociologists don't know because they usually just guess.

Most people try to smooth out the rough edges and tell you everything was peaches and cream and it was a great thing, which is nonsense. People worked hard and people struggled and people looked to make a living and to better themselves economically. That was a prime target, you might say, and not an ignoble target at that.

HARRY CON

My brother was born here and my father came here when he was about fifteen years old, with his brother—in the early 1900s they came over. It's different now [from] when we come in. We come by plane, we come with expensive camera or expensive tape recorder, you know, and then when we arrive, we have a nice car, our friends, our family waiting for us. In the old days, he just came alone. All he had was a bag and he walked off the ship. But he was fortunate: he had two brothers here already to look after him. He and his brother worked for the CPR for a buck a day and had to walk miles every morning to go to work. They had to work about ten to twelve hours a day. Then he worked in Port Moody, in Port Hammond, all different shingle mills. He was a contractor for Chinese labour in the shingle mill business all

Harry Con was born in Vancouver in 1922. He has long been active in the Chinese community and in Strathcona, serving as first president of the Strathcona Property Owners and Tenants Association, as a member of the Chinatown Planning Committee, and as an executive member of the Chinese Freemasons, the oldest Chinese fraternal organization in Canada.

Harry Con in his store on the corner of East Pender and Columbia Streets, 1978. TOD GREENAWAY PHOTO

his life, and he taught young people to saw shingles, pack shingles—he was a good teacher.

In the old days most of the Chinese people could not speak English, and there was no union for them. My father was in that trade all his life, and he was one of the few people that learned a few words of English. He could communicate with the foreman, and also with the managers' staff, and he also married my mother—she is Canadian-born, so she helped along. They needed a person like my father to train Chinese labourers and to hire people to work there. Of course, my father didn't get any special benefits out of the whole thing. His job was actually worse than a permanent sawyer or a packer because if anybody got sick in the mill he had to take over. So night shift, poor guy, sometimes he worked eighteen hours a day, worked two shifts because they're short of labour. So that's why Capilano Timber employed my father as a contractor for so many years. And then in the logging camp in Hatzic, the company provided a shelter, see. But the board was like a commune: they purchased so much food, and they transported it from Vancouver to the camp, say $400 worth a month. And then, say they have fifteen persons—they divide the fifteen into $400 and they take off their paycheque that much. That's the way they worked in the camp. The mill is gone now. It was down at the foot of the PNE [Pacific National Exhibition Grounds]. They had a truck to haul them down to work every morning, and haul them back home in town. They met at our house every morning when I was going to high school. My father was working late work in the early years, so I usually took the workers down before I went to school.

In those days my parents, or any other parents, would like their children to learn some Chinese culture, because they felt discriminated against, they felt Canada's not for the young people. So my parents took me and my sister back to China to study Chinese. I lived in China about nine years, and I came back around 1934.

[When I returned] I went through the Hong Kong immigration, and when we landed in Vancouver, my father and mother went down to the Immigration Office to pick me up. Well we landed down at the foot of Burrard Street, that old immigration building. They called that the "pig house" because all Chinese people who returned back to Canada in the old days had to stay there for weeks, they had to go through the investigation. One of my relatives from the east, when he first came to Canada, he had to stay in there for over a week. You know, it's just like a jail. And then wait for his father to come down and pay $500 head tax, and *then* he was free to go. In the old days, they all discriminated, and that's the law, so what can you do? I think the conditions at that building were as decent as they could be, I mean, not as bad as probably some of the places they *lived* here. Today we think of it as bad, but in those days, in the 1930s, 1920s, the living conditions were not that advanced, you know. But there they had a room, they had a bed to stay— that's not so bad. And they had three meals provided by the government.

Chinese people were not wealthy, they were not rich, like the new immigrants now. They all lived very conservatively. They always saved for a few dollars they sent home. Therefore they didn't own a home here. And mostly all bachelors, you know, in the old days, because they could not apply to get their family over. So therefore, they lived as economically as they could, to save a few dollars and return home. Every so often, they went back home, and had to return, you know. My father, when he returned back to China he had to return to Canada in two years otherwise he couldn't come back.

I learned my Chinese in China, the basics. When I came back here, I still went to Chinese school. Actually when I came back, I couldn't speak English, I had to start all over. I was about fourteen years old and I went to Strathcona School, started Grade 2 at fourteen. I was the oldest student in the class.

In the 1930s they tried to close the Chinese school. Because in the opinions of the whites we were just like today they talk about East Indians, they say they're "hardcore"—they do not integrate with the white society because of their culture, and that comes from the schools. I remember many of the School Board suggested we should close the Chinese school. But the thing is, it works just the opposite, if you give it a chance. I'm the second generation, and they had to push me to learn Chinese—my father had to take me back to China. But when it comes to my children, they all speak English now and I think, in the future, my grandchildren are going to have a rough time trying to speak Chinese. I feel it makes no difference now. We recognize ourselves to be Canadian—so, naturally, you should know the language here. That's the most important tool if you want to make a good living here. But on the other hand, it's good to know your *own* language. I like this word "multicultural." Canada today, is like the United Nations, we have all kinds of people in it. And we should understand each other, so that we can wipe out all this discrimination. Chinese culture is basically built by strong family connections. Chinese in Canada never had to send old people to old-age homes, or worry about old-age pensions. The old folks were all looked after by their own children. But I remember one time one social worker came to Chinatown and he said, "Now, you Chinese people are too dumb. The government will provide money [for the old folks], why don't you go and ask the government to look after that?" And they're teaching *us*? You see, one thing good about multiculturalism is we could take the good part of the Chinese culture, and spread it around to the other sides.

Before the Second World War we could not practise as lawyers, and many other professions we could not get into. Many department stores would not hire Chinese. Government agencies would not hire Chinese. During the Second World War, I had just graduated from high school. Many of us young people at age nineteen to twenty-one were the age of conscription. We knew that, and when the government announced conscription there was a general public meeting at the United Church at Dunlevy and Pender Street to have a debate on whether we should answer the conscription and join the Canadian

Army, or should we just ignore it? Because after all, even though we were born here, we didn't have full rights as Canadian citizens. But at that time, many of us were thinking, you know, of a better future, not only for us, but for future generations if we answered the call. If we joined, then it would be the German Reich, you know, guaranteeing that our government give us full-fledged Canadian citizenship. But if we didn't, well, maybe the government would have the right to say, "You guys didn't serve in the war, didn't answer the call, and you don't deserve it." Maybe this discrimination would be therefore permanent. So for that reason, we voted to answer the government's call. And I remember, during the interview with the Canadian Army officers, they understood our point of view, and the officers that interviewed us, they all said, you know, if we joined, then after the war we would have our right to vote, have our franchise back.[68] So most of us felt, you know, we should be heroic, join and go overseas, and get the experience.

We served in southeast Asia in the so-called Secret Service, Force 136. My group served around Burma and down Malaya, that territory. And mostly as paratroops and wireless, or intelligence interpreters because in Malaysia, in Singapore, 90 percent of the population there are Chinese. So they did need us, Chinese-speaking Canadians, to serve over there. I think there were almost 200 from British Columbia.

In 1945, I was discharged and I worked for the *Chinese Times* as a translator of their news. And the Chinese Freemasons started a Chinese school at Carrall and Pender. I taught there, and I became principal there for five, six years. I think there'd be about five schools at that time. There was Chinese Community School, there was Mon Keong, there was Wah Kiu [Chinese Public School] and there's the Chinese Presbyterian Church School and the Chinese Catholic School. The Chinese Public School was run by the KMT [Kuomintang] people, the Chinese nationalists. Our school was the Chinese Community School and it was sponsored by the Freemasons. Now we were the only school that was free, no charge. It ran almost fifteen years. Then, due to a city fire bylaw, we had to close.

The Freemasons were originally from China.[69] During the gold rush era, they came up from California and they settled up in Barkerville, near Quesnel. At that time, there were gold mines up there, and a lot of gold miners were Chinese, and therefore the first branch was set up in Barkerville [1863]. At that time, China was under the Manchu Dynasty and the people from the Ming Dynasties naturally were against the Manchu takeover, and so they split overseas to do their underground work for China. Why they did that is because in the early days, the white society and the Canadian government did not accept us as today. So their only hope is, they said, one day they'll go back to a China which is returned to the Chinese people. So the Freemason people in the early days went underground and they supported the revolutionists against the Manchus.

Part of the force of the reform group joined forces with the Freemasons

Chinese Times newspaper office, Carrall and Pender Street, c. 1936. CITY OF VANCOUVER ARCHIVES, BU N157.2

who later on helped Dr. Sun Yat-sen to push ahead the revolution. There were many Chinese Freemason buildings mortgaged for that cause. Without that money, you know, Dr. Sun would not have succeeded. And when he came here [c. 1911] he was protected by the overseas Freemasons here in Canada and also in United States. Of course, one of the reasons why the Freemasons helped Dr. Sun was because when he was in Hawaii he became a Freemason member. But unfortunately, after the revolution was successful [1912] then he tried to reform the Freemasons. What happened was, he took some of the Freemason members out and built another political party called the Nationalist Party [Kuomintang], and tried to wipe out the Freemasons. This created friction between Freemasons and Nationalists. But today, we are a Canadian organization—in 1971 we got a national charter—so we want to get out of Chinese politics. We want the Freemasons to get more involved in the Canadian way of life, to try to encourage our members to become Canadians, and try to build a stronger root into Canada.

The Freemasons were always more or less a fraternity organization, they always tried to help other members. The Chinese were being discriminated against and all the new immigrants that came here needed help. You were on your own, you'd come to a strange land, and you had to find work. So the Freemasons was formed to help people who came here when they were unemployed and wanted a place to go have a bowl of rice to eat. And they tried to help each other to find employment.

There was no manpower agency and no unions, so the Freemason organization did all that kind of work. That's why it was formed. And to give the membership a place to go on the weekend, when they didn't have to work. They could come to sit down, have a chat, get somebody to help them write a letter home. And when they couldn't find jobs for them the Freemasons looked after people. They had rooms for them to live in in the Freemason building, and a communal kitchen that all the members could use. If a member dies without any money, we raise money through the membership and bury him.

In the early days, people were sent back to China to be buried and the reason why is because they felt this was not their country. They worked hard, and their family could not come here, so when they died, they wanted their bones sent back where their family was. The white people said that the Chinese are hardcore people and they will not integrate, and even their bones they want to send back home. Actually, it was a condition that was forced onto us. The people came here because they could not make a living in China but they hoped some day they would return back home to be united with their family. If the government in those days had had the same idea as today, probably the Chinese people would have contributed more to this country. In my father's days, if he didn't have to send me home, if he didn't have to send money home, all the money would have been invested here.

Now, with all the family here, they don't have to worry about the other side, all their worry is here. Their children, their grandchildren—now they have roots here. In my father's generation, they said, "Although the tree might grow a thousand feet tall, the leaf will always fall to the ground." That means, when you come to this Canada, this foreign land, it doesn't matter how rich you are, sooner or later you have to return home. But today's philosophy is different. Today we say, the roots we plant here are growing. Now we are here, our sons are here, our grandsons will be here, and their grandsons, because we have roots.

DR. SO WON LEUNG

Dr. So Won Leung was born in Canton, China, in 1916 and immigrated to Canada in 1922. In 1946, following early doctors in Chinatown—Dr. Phillip Chu, Dr. Edward Gung, and Dr. Yip—he established his medical practice in the area.

We came to Canada in 1922, just before the period when there were no immigrants coming. There were only five immigrants who came to this country during the period from 1923 [when the Exclusion Act was passed] up until 1947.[70] Three of those happened to be the other members of my family—my mother and my two brothers. We came with the Methodist church; my father was a missionary. In spite of that, they only allowed us a permit which had to be renewed every year. In 1938, I entered the University of Toronto to take my medical training.

I started my practice right here at Hastings and Main in 1946, right after the war. The people that we looked after were more of the older people, of course. There were very few families as such. Hygiene and sanitation, of course, were part of the work in those days because many of them were married "bachelors" living in communal places. In some of them the hygiene was very good because some of those older people were very meticulous, but then, of course, you have those who are not. But most community-living quarters for the Chinese in those days were kept very clean because they took turns doing the work and everybody had their job. Today everybody looks to the government to do everything; that's a tremendous difference today.

Traditionally, in any country, if you don't have the vote, you just don't feel that you should go and fight for that country. British Columbia was, I suppose, the only area where this did happen because of the fact that the Chinese did not have the franchise.[71] So I can understand that there might have been some problem here. But throughout the rest of Canada, many, many of the Chinese volunteered.

I joined up back east and when people heard that I'd joined, they asked me why I did. "Why don't you come out and practice? You can make a lot of money during the war years." But it's individual, and I felt I wanted to. I wasn't a Canadian citizen, you know. I came here in 1922, and I was not granted permanent landing until 1947. They should never have taken me into the army as an officer, because I was a foreigner! No one ever bothered to ask me, I suppose. I was here on a permit which was renewed *every* year for twenty-five years. And then when I wrote them and said, "I've now joined the army. If I should be sent overseas, what am I supposed to do?" the only reply was, "You must surrender your temporary permit to live in Canada when you leave this country." I mean, it was ridiculous.

It was good for the *politicians* to use the Orientals as an issue. If you look at the newspapers of those years, you'll find all these inflammatory speeches by the politicians. They're the ones, actually, who caused most of the trouble— the pamphlets being written by them and the speeches they made, and so on. That didn't happen in any other province. None of the other provinces had discriminatory laws as they had in British Columbia, and mainly because the Chinese and the Japanese could be seen here.

We, amongst many other people in groups, acted to get the franchise. I was president of the Army and Navy Veterans for a couple of years. We made briefs to Ottawa, we helped to arouse the interest of the people in the elections that were held and took a very active part in the elections so that the people could become more involved.

There's been changes here in Chinatown, as there have been in the whole city, really. I think there were about 8,000 Chinese here in 1946 or 1947. Now there's probably 60,000 in the Lower Mainland. And I think the changes are mainly due to the fact that there are a lot of families. The community now is not just a community of bachelors.

RAY CULOS

Ray Culos, son of Marino Culos and Phyllis Minichiello Culos, was born in Vancouver in 1936. At the time of this interview, he was chairman of the British Columbia Library Development Commission.

My grandparents and other immigrants wanted to have the type of work that would provide them with the things that are regarded as important—satisfaction, career objectives, and just some sort of an intellectual competence. And when you're told that the only job that is available is laying track, if you have no education to begin with and they offer you a steady wage, that seems very attractive and the old people really did regard that as exceptional. That's why Italian people and most other immigrant or ethnic groups were law-abiding, because they saw in our system the means by which they could plan for the future of their families. But where you had a person who had potential, who understood the prospects and possibilities in our society, and being an Italian or of Italian origin from an area of this city that wasn't considered to be acceptable to a large number of other citizens,[72] then the fight was a difficult one and sometimes frustration resulted. That first-generation Canadian probably was a very frustrated generation.

My grandparents on one side of my family never really did assimilate completely. They just longed for the life that was denied them. My grandmother was eighty-nine when she died and she never left the old country, mentally—that's a hardship that a second-generation Canadian can't hope to understand fully. My grandfather lived here for over forty years, and he couldn't tell you where he was going in English if he boarded a streetcar. But then his grandson received a formal education. It's just that that's the process. But for those [first] people, it was tough.

My grandfather Minichiello purchased the Union Grocery store from another immigrant Italian in 1911, and for approximately four to five years they transported groceries that had to be delivered either by hand or cart. My uncle, his brother, told me that it was on April 10, 1916, that he threw in *his* $300 and my grandfather his $360, and they purchased a 1916 Ford for 660 bucks. And he said that when they bought that building on Union Street, they were inundated by the rats, the insects, and the cockroaches. My mother, the first born, was in a crib up on top of a dresser so that she'd have a better chance.

We had one house only, all those years that we lived there, and that was on Union Street. The address was 748 Union, and it was the house in which my paternal grandparents lived prior to the time when my parents were married. The first several years up until about age thirteen, I was completely happy with everything that I saw, because the family unit was well-preserved and we were insulated, I guess, from outside pressures. The family would often be together and there could be thirty or forty people celebrating a festive event, with the music and the wine and the congenial atmosphere that is typical of an Italian function. I was very proud, because my father was among the leaders of the community. My mother is also recognized as a leader in the community, so they always figured in church functions, the Italian movement, and picnics.

When I went to high school, I was exposed for the first time really to a greater understanding of what was available to me as a person, as far as education and social involvement were concerned. It was a real transition period. I didn't like what I saw, because I started to compare myself with other people socially and economically, and it didn't always turn up that what I had was as good. I had a chip on my shoulder. But we were very industrious, we kept busy, we were involved in many things. Most of the boys my age stayed with that Italian influence, and we did such things as deliver papers and work for the old Italian people who had the shoeshine stands.

Where I took up this shining-shoes business was at the Broadway Hotel, which is at Columbia and Hastings, and that would be around 1950 when the whole area was inundated with single people and transients. You could see a lot of things happening right before your eyes. But we worked, we all made good money, even in those days. So then, I guess because of association and by a need to identify, I stayed with that group. The Boy Scouts were out, for example. We were the blackboard jungle type. And I don't know really why, except that maybe the area was populated by many families that had problems, and then you run around in packs. It wasn't until 1949 that Rufus

The Minichiello family in their delivery truck outside Union Grocery Store in 1916. RAY CULOS COLLECTION, COURTESY OF ROYAL BC MUSEUM, BC ARCHIVES

Gibbs donated the old synagogue building as a boys' club. We never did get away from the East End—we didn't have cars, my father never owned a car until about 1951, so we didn't have access to other areas of the city. I was typical of the kids who were ambitious, aggressive, and enthusiastic, a young person on the go and there was nowhere to go. You just bounced off walls down in the East End.

The family unit was so important and so firmly established, that there was *no question* that you wouldn't comply with the wishes of your parents in the main things. We all went to Mass. I was an altar boy for years. But we would still do the things that we wanted to do when we were back on the street, and there was never a conscious effort to relate the two. They were just two different things.

In 1940, when the new Sacred Heart School was built, the priest, Father Bortignon, made an appeal to the Catholic population to send their children to the Catholic school. We were told then that it was considered a sin by the church not to send a Catholic child to a Catholic school, if one was around. My recollection of it is that it was less than satisfactory on all counts. The teachers very definitely were not prepared to teach the sciences as we are taught today. And so there was an incomplete education, even if you were good. The church was in the basement in those days, and so they could call upon the boys who served as altar boys to be available for the funerals during the week. You got your marks for being good in religion. School didn't matter a great deal to people like myself, because the street education dictated how you were going to react to things. The nuns were our teachers, and some of them were quite strict, and corporal punishment was a means of getting to you. Mind you, they probably were frustrated too, because we were hellions. But they *did* help a group of young kids who might not have had the direction or the religious instruction that in all likelihood saved them problems as they grew up.

In the train yards, they would shunt these boxcars around, and there would be the odd time when you could pick up a watermelon from a boxcar that had been opened—some of the split watermelon would be lost and you'd pick those up. And next summer somebody would remember that and break off the seal which permitted you to get into where this good stuff was. That happened. But what did we do? We went to the State Theatre—that was the old Royal Theatre, turned State Theatre, turned Queen Theatre, next to the Roosevelt Hotel on Hastings Street just west of Main. It was burlesque, and on the pretence that we were out looking for new subscriptions for the *Sun* newspaper on a Wednesday night, we would end up in this place. We would be from twelve to fourteen. There was a pool hall directly across the street and we would gravitate there.

We did things that were on the borderline of being wrong, I suppose. But I don't remember anything so serious that we would be hauled in front of a judge—it was an attitude. I can remember wearing those outlandish clothes.

Class on the steps of old Sacred Heart School on East Pender in the 1930s. RAY CULOS COLLECTION, COURTESY OF
ROYAL BC MUSEUM, BC ARCHIVES

I had a hat that was right out of the *Li'l Abner* column, great big hat, and
long fingertip white jacket with great black "strides." I had a thirty-six [inch
circumference] at the knee, and twelve or thirteen at the ankle! And then
adopting a posture that suited the clothes.

I remember the teacher in Grade 9 at Britannia, in that course in which
we would just talk about planning for the future, and he said, "You don't want
to end up being a bootlegger like you see on Union Street." In his mind, that
was really down—and I was from Union Street, and I knew bootleggers. And
so, consciously, I accepted being part of what he considered "undesirable,"
and although I was not directly a part of what he was talking about, I assumed
that I was part of it. I submit that temptation was there, and the people who
didn't have good luck, they got caught. I can certainly recall several instances
of young people being brought before the courts, and there were a couple of
Vancouver City Police detectives that knew how to handle the situation and
kids would be roughed up a little. They reacted to this, 'cause they understood that this was the game.

We just lived right in that neighbourhood, did everything in that area.
We'd swim down off the docks down in the harbour. Crystal Pool was a long
way away, and as a matter of fact, I never knew where the West End was

until I was much older. False Creek was a great play area. We played in the garbage, literally in the garbage. There were characters around there, hoboes living in that dump in paper and tar shacks [1940s]. We got to know one, "Murray the Hobo," and he looked like the tail-end of the Depression-type hobo that may have run the rods. He would go up Hawks Avenue to the Montreal Bakery, where they would permit him to pick up the ends of the bread that didn't bake well and he'd have a sack and he'd take that away. We didn't fear him, but we had a respect for him, and I think that he was not well mentally.

Delivering papers at age eleven and twelve, you'd see some really outstanding things, the drinking and the prostitution and there was a lot of fronting going on there; for example, there was many bookmakers in that Hastings East area. The prostitutes would come to one central point with the merchandise that they had just stolen, say, from Woodward's. And we would witness this, being very young, and know where it was at, and we couldn't be fooled by adults or our contemporaries, because we became educated on the street. Many of the things which I faced probably still exist today, but I came away with the feeling how lucky I was, because there *was* a way out for me. And there isn't for everyone who finds himself down there.

It was an area where immigrants resided because of the direction that somebody placed on them—you didn't want all these people in the West End, right? The Anglo-Saxons who found things difficult for any number of reasons would also live in the East End. And for them it was a tougher struggle than it was for a person who came from a good home—*we* were only there because of the social and economic problems. My understanding of their problems included broken homes, alcoholism, and a good many uneducated people and pensioners.

On Prior Street, there were great rows of tenement houses—single rooms for pensioners. We thought, when we were young, that these people didn't deserve anything better, that it was pretty obvious they'd done something wrong, and they were less than desirable types. And perhaps that's how a lot of people thought about the Italians and the Chinese. But many of the people that lived in those tenements were retired people, and in the late forties and early fifties no one was able to retire on a pension that amounted to anything, and many of them didn't have pensions period. No hot water, no toilet facilities, and the heating was below standard, to say the least. I remember one woman, I guess the manageress, apologizing for the condition of the one toilet on that floor, that they were going to clean it up, they had poured lime all over the area because I guess it was inundated with bugs. The conditions were appalling. They were economically unable to find a place, their rightful place—they found a place, all right, where they were shoved to.

MIKE HARAHUC

I came to Vancouver in 1948 and I liked it. In the wintertime you use the same clothes as summertime. I worked for two years and I bought a house on Union Street, a little place and a good house. For two years, I didn't have to pay rent so I had money in my pocket. I painted the house, fixed it up—it was a little bit crooked from the street. They had shored up the street, there were posts that were rotten, started pressing against the house, put the house a little bit crooked. Every door was hard to close. When I bought the house, I told him I would have given him more but everything was crooked. I worked night shift—in the daytime I fixed everything up, straightened up doors, windows. I moved here because it was close to work, longshoring.

I started work at Ballantyne Pier, first day. I loaded lumber, sometimes big lumber thirty-six feet long by fourteen. Six men would carry it, sometimes

Mike Harahuc was born in the Ukraine in 1901 and immigrated to Canada in 1928. He lived on the prairies for twenty years, where he worked as a farmer and in the building trades. He moved to Vancouver in 1948. The interview was conducted in English and modified into standard English syntax by the editors.

Stevedores on the waterfront in 1932 loading cases of salmon at Ballantyne Pier. LEONARD FRANK PHOTO,
VANCOUVER PUBLIC LIBRARY, VPL 2706

your eyes go out—it's too heavy and if you drop it, you've broken somebody's legs. It was hard hard time. I carried 200-pound bags of wheat all day, not one day, sometimes a full week. Made stacks forty feet high in the boat. I had the 200 pounds on my shoulder, I'd step on the wheat sacks and my feet would go down. Anyway, I'd carry it down, nobody to take it from you, you just swing it from your shoulder. I got it from experience to go easy. First time, oh, I wanted to put the sack straight, but it took time and another man was coming behind me, waiting. As you got experience, you just threw it.

I knew lots of longshoremen who lived in the neighbourhood, close to work. If you got too far from home, you stayed all day down there, you didn't want to spend your money going home, going back, going home. I wanted to join the union but it was hard. The union men would have a friend and bring the friend down and ask the foreman to take that man into the union. I didn't have a friend down there to help me. But I didn't care, I had seven or eight years and I wasn't paid union wages but I didn't pay dues either. There wasn't enough union men so they took spare men then.

YIP TING YUEN & GARSON YUEN

Yip Ting Yuen was born in Hoishan, Kwangtung province, China, in 1894. He first came to Canada in 1920. His son, Garson Yuen, was born in China in 1939. The interview was conducted in both English and Hoishan dialect with Garson acting as interpreter. Translation was by Kwok Chiu of Strathcona Property Owners and Tenants Association.

YIP TING YUEN: I came over in 1920 to join my father who had a laundry then at Walhachin, this little place near Ashcroft. I came by steamboat and it took twenty-six days. I was travelling third class, on the bottom deck. I couldn't eat anything because I'd go down to the toilet and puke it right away. The toilet was awful dirty, oh gee. I had a CNR ticket from Vancouver but they put me on a CPR train, nobody checked my ticket, and then later they said I was on the wrong train and they sent me back. I didn't know where I was, I didn't know anything then, so they sent me down to Chinatown. It happened that one of the people from my hamlet was going back to the Interior, so we took the train together that night.

I came over as a businessman because at that time only businessmen were allowed to come in without paying the head tax.[73] My father made the arrangements with agents in Hong Kong. He paid them $1,200 Hong Kong money and they took care of everything, my passage over, and the business documents. But when I get here and the immigration people found out that I was working in a laundry, they said that wasn't a business. The same thing happened to my brother who came over three years earlier, although he didn't pay the agent's fee. They locked him up at Customs and my father had to pay $500 to get him out. Later, they changed the regulation and I had to pay again in 1922. By that time I had bought a restaurant in Indian Head, Saskatchewan, but government officials came and said I still had to pay the tax.

GARSON YUEN: When he was in Saskatchewan, they closed up shop for a while and he went back home to China and then I was born. Every time he'd come home my sisters or brothers were born. After the war, they allowed people to bring their wives and unmarried children to Canada, and he started making application. At first, he wasn't going to bring us over. A lot of Chinese people had that idea: either they hadn't thought about it any other way or they still thought they would make their fortune and settle back in the old country. But we came over in 1950 on an American war-carrier. He was already running the Mount Shasta Cafe then.

When he came back out to Vancouver in 1945, he wanted to semi-retire, but the only thing he knew was what he could afford, so with a relative he bought the Mount Shasta Cafe on Hastings. It was a gold mine. We had to lock people out, that's how busy it was. It used to be a hangout for a lot of people, post-war immigrants, single people who had struck out on their own. Especially in the wintertime. Summertime, they went to logging camps, worked in the mines, or else they went fishing. They were cooped up in camp for four or five months, so the thing they did when they hit town was go out and socialize. They'd meet their friends in the Mount Shasta, and we were open twenty-four hours a day, 365 days a year. It would get so full we couldn't manage it. People were standing around the aisles, drinking coffee and so on, especially when it rained. They'd have something, they'd pocket the bill, hang around for a while, then sit down for another coffee, maybe later on they'd pay. If we'd had a little business sense we would have got one of those new cigarette machines that came out at that time. But as it was, he was kept busy selling cigarettes and pops to go, and I was helping out, or my brother, around the fountain, making milkshakes and hot chocolates and ice cream, sometimes taking cash, and then going down to the back to look around. People were being, you know...

YIP TING YUEN: Crazy!

GARSON YUEN: At night time it got so busy we put about three locks on the door to keep people out. Rainy days people kept flooding in, or nice days people stayed outside, hung around, sometimes fifty to a hundred people just hung around there till three or four o'clock in the morning.

YIP TING YUEN: At that time meals were cheap, you know, twenty-five cents for a meal—stew, roast beef, chops, fillet of sole.

GARSON YUEN: Those people were post-war immigrants that hadn't got a family yet but they were making a lot of money. They didn't know what to do with it, they didn't know how to handle it. Sometimes they even had money stashed away in their socks and when they had a few drinks they forgot that they had money in their socks, and they'd know that something was bothering them so they'd take it off and shake it, throw the money away. Things like that.

Hastings Street was busy then. A block down was the Common Gold Cafe, they were open twenty-four hours a day. The Blue Eagle was open twenty-four hours, in that same block, and so was the Peter Pan on Granville. Those were the only four places that were open twenty-four hours a day then. A block down the street it was a different crowd, usually dope addicts. They weren't troublemakers or belligerent, but we didn't want them as customers because they scared a lot of people away. They usually had a lot of time to spare, they'd just go in and sometimes they'd doze off, and they didn't usually eat that much, just drink pop, something sweet, especially when they needed a fix. You can only cater to one type of customer, and we didn't want to cater to addicts, that's all there was to it. The people we got were very free, easy-going, easy-go-lucky people. Maybe they tried to hide their misery behind their drunkenness, but I didn't have any trouble with them. When I first started there I didn't know them, and I knew that people had a lot of fights, but when you start to know the people there's no problem getting along with them at all. We got a few rumbles but we never did get a lot of bad fights. It's because the old police station was behind us, on Cordova Street. Even policemen off-duty sitting in the back, they didn't bother. There'd be a rumble, because at times people get drunk, and I just took them out.

YIP TING YUEN: Nobody ever hit me and I never hit anybody. When there was trouble, I always said, "Let's talk it over. There's a whole bunch of us. What you going to do that for? Let's talk it over."

DOROTHY NEALY

Dorothy Nealy was born in Winnipeg in 1917 of an Indian mother and Black father. She grew up in the Ukrainian–Polish district of the city and moved to Vancouver in 1944.

When I came here, this district was Negroes, from Main to Campbell Avenue, like you see the Chinese here now. Whole apartment blocks that were all full of Blacks. In '44 it was a ghetto. They had never realized that they could move out of this area, because if they went someplace to rent a house, they wouldn't refuse them and say, "We don't want you here because you're Black"—they'd just mention some exorbitant price for the rent, you see. And they knew they couldn't handle it 'cause the first thing they'd ask them, "Where do you work?" Well they worked on the railroad, you know, and they just earned a certain amount of money. And then they had four or five kids to support, so they couldn't pay rent like they can now.

When they realized they could get other jobs, then they quit the railroad. Some of them went longshoring, and some of them started driving trucks. There must have been at least 400 people lived down here. And now there's only a handful of Black people left in the neighbourhood.

In 1938, when I came out here for a visit, they had a terrible riot down in Hogan's Alley. Apparently, some college kids came over here, slumming, and one of the girls got stuck on a coloured fellow, and she came back down to the East End, to the night spots. They had dance halls and cabarets all over, you know, and she liked to dance. I mean, there was nothing, she wasn't a prostitute or anything like that. She was just a nice young lady. Well, the white men just used that for an excuse. They said she was down here someplace and they were going to put a stop to it. They came in three carloads and they went down Hogan's Alley. So they sent out a call, the Black people did, and they came from all over here. Well, they almost killed them, and there was about eighteen of them, they just beat them insensible. And they never came back down here. But every now and then, a gang would come down here, just for kicks. Even now it happens once in a while, at the Stratford—bunch of white kids come down. And they'll call somebody a "nigger." Out of a clear blue sky, you know. And the fight is on. You can't wait for police protection, because, if the police come and drive them off, they're only going to come back again. We just settle our own accounts. We *have* to, because I think in their subconscious mind they feel a white supremacy attitude, these kids that come down, you know. So the only way to let them know that one man is just as good as another, is just to beat the shit out of them. And then they'll let you alone.

Fountain Chapel was really the whole hub of this ghetto. If you wanted to meet anyone, the thing to do was to go to church. And that little church would be just packed to the doors. They had a beautiful choir. The preachers didn't stay here long, they were mostly American ministers.

Ten or twenty years ago, we didn't know anything about Africa. We were all Canadians and all we knew was British history. Like, I never knew Hannibal was a Black man till after I was grown and married. What I was taught was about all the great explorers and the seafaring men and how the British Empire was won. But we didn't know at *what cost*.

It's just in the last few years we've really become aware of what's happening. And then we started reading. There was a time we couldn't even get these *Ebony* magazines in Canada. We had to get the American railroad porters to bring them in. When the BCAACP [British Columbia Association for the Advancement of Coloured People] first started out, over twenty years ago, it was the NAACP [National Association for the Advancement of Colored People (American)], and then they changed into the BCAACP because we're all Canadians. They more or less felt like our situation here is quite different, because, in the United States, the Americans are so blatant about the racial prejudice. You can fight it, because they call you "nigger" and they segregate you out loud and clear. But the racism in Canada is so subtle, and so elusive you can't really pin it down. Like finding jobs. They'd tell you, "Oh, that job was just filled fifteen minutes ago, and if you had of come a little earlier you could have had the job." They would no more have hired you than shot themselves.

But when I came to this East End in 1938, oh! I thought I was in something like Hollywood, because every door was sitting wide open, and you could walk right in, you know. It was just like walking in the beer parlour today, but these were bootlegging places. And they all had music, and they all had something to eat—fried chicken, hot tamale, bowl of chili.

I think the first big shakeup they had here was when [Gerry] McGeer became mayor. And they said, "McGeer's put the lid on Vancouver and he's sitting on the lid." Because before that, these people ran these places like they had a licence, but they didn't, you know. Like all the sporting houses—they had to pay the police, because if any strange women was hustling out in their block, in front of their house, they phoned the police and had her arrested.

Dorothy Nealy at home, 1977. TOD GREENAWAY PHOTO

They had so many houses on Union Street, and all up and down Gore Avenue. They had all kinds of women. Some of them had Chinese, Japanese, white, coloured, all nationalities. None of them specialized. Because the girls were moving from place to place across Canada, or going into the States. One girl would say, "I'm tired of Vancouver. I'm going to see if I can get in a house in Calgary." So they'd contact a landlady in Calgary, which was wide open too. Or they'd go to Nelson, or Prince Rupert. Some went to Toronto. All the landladies knew each other, clear across Canada and down through the States. I've heard the girls saying, "I'd like to go to Kimberley. I've got a friend, she told me she made a lot of money up at Kimberley." And the landlady would say, "Don't go till I get someone to take your place." Some houses had two girls, some had five. Well, they got tired of living in a house maybe for five or six months or a year, you know. Maybe she'd want to go to Kimberley, and they'd phone the landlady in Kimberley, say, "Can you send me a parcel?" "Yes." "Well, I can send you a parcel in two weeks." "Well, I'll send you mine in two weeks." So that meant that when that girl came, the other girl left, so the landlady wouldn't be out of a girl.

And then when the heat was on, well, the girls would disperse. Like a new mayor or a new police chief, they'd come in and they'd close all the sporting houses and raid all the bootlegging places, and then everybody'd have to scatter, especially the girls. The landladies stayed and they would try and get them places to go to in different parts of Canada. 'Cause the police chief as a rule, he gave them thirty days' notice. And then maybe the sporting houses would be closed down for a month or two months. And then they'd make a donation, to the firemen's or the policemen's—some benefit organization that they had going, you know. And then they'd have a talk with the police chief, or the mayor. Then pretty soon they'd start to get one girl, then they'd get two girls, then they'd get three girls and start all over again. The sporting houses, they finally closed down in the fifties. But the bootleggers, they never really shut down until the last few years.

Practically every Black woman in Vancouver worked for Mrs. Pryor's Chicken Inn sometime or other. Some of them has worked there for years and years, from the time she started. And when she first started [c. 1918], she couldn't afford to pay wages, so everybody worked for their tips. The Chicken Inn was just like sitting in your own kitchen, you know. It was kind of primitive: she had plain tables and chairs, with oilcloth on the tables, and she had ashtrays there for a while, glass ashtrays, but everybody kept stealing them, so she just put sardine cans on the table. The food was very good. She sold hot tamales and chili and fried chicken and steaks. Her coal and wood range was about the size of that bed, a huge great big black monster. I think there was about eight eyes in it. And she had those big black cast-iron frying pans, and they were huge things.

I was the day cook. I'd come on at two o'clock in the afternoon and work till ten o'clock at night. I'd go out and chop kindling and get two or three cardboard boxes of kindling, and bring in several scuttles of coal, and I'd start the fire and I'd make the soup, and then sometimes I'd make the biscuit dough, or the cornbread dough. In the daytime it was usually very quiet, but if it got busy she was there, 'cause they lived upstairs. And she'd come down every day, sit and talk with me, and when it got crowded she'd cook and I waited table.

Then there was a lot of poultry houses too, in this part of the East End. I worked for three years at Visco Poultry packing house in the 300-block Keefer. We used to dress chickens and turkeys and geese and ducks. And then there were two places on Georgia Street and a lot of places on Pender Street where they killed and cleaned chickens. The trucks would come in and the chickens were squawking and the ducks were quacking and there'd be trucks lined up and down the alleys, waiting to be unloaded. Chickens were killed by hand, and then they went through a scalding tank, then they went through a buffing machine which buffed the feathers off them, and then they were on an assembly line and every one of us had a job to do. My job, 'cause I had small fingers, I'd slit a hole in the chicken and draw the craw out, and I'd do that all day long. I know there was twenty-two of us Negro women working there, several Japanese, Chinese, East Indians—not very many East Indians. They stuck to the mills in those days, and they didn't allow their women to go out working, like they do now.

There was the New Station Cafe, on Main Street between Union and Georgia, and it stayed open twenty-four hours a day. It was world-renowned—anything you wanted to find, go to the New Station. People would come from all parts of the city, used to come off the ships, the merchant seamen, and they'd stop you, "Where's this New Station?" You ordered something to eat, and you had your bottles with you, and you drank, and you met people and laughed and talked and danced up and down the aisles. Chinese owned and operated that restaurant. I don't know how they stood it, but they made money, and I think their whole attitude was, well it was no Chinese making a fool of themselves. If you started a fight, well they'd just call the police, and the police came with the wagon and threw in whoever was going in there, and the party went on. They had a jukebox in there, and they had one of those pinball machines. And they had two rows of booths and then they had a long counter. If we went to the New Delhi [Cabaret], well they closed at four o'clock in the morning, and everybody would just pour out of the New Delhi, those who were still on their feet, and we'd go down to the New Station. And they'd be walking bootleggers, up and down the aisle. Then you'd just call them, "Give me a mickey." They'd give you a mickey, you'd call the waiter, "Give me a Coke, 7 Up, glass of water." And you'd be pouring, and if the police came round, you'd just put it down, and they'd come round with the flashlight, "Is that your bottle?" "No, *I* didn't...is that a bottle under there?" 'Cause you had to pay a fifty-dollar fine, you know, if you claimed a bottle, and nobody claimed the bottle.

As soon as they walked out, "Well, they've gone to Hastings Street." Well, call the bootleggers, and the bootleggers would have their booze stashed around out in the garbage cans and different places. They'd go out there and open the garbage can and come up with a half a dozen bottles, then serve everybody and the party would carry on. We got a thrill out of the cat-and-mouse game with the police, you know. We were always trying to find some way of stashing our liquor. Like one time we were in the New Delhi and they says, "The law's at the door." So I took the two bottles of whisky and I put 'em in the toilet waterbox, and came back proud as punch, thought I had defeated the police. They searched the building. Finally they went to the bathrooms and opened them, took all our whisky, and we'd been just so smug 'cause we figured they wouldn't *think* of looking in the women's room.

When I first started working at Canadian Fish, there was whole families of Indians, the mother and the father right down to the grandchildren, all working. This lady, she worked there for so many years she was the top seniority woman, and to me she looked quite young. So I said to her, "How could you get so many years seniority? You must be sixty-five or seventy!" She says, "No, I came in here as a child." She says, "When we started, my mother stood me on the box and I put labels on the cans." Then she said, "That's the way we worked in *all* the canneries." Steveston, Queen Charlotte canneries—they did that throughout British Columbia, years and years ago.

And then, in the early days, the Chinese used to contract. One Chinese, he'd be like the foreman and he'd hire all the Chinese and they would pay him by the month. They weren't paid by the hour like the rest of us. But now the union has stopped all that. They're more integrated in the everyday workings of the cannery, they run the machines, or they're mechanics, or engineers. They're qualified.

On Dunlevy Street, before they fixed up the neighbourhood, there used to be a row of houses from Union to Hastings, and on both sides of the street the old Chinese men all summer long, they chopped wood in stove-sized pieces. And they'd pile them up on the side of the house, they'd fill the basements, then they'd fill the side of the house, and then they'd put pieces of tin to keep the rain off of it. They'd do that every summer. One old man, when he told me he moved into the housing project, "Oh," he says, "I miss the house. Nothing to do. Just sit down. Nothing to do." But they'd all talk and they'd stop and smoke their cigarettes and their pipes and they'd laugh and talk, and then they'd go in and have a cup of tea and they'd come back out. And they were there from dawn to dusk. They chopped cords and cords of wood, *all* summer.

When we heard of city council's plans for the neighbourhood, we were horrified, we just screamed. They intended to put high-rises all over here, like the West End. But the people that lived here, we just took up a petition. We got thousands and thousands of names. And we stopped them. The Vancouver Resources Board met with city council and they met with different organizations. They met with SPOTA [Strathcona Property Owners and Tenants Association]. You see, it wasn't just SPOTA that fought for this East End. There was the churches and all kinds of people got involved. The whole neighbourhood got involved. Because *we* were satisfied with our neighbourhood. But the people from outside came in and told us we shouldn't have these houses, we should live in housing projects, we should live in high-rises. But what was wrong with living here? *They* didn't live here, I don't know what they were so worried about. As I said, I've lived here for thirty-three years. I wouldn't want to live anyplace else. But somebody comes over from Dunbar district, looking down their nose at this end of town. It's just like the Christians going to Africa, trying to convert you to Christianity when you already have your own tribal laws and religions and everything else. And that was their attitude when they came down here.

They interviewed every individual and they had all kinds of books. And they'd go from room to room. First thing they'd ask, "Wouldn't you like to move out of here?" We'd say, "Move where?" "Well, out of this neighbourhood." No, nobody wanted to move out of here. It was just like a village, just the same. You went out the back door, you stood on the back verandah, and somebody'd wave at you, over there. Even if you didn't know them, you'd wave back. And when you walked down the street, you nodded your head.

Fish wharf at the foot of Gore Avenue, 1931. LEONARD FRANK PHOTO, VANCOUVER PUBLIC LIBRARY, VPL 2787

Sometimes you said, "Hello," or you just nodded your head and smiled and kept going. That's the way we lived.

COMMUNITY ATTITUDES TO URBAN RENEWAL

From interviews with Fred Soon, Ramon Benedetti, Harry Con, Mary Chan, and Shirley Chan.

Yun Ho Chang and Lo Po Yin. STRATHCONA PROPERTY OWNERS AND TENANTS ASSOCIATION

FRED SOON: I had a house in the 600-block Pender Street. City Hall wanted the land, and at meetings at the Chinese Benevolent Association, one of the questions I asked was, "How is the City Hall going to pay us for the house and land if we are going to be vacated?" City Hall people said, "Oh, you'll be well paid, you don't have to worry," so I didn't pursue it much further. But that was the kind of blanket promise you can hardly rely on, as I found out later.

The government just ran over us and didn't respect our right to speak up [but] I made representation to the City Hall. They sent a negotiator, who came to my house three or four times. Every time, he offered me maybe $300 or $400 more than the price they offered before. When they tried to expropriate me in 1965, they pinned the notification on my door. They didn't even have the courtesy to see me and hand it to me personally. They merely nailed it on the door. They said there was nothing I could do about it, my house was under the expropriation law, but I could always talk with the negotiator.

Negotiation? What a farce! The land was earmarked for expropriation, so the market value was very low. What I needed was replacement value, not market value. My first lawyer advised me to go into arbitration. I didn't want to go into arbitration, because once you agree to arbitration, you can't go any further. And I was still left with a dilemma that I couldn't solve. I wanted replacement value for my house, and that's all.

I had hoped to prevent them from demolishing the house. I had every intention of doing that. But then my wife saw that all the houses left and right of us were going down, hammers and bulldozers all buzzing around, and she was almost going crazy. Finally, I found a house approximately the same size. Immediately, I went to the City Hall and gave them the proposition: "Will you pay for that house?" They shook their heads. We bought the house anyway—borrowing money privately. When we moved, we didn't give the first house to the city, we just left it, and I had every intention of guarding it. One day, during 1967, eighteen months after we moved, the bulldozer came around and demolished it. I was so surprised. I got off work and all I saw was the whole house demolished. Previous to the demolishing, I engaged a second lawyer, and I told him that I was not agreed with the way the city was giving me remuneration for my house, that I would rather keep it because I would like to go on living in the Strathcona area.

In 1968, I discharged that lawyer and engaged another. A short time later, he told me: "Your case is finished. I represented you at the courthouse, and the city had their own representative, and they kept on saying they could pay you $6,600, and so I accepted it on behalf of you." I certainly did not agree. I paid him a retaining fee, I paid the interim charge for his appearance in court, and I discharged him. So now I had used up three lawyers and I couldn't afford a fourth one. So I thought I had better apply myself as a lawyer, and I made quite a noise at City Hall.

The city had no right to initiate that program of urban renewal. It should come from the people, from the grassroots. And they didn't treat the inhabitants as people. They had no housing rehabilitation program that suited the people. Their main purpose was to get them out and get their land. They should have realized that people come first. If they say "urban renewal," they should renew the house. But what they wanted to do was really paradoxical: they wanted to destroy the house.[74]

RAMON BENEDETTI: One Chinese man, he got $5,200 for his house and his twenty-five–foot lot. Now this man's home meant a hell of a lot to him, and he was an elderly man that had no place to go. Where are you going to go when you're fifty? Who's going to give you a mortgage, huh? But at that time, you know what they did? They bulldozed your place down and then you went to court for a settlement.

I remember the first meeting we had, and I says, "All right, arise! You people, arise! To arms, it's time! These guys are bulldozers. They're rolling over us, you know."

I've got to take a deep breath—those city planners, they were all up there, sitting up there, as smug as bugs in a rug up there. And who are us lowly people to complain, to stand up against these sneaking, conniving, side-winding, backstabbing claim-jumpers? How do you fight these people? Where do you start? So you got up and you said something, and that was it. And then the next guy stood up: "Sorry, you've already said your piece." You never got a chance. And you didn't get any answers out of them. I mean, this is the feeling of frustration that I had. I felt so helpless.

And then we started. "Hey, man, let's get together. Let's stop this." Do you know that they were paying you for your land only? The land value. You got nothing for your house. So where do you go?

So then we got together—myself and a bunch of people. We said: "Okay. You want my place? Fine. I've got a six-room home here. Find me another one. We don't want money. We want a house for a house." They said, "Oh, well, we can't do that. We'll put you in a low-income housing project." I said, "You can take the cement cubicle and stick it in your ear, man." You know. "You want to take my house and put me in one of them cubicles? *You* go in there."

And then we started to gather a little momentum. Then we got the Chinese worked up—some of the Chinese that were sitting back—and then, really, they got going. And you've got to hand it to them, because they got the ball rolling.

HARRY CON: In the early 1960s, when the city started to have this urban

Group of concerned residents at a SPOTA meeting.
STRATHCONA PROPERTY OWNERS AND TENANTS ASSOCIATION

Fred Soon's house on East Pender Street before demolition by the city. FRED SOON COLLECTION, COURTESY OF ROYAL BC MUSEUM, BC ARCHIVES

Fred Soon at a neighbourhood meeting. STRATHCONA PROPERTY OWNERS AND TENANTS ASSOCIATION

renewal program, the Chinese people asked the Chinese Benevolent Association to help, and they did form a Chinese Property Owners' Association at that time. This was the older-generation group. They were under Mr. Foon Sien. He was one of a new breed who could speak English and who could communicate with the politicians and with the white society, and he did a lot of speaking for the Chinese after the war.

They hired a lawyer and went up to City Hall and presented a brief. After they finished, the lawyer argued with city council but they voted against it. The city got financing from the federal government to go ahead with the urban renewal first phase and then the second phase.

In December 1968, they had this meeting organized by a group of residents. I remember there was Mr. Walter Chan and Mrs. Chan and there was Bessie Lee and Mrs. Lilyan Luk and Mrs. Margaret Mitchell, who was the area social worker who helped to organize this meeting. That night I didn't actually have the intention to go to a meeting, but I thought: oh, hell, maybe I should go, maybe I'm involved, maybe I *have* to go. I did attend and I was elected to the committee that night. So from then on SPOTA was formed.

The Sien Lok Conference [in Calgary, 1969] was the first national conference to talk about how urban renewal was damaging the Chinese communities all across Canada. After the conference, we decided to send a delegate to Ottawa to meet the new housing minister, Mr. [Robert] Andras, and we presented our view. Then he came out to Vancouver, and he met with us to iron out the program, and he also talked with the provincial people and the city people. Probably a lot of things made us fight, you know. There was no Chinese Cultural Centre then.[75] And the Chinese Benevolent Association was not very active in those fights. But, by 1969 we did have the government backing us on a rehabilitation program [as distinct from urban renewal— i.e., rehabilitating existing homes instead of demolishing them and building public housing units].

And then this Georgia Viaduct was built. See, in the original plan, they were using Union Street as a one-way freeway and then Prior Street the other way—one going and one coming back. The famous saying in those days— and we used it as an example, telling the council: "If you'd like a freeway to go through *your* living room, then go ahead." Anyhow, we put on many protests, and we got it stopped.

MARY CHAN: By 1949, when we first moved into Strathcona, there were a lot of Chinese people who were bringing their families, and that raised the prices in the neighbourhood because people wanted to live here. We didn't know anything about demolition when we bought [our house in 1953, or 1954]. We learned a few months after. There were lots of Chinese buying homes for sale in the neighbourhood, and they didn't realize, either, until after they'd bought.

SHIRLEY CHAN: I remember after they learned about demolition of old houses, my parents further invested a lot of money into renovating the house so that it would *not* be demolished, but did not realize it was slated for blanket demolition. So that was their second error.

MARY CHAN: I started with the Chinese Benevolent Association to fight urban renewal in 1956 or '57. There were big meetings and everybody put some money in and we hired a lawyer. But after the money was gone, then he didn't do anything. Shirley used to help me translate when we went door to door to get people to sign petitions.

SHIRLEY CHAN: I was about nine or ten then. I grew up with it. But it wasn't until I was a university student, 1968, that I got involved. Prior to that, I'd say I was politically unconscious. I was a student at Simon Fraser. And there was a meeting one night at First United Church, and I came home and Dad asked me if I would go—Mother was already there. So I went to the meeting, and I just heard the incredible anger that the community was feeling, and the frustration. I heard people saying, "All I want is a fair shake," and these were my neighbours. Or I heard Mr. and Mrs. Wong say in Chinese, "We worked very hard to build ourselves a nest, and now you're going to take it away from us." So that was enough. That was how I got involved. And from then, it was just phone calls and trying to make contacts and meetings.

The Hellyer Task Force was meeting, and we put in an appearance for the community. They were asking for a better deal for the people; you know, a little more money, a social worker under each arm maybe. And the people didn't want that. It was a question of not just relocating, getting another house for a house, but it was a house of the size that an extended family could live in. It was a house where your life patterns wouldn't be disrupted.

Community leader Harry Con, with provincial politicians Grace McCarthy and Herb Capozzi at a SPOTA banquet. STRATHCONA PROPERTY OWNERS AND TENANTS ASSOCIATION

That first appearance at City Hall, I was used as someone who would speak for her parents, and there was a tremendous discussion as to whether or not I would be allowed to say anything because it was out of order. They allowed me to speak, and I just sort of spoke up and talked about the situation of my family, and the fact that the community was a Chinese community and that was important to them.

Then my first television interview was arranged through my psychology professor, who used to work as a researcher for CBC. I suppose with that I started to make contacts and from there became the English-language public relations officer for SPOTA.

We found people who had ears. They heard that what we were saying was not that we wanted relocation assistance, but that we wanted urban renewal to be stopped and that we should be allowed to stay. Darlene Marzari put us in touch with community workers like Margaret Mitchell and Jonathan Lau.

These people were willing to help us achieve what we wanted to achieve, rather than telling us what we ought to achieve. And there were people like my mother who would go and do the legwork, right? Pound the streets, knock on doors, ask people to come out for meetings, collect money. And so the idea of the block captain developed.[76]

All of this happened, not so much out of the Gibbs meeting [a 1968 public

Federal cabinet ministers Ron Basford and Robert Andras at a SPOTA banquet. STRATHCONA PROPERTY OWNERS AND TENANTS ASSOCIATION

Mary Chan at a community meeting. STRATHCONA
PROPERTY OWNERS AND TENANTS ASSOCIATION

Pat Canning and Jonathon Lau in discussion.
STRATHCONA PROPERTY OWNERS AND TENANTS ASSOCIATION

This interview was conducted in the SPOTA office with Bessie Lee, then president of SPOTA; Tom Mesic, past-president of SPOTA; and Ann Chan and Mary Chan (not related), both long-standing members of the executive. Bessie Lee acted as interpreter for Mary Chan when required.

meeting at the Gibbs Boys Club]—that was one stage at which we founded the organization and we agreed what our common goals were, and we in fact elected *three* co-chairmen so that the burden would be shared: my father, Harry Con, and Sue Lum who lived around the corner. So that was one way of finding that the community was together. But the other way was sitting in living rooms over many cups of tea and coffee, and talking about what we should do next, developing the strategy of block captains, and having people go from door to door on a regular basis to talk about recent developments. We felt that was necessary so people could be part of what was happening, and, gee, they felt exactly like us. I mean, that was the beauty of it, learning that *we* weren't the only ones who felt that way about urban renewal. There was no question that I was a follower in my parents' vision for their home, for their community, 'cause *they* struggled for it, they struggled to make it.

MARY CHAN: My husband said we must have faith and work together, and if the CBA doesn't want to fight for it, we will. He said the Chinese have to *show* that they're capable of winning the fight with City Hall, and we mustn't look down on ourselves as a people—we *can* do it.

SHIRLEY CHAN: Father provided the motivation and the brains. Mother provided the legwork and the willingness and the energy and the contacts. There were some painful times, and I remember tears and I remember exhilaration, and I remember saying, "Well, we've got to say it's a victory," or "We've got to say it's a loss." Because until people *see* things in terms of a struggle, they won't act. There were a lot of struggles, and there were things that we lost and things that we gained, but ultimately I think it's a good place to live.

STRATHCONA PROPERTY OWNERS AND TENANTS ASSOCIATION (SPOTA)

ANN CHAN: It's been almost twenty-five years since the city said the blights was on this neighbourhood and started tearing down houses. "Slum clearance" they called it. And they bought all these houses and then just left them for quite a few years. And then people would get real mad. "What's the city going to do? Why don't they do something?"

BESSIE LEE: The city announced a public meeting down at CBA and they presented a beautiful plan—you know, "Vote for this and clean up your neighbourhood." There were dilapidated rooming houses then, the old kind with outhouses, and on Campbell Avenue there was a lot of row-housing with a lot of fires happening. And vegetable farms with sheds near where the Raymur high-rise stands now. So when they showed this plan to upgrade the general area, of course I voted for it. The first phase, they built the MacLean Park Housing high-rise [finished 1963] and then they started tearing out the homes. Skeena Terrace Housing [on Cassiar Street, the eastern edge of the city's East End] was developed first for the local people to move out to. But none of the Chinese would go out there to live and they all looked for other areas to move out to. So when they finished MacLean Park, a small percentage of the residents was from the local area but the larger percentage was from the outside. And then I realized that something wasn't right. When they put up Raymur Place Housing Project [finished 1967] some people from the community went to live there because they had no alternative, their homes were purchased and they had nowhere else to go. A high percentage of people owned their homes outright and that meant they would have to go into debt to buy a new home all over again.

Mary Chan: When the city first started buying houses, they chose the most rundown houses to buy, and after that they started buying the better homes but they would negotiate for them and the price wasn't very good. All the time they'd come over, "You want a better price?" I said, "I *don't* want to sell my house, that's that." Then they'd say, "Really? I'll give you a higher price, just say how much more you want." They'd try to buy a whole block.

Four blocks of homes demolished in 1968 for construction of a housing project. VANCOUVER PUBLIC LIBRARY, SPECIAL COLLECTIONS, VPL 3235

They'd say, "Look there are only three or four houses left, there's nothing else you can do. You won't have any lights if you live here." So then Sue Lum, me, and Mrs. Mah, we went around and we said, "They want to buy the whole block and one person signing will give them the block. So when they come back and talk, say 'No way. Talk to the people next door.'" Next door says, "No, when the next house sells I sell." That way we were strong, we had a strong block.

BESSIE LEE: I stopped by at this large meeting at Strathcona School [November 1968]. Well, the city planners were down there explaining the beautiful concept of this urban renewal project and they asked for questions. So I asked a couple of questions and I got just a very negative attitude—"I can't give you an answer on this," or "There is no answer to that." I got more angry each time I asked a question and I said, "What are you down here for?" Margaret Mitchell [community development worker from Neighbourhood Services Association, now Vancouver East MP] happened to be sitting near me and she said, "Look, if you *really* want to find out more and do something about this, give your name to that girl over there." So I said, "Why not?" and I went over and gave her my name. Before I knew it, she contacted me. "Would you like to come to our little meeting and would you bring someone?" Well, that "little meeting" was not just any little meeting: it was the preplanning of the first huge public meeting, the one that was held at the Gibbs Boys Club [December 1968]. We discussed tactics: What can we do to ensure that this organization will be successful? The majority of people going to those early meetings were mainly Chinese-speaking and they had to rely on the services of a lawyer. So we decided right then and there to get English-speaking or bilingual people into the group to make it strong.

MARY CHAN: We went door to door to collect money—one dollar, two dollars, anything, so we could put it in the Chinese papers, and we told people, "Meeting! Meeting! Hurry up and come out! If you don't come, they'll tear all the houses down."

BESSIE LEE: Mr. Chan was chairman of that meeting but he was such a gentle-speaking person it was very difficult to hear him because there was such a madhouse, just a full house, it spilled right out onto the street. People that you didn't think would come turned up because their home was at stake. So we called for nominations right away from the floor. Harry Con was nominated for president, and Walter Chan was nominated for president, and Sue Lum was nominated for president. And all of them said, "I can't do it." "But if *you* can't accept, and *you* can't accept, and *you* can't accept, then we'll have no leader and we're not going to be strong. If all three of you accept, then you can lend each other strength, and if one is short-handed in doing something, the next person can take over." So we had three presidents in the beginning, and we had two secretaries and two treasurers [English-speaking and Chinese-speaking]. At the next meeting, a *lot* of people came out to support us. I think we had the largest membership around that time, as much as 600 members.

Chinese Consul and members of the SPOTA executive on the steps of the SPOTA office. STRATHCONA PROPERTY OWNERS AND TENANTS ASSOCIATION

Joe Wai talking with Mike Harcourt. STRATHCONA PROPERTY OWNERS AND TENANTS ASSOCIATION

TOM MESIC: The shape the housing was in and the conditions of the streets, that's what crystallized that meeting. The streets hadn't been paved for fifteen years and you couldn't get a permit to fix anything.[77] They had wooden blocks on the roads and they would patch them. Strathcona was always in the process of being patched, it was a patchwork effort. Most people wouldn't invest any real money in their houses, because if they were going to be expropriated why invest? And then the influx of people into the new housing projects was mostly one class: single parent and low income, which created difficulties in the area.

BESSIE LEE: It was like Custer's last stand here. Families wanted to keep their culture, send the little kids to Chinese school here, so that the grandparents could still relate to the children when they came home.

TOM MESIC: Shirley Chan played a great role because she was uninhibited. Here was this young Chinese girl, she was only about eighteen or nineteen, and she wasn't afraid of politicians, she treated them as equals. And that was sort of a challenge to City Hall.

Margaret Mitchell and Julia Lee conversing at SPOTA meeting. STRATHCONA PROPERTY OWNERS AND TENANTS ASSOCIATION

BESSIE LEE: It was Margaret Mitchell who was able to guide and assist Shirley to utilize the services of resource people in social services and young lawyers,[78] and that enabled the organization to manoeuvre on the political scene. But the groundwork organizing was done by Mr. and Mrs. Chan and Sue Lum going out into the community, and by an older group, Mr. Wong Yuen and Mrs. Sam Lum and Louise Fung. And Jonathan Lau provided translation at all our meetings and he made sure the right articles got into the newspaper with the right timing. He used to walk the streets just to talk to people to keep their morale up and inform them of what's going on.

There were always meetings, just about every night. We'd meet at Shirley's place, meet at the Pender Y, meet at Harry Con's or over coffee in Chinatown—"What are we going to do? The city is planning this" or "The government is planning that." The hardest thing was getting recognized by the city. They questioned SPOTA's legitimacy even up to when the Working Committee was formed. "Do you truly represent the community?" After so many hundreds of signatures on so many proposals and briefs! And we had accountability too: that is, every time we had a new proposal, a new concept, we always held a public meeting. We had a public meeting about once a month for the first two years, and that took some organizing.

Shirley Chan at SPOTA meeting. TAMIO WAKAYAMA PHOTO

The federal Minister of Transport was in charge of housing then [1968–69] and that was Paul Hellyer. He had put a freeze on urban renewal programs because when he came across Canada to listen to reports, he found out that people living in housing projects were unhappy. Shirley and Mrs. Chan, Sue Lum, and Fred Soon attended those Hellyer Task Force meetings [November 1968] with Penny Stewart and Darlene Marzari who arranged a meeting with the Central Mortgage and Housing people and the minister. They took them around Strathcona, pointing out that the houses weren't all bad, that there was a lot of good strong substantial housing left in the

Lo Po Yin. TOD GREENAWAY PHOTO

community. From then on, demolition was stopped completely until a new way was found which would involve rehabilitation [of existing houses]. And from that point, a committee was formed [in the fall of 1969 with representation from the three levels of government, plus SPOTA] to get the concept ready for the actual rehabilitation project. But at these committee meetings they made sure that we would not understand things by bringing in a lot of experts. We learned that in order for us to be well-protected we had to make sure our own consultants were there.

TOM MESIC: Harry Con was always saying, "We're just citizens. Now could you explain it in Strathconanese instead of your jargon?" And the chairman would have to start over again and explain it to Harry because he was just a layman and a Chinese and didn't understand things! They were always giving our proposals back to us, saying, "This can't be done. You can't get an outright grant. It's never been done in Canada." The process took so long—it dragged on for about two and a half years in negotiations—I don't think anybody on the executive at that time expected the grant and loan to be finalized. We expected that we would secure the area, but I don't think we expected to get any grant and loan.

BESSIE LEE: When it got to the stage where we could form the Strathcona Rehabilitation Committee, Robert Andras [federal Minister for Urban Affairs] came out to Vancouver and met with us privately before he met with the city officials. When they found that out they were really angry because they still thought they were going to get their way, you know. So then at the meeting at City Hall in the afternoon he stood up and said that he would not allow the program to proceed without the community having full participation in the planning.[79] So we were recognized as the fourth level of government for this area, and that was the first time this ever happened anywhere. We didn't think it was special because we had worked so hard for it.

TOM MESIC: Prior to our housing concept being accepted by the provincial government in '72, we had pushed for two years that SPOTA form a corporation to develop non-profit housing. The new NDP government accepted the concept. Phase one was co-operative housing, and phases two, three, and four were condominiums and single houses on individual lots. A tremendous amount of time and energy was put into this project by the executive of the Strathcona Area Housing Society, for which they have never been paid. It's remarkable that any citizens' group could put up with that for five years without falling apart.

BESSIE LEE: Because of the houses that were removed, we needed to build new ones which would provide non-profit housing for needy families and also get rid of vacant lots that had been used for dumping.

TOM MESIC: We've had problems of traffic, problems of new housing, problems of new immigrants, and a history of these different fights with the city. And because of the community's location, being so close to the downtown core, we'll always have major concerns of this type.

BESSIE LEE: We have to remind the city that when they decide to change things in a community they must always consider the total planning of that community and the concerns of the people who live in it.

Emery Barnes and Mary Chan at opening of SPOTA Housing Co-op. TAMIO WAKAYAMA PHOTO

ACKNOWLEDGMENTS

With many thanks to:

Brad Cran, 2009–11 poet laureate of Vancouver, for facilitating the republication of *Opening Doors* some 30 years later.

Everyone at Harbour Publishing for their enthusiasm in bringing out this handsome new edition.

W.J. Langlois, former director of Aural History and co-ordinator of this project, especially for his encouragement during the interview phase.

Members of Strathcona Property Owners and Tenants Association for support, introductions, and access to their archives.

Those who gave background information, introductions, and references: Myer Freedman of the Jewish Historical Society; Peter Battistoni; Ines Leland; the Benedetti family; Marino Culos; Angelo Branca; Gordon Cumyow; Dorothy Nealy; Max Jaffe; Reverend Len Burnham; Roy Mah of *Chinatown News*; Dr. Maurice Fox; Major Kerr, Wilf Smith, and Lt.-Col. J. Steele of the Salvation Army; Gary Chapman; Deputy Chief Constable R.J. Stewart, Norman Holland, and Nicolas Glover of the Vancouver Police Department; Father de la Torre; James Frew, president of the Superannuated Policeman's Union; retired Constable Bill Mackie; Mr. and Mrs. E. Colchester of the Vancouver Historical Society; Miss Tosell of Strathcona School; Fumiko Greenaway, Wilma Steele; William Murphy, president of Pioneer Schools; Muriel Whalen of the Vancouver Labour Council; Sister Mary Beata of the Franciscan Sisters of the Atonement; the staff of the *Mirror*, Strathcona's community newspaper; Winnie Leung; Harold Lim; Rose Branca; Bill Abercrombie; Vernon Wiedrick; Strathcona branch of the Ministry of Human Resources, especially Mary Segal and Heather Smith; Shirley Ricci; Angelo Tosi; Bill Woo; Gene Barry; Olive Gillis; John Tate; Nino and Rose Salla; Pearl Oates; Louise Kennedy; Louie Valenti; Lena Skehor; Lo Po Yin; Louise Fung; Lily Wong; Elizabeth Martin; William Whyte Quigley; Marie Manieri; Wing Wong; Mrs. Jimmy Koo; Dr. S. Wah Leung; Jack Lee.

Those whose memories were recorded and stored in the Provincial Archives but not used in this publication: Al Izen; Ted Osborn; Reverend Annie Girard of Fountain Chapel; America Bianco; Jeannie McDuff; Phyllis Culos; Doris Lawson.

Vancouver City Archives, Sue Baptie and Paul Yee; Vancouver Public Library, Ron D'Altroy of the Historical Photographs Section, and the Northwest Reading Room; Strathcona School library, for access to school archives; Special Collections, UBC; archives of the *Jewish Western Bulletin*; National Film Board of Canada for use of their film *To Build A Better City*; and the Canada Council Explorations Program for partial funding, Tamio Wakayama of Japanese Canadian Centennial Project.

The editors would also like to thank Roy Kiyooka, Cheryl Sourkes, and Rhoda Rosenfeld for their personal support and criticism.

NOTES

1. Harold Kalman, *Exploring Vancouver* (Vancouver: UBC Press, 1974), p. 23.

2. Edward M.W. Gibson, "The Impact of Social Belief on Landscape Change: A Geographical Study of Vancouver" (Ph.D. Dissertation, University of BC, 1971), p. 74.

3. See J.S. Matthews, *Early Vancouver*, vol. 1 (Vancouver: City Archives, 1932), pp. 2, 3.

4. Paul Yee, "The Chinese in British Columbia," *Vancouver City Archives Bibliography*, no. 3 (1977): n.p.

5. So Eric Nicol implies (p. 58, *Vancouver*) when he quotes W.H. Gallagher's account of the incident from Matthews' *Early Vancouver*, vol. 1, p. 147.

6. S. Osterhout, *Orientals in Canada* (Toronto: Ryerson Press, 1929), p. 29.

7. The Vancouver Trade and Labour Council formed the Asiatic Exclusion League in June of 1907 in response to increased Japanese, Chinese, and East Indian immigration. On September 8, 1907, the League organized a march to City Hall (then at Hastings and Main) where several Vancouver clergymen made anti-Asian speeches. E.A. Fowler, secretary of the Seattle Exclusion League, gave such a rousing speech that a splinter-mob went through Chinatown, breaking windows, and then moved on to Powell Street, the Japanese quarters, for more of the same. The following morning, mobs made another attack but were routed by police while Japanese patrolled their own streets in self-organized militia. All Chinese domestic help, plus cooks and waiters, went on strike. Prime Minister Wilfrid Laurier sent a cable of apology to Japan, although none was forwarded to China. See James Morton, *In the Sea of Sterile Mountains* (Vancouver: J.J. Douglas, 1974), pp. 203–205; and Ken Adachi, *The Enemy That Never Was* (Toronto: McClelland and Stewart, 1976), pp. 63–85.

8. Chinese and Japanese students were effectively barred from studying either law or pharmacy by a law that required the names of students of these professions to be registered on the voters' list. Since neither Japanese nor Chinese were given the franchise until after World War II, they could not enter either of these professions.

9. It was only during the course of Deputy Minister of Labour William Lyon Mackenzie King's inquiry into losses sustained by the Chinese population in the 1907 Race Riot that the federal government became aware that opium factories existed in Vancouver, Victoria, and New Westminster—and existed legally, since there had never been a law made against them. Two factories in Vancouver each presented bills for damage suffered and stated, on inquiry, that they had been operating for ten and twenty-one years respectively. Each was making about $180,000 yearly gross. Francis Hardwick, ed., *East Meets West: The Chinese in Canada* (Vancouver: Tantalus Research, 1975), pp. 55–58.

10. This rescue home was initiated in 1886 in Victoria by the Methodist Women's Missionary Society in response to a considerable traffic in imported Chinese slave girls, from 100 to 200 a year, according to Rev. E. Robson as quoted in S.S. Osterhout's *Orientals in Canada* (Toronto: Ryerson Press, 1929). The society contested in court for guardianship of the rescued girls and gradually developed into a school for Chinese girls.

11. According to Adachi, *The Enemy That Never Was* (p. 228), "Some 980 boats...remain(ed) idle for six weeks, swinging at anchor and, in many cases, damaged and lying waterlogged on the banks of the Fraser and awash at high tide, their engines sludged with silt."

12. "The BC Security Commission expected the Japanese to support themselves, so all property owned by Japanese was liquidated to supply funds for this purpose. Food and clothing allowances were made available depending on income, but food was very expensive and wages were kept low because of public pressure—the Canadian Government

spent one-fourth as much per evacuee as did the U.S. Government during the war years." The Japanese Canadian Centennial Project, *A Dream of Riches* (Vancouver: Japanese Canadian Centennial Project, 1978), p. 93.

13. See Ivy Kaji McAdams interview on page 146.

14. Other early English settlers in the neighbourhood remember cattle or sheep being herded along Pender Street or Prior Street and wandering into front yards and up onto porches on their route to the P. Burns and Company slaughterhouse at the foot of Woodland Drive.

15. The bascule span was added in 1909 to an already existing trestle bridge, Vancouver's first big bridge, erected in 1876.

16. Indeed, this was one of the larger demonstrations at Powell Street Grounds, with an estimated 4,000 to 5,000 men gathered there. A public free-speech demonstration took place protesting the police department's earlier decision to disallow street meetings and public demonstrations. Batons and mounted officers' whips were used as "mounted police lined up at the west end of the grounds and the east end of the grounds (and) simultaneously raided the field." No mention was made in the newspaper account of Mayor Taylor reading the *Riot Act*, but there were some skirmishes over who should take the orator's stand: R.P. Pettipiece, a well-known socialist and later civic alderman, or the deputy police chief. This was a period of unemployment, and the news account states that the pockets of the arrested men contained only a few crusts of bread and one ten-cent lottery ticket. *Daily Province*, January 29, 1912.

17. The tidal flats of inner False Creek (from Main Street to Clark Drive) were filled in, 1915–21, for the yards of the Great Northern and Canadian Northern Pacific (now CNR) railways. The Canadian Northern Railway acquired the land from the City of Vancouver in return for draining, filling, and construction of the terminus plus a large hotel, etc., and the work was done at the company's expense.

18. The Societa Veneta was founded by Angelo Branca's father, Filippo Branca, as an alternative to the Sons of Italy.

19. Sacred Heart Church was established in 1905 on the site of a Protestant church on the corner of Campbell Avenue and Keefer Street, which was sold to the Catholic Diocese for $1,500. Angelo Branca's baptism in 1906 was among the first recorded at Sacred Heart.

20. In 1934, local boxer Jimmy McLarnin won the world welterweight title.

21. There are various local anecdotes about the exploits of this team of detectives, including the following from Peter Battistoni: "In Chinatown they used to have all these underground little coves. And this Ricci, he used to go down to these opium dens, and the Chinese got smart one time and they figured they would block him in there and nobody would find him. But he had strapped a small hatchet on his leg, and if he didn't have that hatchet he would of been dead underground and nobody would know it, never would find him either. There was lots of opium parlours in them days down in Chinatown. And I guess there was a lot of white people that used to cater to these opium dens."

22. Mr. Branca's argument for reclaiming this land, while unorthodox, was certainly convincing: he took up a heavy stick and beat the bushes, immediately sending a swarm of rats toward his dignified guests.

23. In August 1921, the Asiatic Exclusion League met with clergymen, businessmen, World War I veterans (many of whom felt that Chinese workers had taken their jobs in their absence), and representatives of six trade unions and the Vancouver Trades and Labour Council. They began an anti-Asian campaign which eventually led to Ottawa passing the *Oriental Exclusion Act* of 1923. This act effectively prohibited immigration for all Chinese except consuls, merchants, and students. Those men with families still in China (the vast majority) were unable to bring their wives or children over until 1947, when the act was rescinded.

24. Kang Yu-wei, supported by the Pao Wang T'ang (Empire Reform Association, pro-Manchurian), and Sun Yat-sen, supported by the Chih Kung Tang (Freemasons, the oldest Chinese association in British Columbia, formed in 1863 in Barkerville), were both competing to raise funds and political power among the overseas Chinese. The split between the two supporting groups was serious in Chinatown and lasted until the former association vanished with the 1911 rebellion. Later conflict occurred between the Kuomintang (the Nationalist Party originally formed by Sun Yat-sen

and later the ruling party of the new republic) and the Freemasons, who felt that their support of Sun Yat-sen in the making of the revolution had not been honoured with participation in the new republican government as promised. The conflict reached its climax in the twenties in Vancouver. W.E. Willmott, "The Evolution of Community Structure among Chinese Canadians," with C.P. Sedwick, in *The Canadian Forum*, September 1974. W.E. Willmott, "Approaches to the Study of the Chinese in BC" *BC Studies*, no. 4 (Spring 1970).

25. The Chinese, drawn into British Columbia by the gold rush of the nineteenth century, first settled in the Vancouver area on the tidal marshes of False Creek, on the opposite side of the isthmus from Hastings Mill. This first settlement of squatters was quickly enlarged with the influx of thousands of unemployed railroad workers once the CPR was finished in 1886. See Edward Gibson, "The Impact of Social Belief on Landscape Change: A Geographical Study of Vancouver" (Ph.D. Dissertation, University of BC, 1971), pp. 70–71.

26. With the outbreak of war, the federal government invoked the *War Measures Act* to render fascist organizations in Canada illegal. A number of Italian-Canadians were arrested and sent to a prisoner-of-war camp in Petawawa, Ontario. However, appeals began to be heard almost immediately by a committee headed by Justice H.A. Fortier and Justice Handman. "Within a few weeks interned people were being released. When the war ended only those who had refused to make an appeal were in the camps," A.V. Spada, *The Italians in Canada* (Montreal, 1969), p. 126.

27. A common method of washing terrazzo or hardpan dirt floors in Italy continued here. "In those days people were so clean that every Saturday you would find nearly all the women with a hose washing the whole house. The husband would drill holes in the floor so the water would run out, and they'd open all their windows."—Peter Battistoni

28. Italians arriving after 1922 (when Mussolini came to power in Italy) had to report to the RCMP during World War II; those arriving prior to 1922 but who had not taken out Canadian citizenship also had to report. Canadian-born wives of those who had to report were also required to report.

29. The Venice Bakery was reopened after the war and eventually sold in 1959 to Gordon Schwandner, a German immigrant. Retaining the name, Mr. Schwandner developed "a small bakery employing five people with two delivery trucks" (*Vancouver Sun*, January 17, 1967) into a large mechanized operation based in North Vancouver, one of the major bakeries of the city.

30. The original MacLean Park occupied the block bounded by Jackson, Georgia, Dunlevy, and Union, and was, as early as 1911, a supervised playground. Now MacLean Park occupies the block between Keefer, Heatley, Georgia, and Hawks, originally a block of homes which were demolished in 1960 to make way for the replacement park.

31. J.S. Matthews gives a vivid description of how the water impinged on the roads of Vancouver in the late 1880s. "The tides of Burrard Inlet still seeped onto the low land beneath the stilted board walks of Water Street; a walk from Water Street to Pender Street at high tide usually meant wet feet; skunk cabbage grew in the muskeg, and the rotting debris sometimes gave off queer effluvia. At the False Creek end of Carrall Street, an indent brought those waters—and floating logs, almost to Pender Street." J.S. Matthews, *Early Vancouver*, vol. 1 (Vancouver: Matthews, 1932), pp. 27–28.

32. This 1917 incident did much to give the neighbourhood its reputation for crime, because Bob Tate's other victim was Chief of Police Malcolm McLennan, who was murdered during the police attack on the house at 522 East Georgia. These murders were referred to by many early residents and they have become part of Strathcona folklore.

33. Mrs. Jean McDuff, who worked for years as a cook for First United Church, recalls: "They were coming every day off the trains. And then they got to know about First United and they came up and Mr. Roddan made this stew. They never sat down, they just came in and we gave them out plates. Some of them were so cold, you know, they could hardly hold their plate. Mr. Roddan would always say to them, 'When did you hear from your mother last?' They didn't write, I guess they were ashamed to. And it would be, 'Oh, years.' And he'd say, 'All right, before you get anything, I'm going to give you pen and paper and just write a wee note telling her you've been in to the church.' [Rev. Roddan] was a real family man. We fed all that was there and sometimes we sent out for bread and stuff. The breadline was every day, we made a stew every day in the morning. They'd come in about eleven or twelve to get it. Mr. Roddan used to go down to

the stores too, and get bread and hustle up stuff. We made a joke about it. I said, 'Oh, never mind, we'll get something, we'll make "ends" meet.' And I meant these oxtails, you know. Mr. Roddan was on the radio twice, morning and evening. He thought the thirties were terrible. He and Roy Stobie, when they went to the jungles [on the False Creek mud flats], they carried the big kettle of stew down, took it in the back of the car, and fed them down there."

34. Since 1913, the church had been known as the Norwegian Lutheran Church. From 1903 to 1913 it was the German Lutheran Church, according to the city directory.

35. According to contemporary newspaper accounts, on October 9, 1922, at 2.30 a.m., Police Constable R.G. McBeath was fatally shot on the corner of Davie and Granville Streets, after boarding a car and arresting its driver, Fred Deal, for drunken driving. Marjorie Earl was the other occupant of the car. After shooting McBeath and Detective R.S. Quirk, Deal escaped but was rounded up by other officers called to the scene. At his arrest, he was unarmed, but a revolver identified as Marjorie Earl's was found on the staging of a billboard in the vicinity. This killing caused public outrage because McBeath was a young World War I veteran who had been awarded the Victoria Cross for heroism in France.

36. Construction of the first Schara Tzedeck Synagogue was completed in 1911, and the house that had stood at 514 Heatley, on the lane, was used as the Talmud Torah, the school. In 1921, a new and larger synagogue was built to replace the old one, and at this date is still standing as the closed-up Gibbs Boys Club.

37. Nathan Mayer Pastinsky was not an ordained rabbi but served as rabbi from 1918 to 1946, and as *shochet* (ritual slaughterer), *mohel* (circumciser), and *chazan* (cantor).

38. Charles Woodward opened his first store at the corner of Georgia and Main in 1892. By 1904 he had relocated and built at the site of the present-day department store, Hastings and Abbott.

39. David Spencer opened his store on West Hastings between Seymour and Richards in 1906 and eventually sold it to Eaton's in 1948.

40. Dr. Dave Tompsett (1888–1971) began practising in Vancouver in 1912.

41. In 1910, the property at the corner of Heatley and Pender Streets was purchased for the site of the present synagogue, known as the Schara Tzedeck, completed in 1911. *Jewish Western Bulletin*, July 9, 1971.

42. By 1920, when a new synagogue was built on the same site, there were more than 250 Jewish families in the city and over half of them lived in an area bounded by Gore and Raymur, Cordova, and Prior Streets. The twenties saw an influx of European families and of Russian Jews who had escaped the pogroms of 1903 and 1905, had settled in eastern Canada, and were now moving west. By 1929, about the time that Jewish families began to leave the Strathcona neighbourhood, there were more than 600 families in the city. *Jewish Western Bulletin*, July 9, 1971.

43. Orthodox Jews did not labour on the Sabbath, which included not lighting fires or lamps.

44. "There was one doctor I used to go to, a really smart doctor. His clientele was mostly white people. This was on Powell and Main. Name was Shima Takahara, and they lived in a better part of town. And as soon as the war broke out, they had to get ready to go, and I guess the house was empty after, and people went in and tore out all the wiring and broke the windows. A nice house, you know. They had no rhyme nor reason to do that."—Peter Battistoni.

45. In 1913, by an act of Parliament, the Vancouver Harbour Commission was created to administer the Port of Vancouver and was granted "wide powers...to acquire, expropriate, hold, sell, lease, and otherwise dispose of such real estate and personal property as was deemed necessary for the development of the harbour." Norman Hacking, *History of the Port of Vancouver* (Vancouver: National Harbours Board, 1978).

46. The original wood-frame building was erected in 1906, and a brick building addition that stood behind it in 1909. When these buildings became too small for the size of the school, the Japanese community erected the Japanese Hall in 1928 to serve as both a school and community centre.

47. Tsutae Sato arrived in 1917 to take up a teaching appointment at what was then called Nippon Kokumin Gakko (Japanese National School), in accordance with the original conception that the Japanese children of Japanese immigrants should be given a traditional Japanese education to fit them for their return to Japanese society. By 1917, there was

already a move to make the school simply a language school extracurricular to a basic Canadian education that would teach the children how to become good Canadian citizens. This was Mr. Sato's policy after he became principal in 1921. Mr. and Mrs. Sato taught for some fifty years at the Japanese Language School on Alexander Street and were responsible for establishing a Japanese library and a Japanese Language Schools Society throughout Canada.

48. Strathcona School is one of the earliest schools in Vancouver. The first building on the grounds was completed in 1891 and was known as the East School until 1900. In 1897, an eight-room addition was completed, which is still standing as a landmark of architectural competence from an earlier era. The North Wing was built in 1915, and then later the first structure was demolished and the bricks were used to build the present Primary Building in 1921. Stanley D. McLarty, *The Story of Strathcona School* (Vancouver: Vancouver School Board, 1961).

49. Miss A. McLellan served as school nurse from 1911 to 1936, when she was promoted to supervisor of school nursing with the establishment of the Metropolitan Health Committee in Vancouver.

50. The popular suspicion of fifth-column activity among the Japanese on the West Coast was aroused by British Columbia's politicians, by incendiary newspaper articles, and by a certain panic in the general populace here after Pearl Harbor. The RCMP, the Navy, and the Army all considered the possibility of such activity unlikely. In fact, early in 1942, Lieutenant-General Ken Stuart said: "From the Army point of view, I cannot see that they constitute the slightest menace to national security." M. Pope, *Soldiers and Politicians* (Toronto: University of Toronto Press, 1962), p. 177. Quoted in Ken Adachi, *The Enemy That Never Was: A History of the Japanese Canadians* (Toronto: McClelland and Stewart, 1976), p. 203.

51. In 1941, over 8,000 persons of Japanese origin lived in Vancouver, largely in the Powell Street area.

52. In 1923 the Buddhist Church relocated to 549 Cordova Street, and in 1936 the Hompa Buddhist Church was erected at 604 Cordova, on the corner of Princess. During the war years the church was dispersed, but in 1956 it bought the former Japanese United Church, which it rebuilt in 1979.

53. When the evacuation began in early 1942, the authorities turned the cattle barns at Hastings Park (Pacific National Exhibition Grounds) into a clearing centre for evacuees. Families were detained here, with women and children in one building and men in another, as they waited to be shipped out to the "relocation" camps being hastily erected in the Interior. "At the end of a 9-month period, from February to October of 1942, more than 22,000 people (had) been displaced from their homes." *The Japanese Canadian Centennial Project, A Dream of Riches: The Japanese Canadians, 1877–1977* (Vancouver: Japanese Canadian Centennial Project, 1978), p. 78.

54. Dr. Maurice Fox (b. 1898) began practising medicine in Vancouver in 1924 and was still in practice in 1979.

55. The provincial government estimated that 30 percent of the people of British Columbia were sick. In Vancouver there were between 28,000 and 30,000 cases of influenza. In 1918 there were 618 deaths and in 1919 there were 329 deaths. Margaret Andrews, "Epidemic and Public Health Influenza in Vancouver, 1918–19," *BC Studies* 34 (Summer 1977), pp. 21–44.

56. In 1947, with the resumption of Chinese immigration, which had been virtually cut off since 1923, the federal government also extended full citizenship to those Chinese who had resided in Canada for five years or more. See Foon Sien's chapter, "The Chinese," in John Norris, *Strangers Entertained: A History of the Ethnic Groups of BC* (Vancouver: BC Centennial '71 Committee, 1971).

57. See letters to the editor in the *Vancouver Sun*, April 22, 1942, and Private Robert Hughes' statement to the judge on being sentenced to hang, April 18. This murder conviction was later converted to a manslaughter conviction in a Supreme Court appeal that laid down a new principle for the judging of murder cases. Hughes' lawyer for his appeal was Angelo Branca.

58. Because of their marginal acceptance in Canada, many Japanese parents registered their children at birth with the Japanese consul, thus giving them dual citizenship, as a security measure. Japanese Canadians with dual citizenship had military service obligations to Japan. Furthermore, male Japanese immigrants aged seventeen to thirty-seven were

not able to renounce their Japanese allegiance, should they have wished to, without first fulfilling their military service. Ken Adachi, *The Enemy That Never Was: A History of the Japanese Canadians* (Toronto: McClelland and Stewart, 1976), pp. 126, 175–77.

59. In May and June 1938, unemployed men occupied both the Vancouver Art Gallery and the Vancouver Post Office as a means of protesting the lack of jobs. On June 20 they were forcibly evicted, and those at the post office suffered gassings and beatings.

60. See Michael H. Marunchak, *The Ukrainian Canadians: A History* (Winnipeg: The Ukrainian Free Academy of Science, 1970), p. 608.

61. Harold Winch was a provincial MLA and leader of the British Columbia Cooperative Commonwealth Federation from 1938 to 1953. His father, Ernest Winch, was also a CCF MLA in British Columbia.

62. See Rosa Pryor, pp. 138.

63. According to Doris Lawson, who worked for Mrs. Pryor for nine or ten years beginning sometime in the forties, "We always had a piano player there. Shebo'd be before Joe Wilson, Shebo and then Joe Wilson and then Mac, and Beau Panky stayed the longest, and Hilda Sing, a white girl who played the piano—she was married to a Chinese fellow. Black fellow, Joe Wilson, he's dead. And Beau Panky's dead. Well, everybody knew Joe Wilson, he was kind of famous, he was a boxer, you know."

64. A. Phillip Randolph was born in 1889 in Crescent City, Florida. From 1920 to 1960 he played a leading role in Black rights. He was head of the Brotherhood of Sleeping Car Porters until 1968 and became a vice-president of the American Federation of Labour.

65. Joe Celona was born in Italy in 1898, immigrated to Canada in 1913, and came to Vancouver six years later. He was shot in an incident in his home in 1933. A year later he was arrested on white slavery charges. At his trial in 1935, he was convicted of living in part on the earnings of prostitution, and of keeping a "disorderly house" (the Maple Hotel at 177 East Hastings, the top floor of which was said to be a brothel). He was sentenced to eleven years, but after serving five was released on parole by the Justice Department. Public outcry resulted in his being returned to the penitentiary to serve the remainder of his sentence. After his release, he turned to bootlegging. He was a witness during the 1955 Royal Commission investigation of charges of bribery and corruption in the Vancouver Police Force. He died in 1958. *Province*, July 9, 1940, and April 12, 1935; *Vancouver Sun*, March 5, 1958.

66. According to another authority, the Fascist organizations set up in eastern Canada in the late twenties were directly connected with Rome. "The Italian authorities in Montreal received orders from Rome to form a local Fascio which was called Luporini. It was followed by the organization of branches from Nova Scotia to British Columbia... Fascism permeated Italian community life...It was, perhaps, the most blatant case of exploitation by a foreign government of all the nostalgic and delicate sentiments of any nationality in Canada. Married Italian women were induced to give the Italian government their marriage rings to be melted and sent to Italy to help in the war against Ethiopia." A.V. Spada, *The Italians in Canada* (Montreal: Italo-Canadian Ethnic and Historical Research Centre, 1969), p. 125. In Vancouver, Italian Canadians were quick to assert their loyalty to Canada. On June 11, 1940, a public meeting in the Hastings Auditorium led to the formation of the Canadian–Italian War Vigilance Association, with Angelo Branca as spokesman, and the immediate voluntary registration of the 3,000 to 4,000 Italians in the city. See the Vancouver *Province* news item quoted in Francis C. Hardwick, *From an Antique Land: Italians in Canada*, Canadian Culture Series No. 6 (Vancouver: Tantalus Research, 1976), pp. 36–37.

67. Harold Winch was a well-known Cooperative Commonwealth Federation-New Democratic Party politician who was an MLA and MP for many years. He was the provincial leader of the CCF from 1941 to 1953. Sam Carr was a well-known communist organizer and editor of the Communist Party of Canada publication, *The Clarion*.

68. Chinese in Canada lost their franchise in 1885 when the federal government passed a franchise bill designed to

give native Indians the vote. At the suggestion of Sir John A. Macdonald an amendment was inserted which excluded "a person of Mongolian or Chinese race" from voting.

69. Not to be confused with European Freemasonry, the Chinese Freemasons or Chi Gung Tong developed from the secret Triad Societies of southeastern China working to overthrow the Manchu regime. In Canada, the Freemasons became more a benevolent society offering support to its members on a communal basis. See W.E. Willmott, "Chinese Clan Associations in Vancouver," *Man* 64, no. 49 (1964), and S. Lyman, W.E. Willmott, B. Ho, "Rules of a Chinese Secret Society in BC," *Bulletin of the School of Oriental and African Studies* 27, pt. 3 (1964).

70. Morton gives the figure as eight Chinese immigrants allowed to enter Canada during those years. James Morton, *In the Sea of Sterile Mountains* (Vancouver: J.J. Douglas, 1974), p. 242.

71. In 1895, the British Columbia government passed an *Elections Act* depriving Japanese of their provincial franchise. The Chinese had been disenfranchised in the 1870s. Since the voters' lists for federal elections were based on those for provincial elections, Asians were effectively deprived of their federal vote as well. This tacit federal disenfranchisement was made explicit in 1920.

72. Or as Marino Culos puts it: "We were just the slobs, you know, and the city didn't seem to care much. For a while the East End was noted that way. We were always the 'illiterates,' the 'incapables.'"

73. In 1885, the federal government set the first Chinese head tax at $50. This was raised in 1901 to $100 and in 1904 to $500 in an attempt to reduce, if not eliminate, Chinese immigration.

74. In 1979, Mr. Soon was in his seventies, and thirteen years had passed with no satisfactory terms having been reached.

75. The Chinese Cultural Centre was formed in 1972 at a meeting of more than fifty Chinese community leaders and representatives from Chinese organizations, who came together to organize community support for the establishment of a Chinese Cultural Centre in the area of the Keefer Street diversion, close to the site of the original Chinese settlement in the city.

76. Block captains were residents who were assigned to keep their neighbours, within a radius of two or three blocks, informed of SPOTA's progress and who carried back opinions and suggestions to SPOTA. This system expanded into other services, such as the city police department's Neighbourhood Watch protection program, delivery of the community newspaper, and representation on local social service boards.

77. Because of its twenty-year urban renewal plan for Strathcona, the city froze property values in the district from 1958 on. "No major redevelopment and home improvement permits were allowed. No regular public works maintenance was carried out. The neighbourhood was left to await the bulldozer." Hayne Wai, *The Strathcona Story* (Vancouver: SPOTA, 1977), p. 4.

78. Penny Stewart, Darlene Marzari, and Mike Harcourt were sympathetic and active supporters of SPOTA.

79. The project was jointly funded by federal (50 percent), provincial (25 percent), and municipal (25 percent) governments.